Extractive Industries and Sustainable Development

An Evaluation of World Bank Group Experience

Andrés Liebenthal
Roland Michelitsch
Ethel Tarazona

2005

The World Bank
Washington, D.C.

International Finance Corporation
Washington, D.C.

Multilateral Investment Guarantee Agency
Washington, D.C.

http://www.worldbank.org/oed
http://www.ifc.org/oeg

Cover photo: Uchucchacua Mine, Oyon Province, Peru. Courtesy of Sidney J. Edelmann, Senior Evaluation Officer, OEG/IFC

ISBN-10: 0-8213-5710-7
ISBN-13: 978-0-8213-5710-1
eISBN: 0-8213-5711-5

Library of Congress Cataloging-in-Publication Data has been applied for.

 Printed on Recycled Paper

Contents

Acknowledgments

Special thanks are due to the members of the advisory panel for the study, who provided unique perspectives and advice:

- James Cooney, General Manager, Strategic Issues, Placer Dome, Inc.
- Cristina Echavarría, Director, Mining Policy Research Initiative, International Development Research Centre (IDRC)
- Arvind Ganesan, Director, Business and Human Rights, Human Rights Watch
- Michael Rae, Program Leader—Resource Conservation, WWF, Australia (formerly World Wildlife Fund, now World Wide Fund for Nature)
- David Rice, Group Policy Adviser, Development Issues, British Petroleum.

The report benefited immensely from the insights of past and present operational staff who kindly agreed to be interviewed and generously shared their insights about their projects: Eleodoro Mayorga Alba, Natasha Beschorner, Mohammad Farhandi, Mansour Farsad, Nelson de Franco, Hermann von Gersdorff, Alfred Gulstone, Richard Hamilton, Marc Heitner, Heinz Hendriks, Charles Husband, Salahuddin Khwaja, Paivi Koljonen, Marie Ange Le, Maria Lister, Charles McPherson, James Moose, William Porter, Emile Sawaya, Robert Taylor, and Chris Wardell.

A number of staff in the WBG's global product groups for oil, gas, and mining; country departments; network anchors; regions; and IFC's environmental and social department provided valuable comments, suggestions, and corrections during preparation of the report and background papers: Ron Anderson, Craig Andrews, Henk Busz, Anis Dani, Poonam Gupta, Michael Haney, David Hanrahan, John Johnson, Charles Di Leva, Stephen Lintner, Jean-Roger Mercier, Helga Muller, Kyle Peters, Anwar Shah, John Strongman, Rodrigo Suescun, Peter Thomson, and Monika Weber-Fahr. Our particular thanks go to Clive Armstrong and Paul Andre-Rochon, who organized staff and management feedback and put it in a coordinated framework.

The authors also are grateful to the 102 stakeholder representatives and 66 World Bank Group staff members who responded to the study surveys, and to the many people they met in the field who shared their views about the sector and its impacts. We also thank William Hurlbut, who provided editorial and document production support for all parts of the report.

Annex C, on the IBRD and IDA experience, was written by Andres Liebenthal and Ramachandra Jammi, with input from background papers prepared by Roger Batstone (Safeguards Study), Melissa Thomas (Governance Study), and Luis Ramirez Urrutia (Revenue Study), and from country case studies prepared by Dominique Babelon and Charles Dahan (Ecuador and Equatorial Guinea), Richard Berney (Kazakhstan), and Sunil Mathrani (Ghana and Papua New Guinea). Soon-Won Pak provided administrative assistance. Maria Mar and Alex McKenzie helped set up the online survey of WBG staff. Aracely Barahona-Strittmatter translated two country case studies into Spanish.

Annex D, on the IFC experience, was written by Roland Michelitsch under the general guidance of Bill Stevenson, director of IFC's Operations Evaluation Group (OEG). Other contributors include Rex Bosson, Sid Edelmann, and Dennis Long, who also completed project-level evaluations, conducted site visits, and helped prepare the report. Margaret Ghobadi assisted with the analysis of trust fund activities. Linda Morra, Head of Special Studies in OEG, provided valuable advice. Pelin Aldatmaz, Nicholas Burke, and Sanda Pesut assisted with data analysis and presentation. Cesar Gordillo, Yvette Jarencio, and Elvira Sanchez-Bustamante provided essential support as program assistants.

Annex E, on the MIGA experience, was written by Roger Batstone , Ethel Tarazona, and Stephan Wegner, under the general guidance of Aysegul Akin-Karasapan, director of MIGA's Operations Evaluation Unit (OEU). Richard Berney, Alberto Pasco-Font, Felix Remy, and Dale Weigel prepared background papers and case studies for this evaluation. Photis Bourloyannis-Tsangaridis and Brian McKenna provided research assistance. Alima Ngoutano-Njoya and Karalee Rocker helped to edit and format this report.

Director-General, Operations Evaluation:
Gregory K. Ingram
Director, Operations Evaluation Department:
Ajay Chhibber
Director, Operations Evaluation Group:
William Stevenson
Director, Operations Evaluation Unit:
Aysegul Akin-Karasapan
Manager, Sector & Thematic Evaluation, OED: *Alain Barbu*
Task Managers: *Andres Liebenthal, Roland Michelitsch, and Ethel Tarazona*

Foreword

The extractive industries—oil, gas, and mining—produce essential inputs (energy, metals, and minerals) for the global economy. Demand for these inputs is likely to increase, especially in developing countries, as people seek to improve their living standards.

The World Bank Group (WBG) finances only a small fraction of the investment in the sector, but its reach—through its access to stakeholders and the influence of its environmental and social policies, guidelines and procedures, and the demonstration effects of its projects—is potentially greater. However, the WBG's involvement in the extractive industries has come under increased scrutiny in recent years from several sections of civil society. At the Annual Meetings in 2000, some nongovernmental organizations (NGOs) presented the WBG with a request to stop supporting extractive industries because, in their view, the industry's adverse environmental, social, and governance impacts outweigh whatever economic and social benefits may accrue to the domestic economy and the poor. Climate change resulting from the use of fossil fuels is also an important concern.[1]

Following the 2000 Annual Meetings, WBG management launched the Extractive Industries Review (EIR) to take an in-depth look at the potential future role of the WBG in extractive industries. The EIR, headed by Professor Emil Salim, former Minister of Environment for Indonesia, focuses on consultations with con-

cerned stakeholders.[2] Its findings and recommendations will be presented to WBG management in December 2003.

Conducted in parallel with the EIR, this study by the independent evaluation units of the World Bank, International Finance Corporation (IFC), and Multilateral Investment Guarantee Agency (MIGA) assesses how effective the WBG has been in enhancing the contribution of extractive industries to sustainable development. The purpose is to provide an objective assessment of the results within the context of the WBG's overall mission of poverty reduction and the promotion of sustainable development. Its findings and recommendations provide guidance for the WBG's future strategy in the sector.[3]

The methodology of this evaluation is outlined in the Approach Paper.[4] This report highlights the main conclusions and recommendations, drawing from the experience of three agencies of the WBG—World Bank (Annex C), IFC (Annex D), and MIGA (Annex E). They are based on a review of the portfolio of extractive energy projects and EI-related advisory services; thematic reviews on revenue management, safeguards compliance, and governance; field missions to evaluate selected projects and prepare country case studies; and surveys of stakeholders and WBG staff. Annexes C, D, and E contain specific conclusions and recommendations for the respective agencies of the WBG.

Definitions

Extractive industries for this review include oil, gas, and mining of minerals and metals. Mining for construction materials, including cement production and quarries, is not included, nor are indirect investments through financial intermediaries.

Sustainable development meets the needs of the present without compromising the ability of future generations to meet their own needs. This requires sound environmental and social performance and economic efficiency. Given that fiscal revenues constitute a major source of net benefits (beyond those for the project financiers or sponsors) obtained from the extraction of mineral resources, the interests of future generations can be protected through the efficient utilization of these revenues for people in the host country.

Revenue management refers to the collection, distribution, and utilization of government revenues.

The World Bank Group includes IDA, IBRD, IFC, and MIGA. In this report, the combination of IDA and IBRD is referred to as the World Bank or "the Bank." The evaluation units of the WBG are the Operations Evaluation Department (OED) of the Bank, the Operations Evaluation Group (OEG) of IFC, and the Operations Evaluation Unit (OEU) of MIGA. These units are independent of WBG management and report to the WBG's Board through the director-general, Operations Evaluation.

Resource-rich and **EI-dependent** are used interchangeably in this report to refer to developing countries whose average annual export value of oil, gas, or mineral products exceeds 15 percent of total exports. This standard has been chosen with reference to the WBG's *Poverty Reduction Sourcebook,* which states, "A country's mining sector can play an important role in poverty reduction strategies if the approximate share of the mining sector is...greater than 10–25 percent of export earnings...." For a list of countries meeting this criterion, see Annex C, Attachment 2.

Executive Summary

How effectively has the World Bank Group assisted its clients in enhancing the contribution of the extractive industries (EI) to sustainable development?

On the one hand, with its global mandate and experience, comprehensive country development focus, and overarching mission to fight poverty, the WBG is well positioned to help countries overcome the policy, institutional, and technical challenges that prevent them from transforming resource endowments into sustainable benefits. Furthermore, the WBG's achievements are many. On the whole, its EI projects have produced positive economic and financial results, though compliance with its environmental and social safeguards remains a challenge. Its research has broadened and deepened understanding of the causes for the disappointing performance of resource-rich countries. Its guidelines for the mitigation of adverse environmental and social impacts have been used and appreciated widely. More recently, it has begun to address the challenge of country governance with a variety of instruments.

On the other hand, the WBG can do much to improve its performance in enhancing the EI sector's contribution to sustainable development and poverty reduction. There are three main areas for improvement:

Formulate an integrated strategy: The WBG has not devoted enough attention to the developmental needs of the poorly performing resource-abundant countries, many of which experienced negative growth during the 1990s. To address this gap, the WBG needs to formulate and implement integrated strategies at the sector and country levels for transforming resource endowments into sustainable development. These strategies should start with the presumption that successful EI projects—whether financed by the WBG or not—should not only provide adequate returns to investors but also provide revenues to governments, mitigate negative environmental and social effects, and benefit local communities. The strategies also will need to address governance squarely and help to ensure that EI revenues are used effectively to support development priorities. They will require, in addition, much better cooperation across the WBG and with other stakeholders.

Strengthen project implementation: The WBG needs to strengthen the implementation of its existing policy framework. Given the potential environmental and social impacts of resource extraction and the controversy surrounding the sector, rigorous implementation of safeguard policies is a minimum requirement for it to operate in a world concerned with sustainable development. The safeguard policies and guidelines also need to be adapted in line with evolving good practice, especially where they are inconsistent or incomplete. In addition, in light of growing concerns about the sustainability of EI development, the WBG needs to define, monitor, document, and report on the economic, social, and environmental impacts of its projects more systematically. Specifically, the distribution of benefits, identified as an important issue for the sector by many stakeholders, needs to be monitored and evaluated explicitly.

Engage the stakeholders: Often in collaboration with other organizations, the WBG has brought together diverse stakeholders in extractive industries to address issues at the local, national, regional, and global levels. The WBG's convening role has been actively sought and has been significant because of its access to all stakeholders, its private and public development experience, and its ongoing involvement with project investment and technical assistance in the sector. But the WBG has inadequately addressed some areas—notably governance and revenue management. The WBG's performance in these areas can be enhanced by improving consultation with stakeholders, including local communities, and by reporting on key sustainability indicators systematically and transparently. The WBG also should vigorously pursue countrywide and industrywide disclosure of government revenues from extractive industries. Such an approach is also likely to raise standards and practices for the sector as a whole.

Acronyms and Abbreviations

AAA	Analytical and advisory activities
AFR	Africa Region
AMR	Annual Monitoring Report
ASM	Artisanal and small-scale mining
ASEAN	Association of South East Asian Nations
CAE	Country Assistance Evaluation
CAO	Compliance Advisor/Ombudsman (for IFC and MIGA)
CAS	Country Assistance Strategy (World Bank Group)
CDP	Community Development Program
CODE	Committee on Development Effectiveness
DGO	Director General, Operations Evaluation
EA	Environmental assessment
EAP	East Asia and the Pacific Region
EAP	Environmental Action Plan
EBRS	Energy Business Renewal Strategy
ECA	Europe and Central Asia Region
EI	Extractive industries (oil, gas, and mining)
EIA	Environmental Impact Assessment
EIR	Extractive Industries Review
EMP	Environmental Management Plan
EMS	Environmental Management System
ERL	Emergency Rehabilitation Loan
ERR	Economic rate of return
ESW	Economic and sector work
E&S	Extractive Industries and Sustainable Development
FDI	Foreign direct investment
FMR	Final Management Response
FRR	Financial rate of return
FY	Fiscal year (July 1 to June 30)
GDP	Gross domestic product
GEF	Global Environment Facility
GHG	Greenhouse gas
GOPNG	Government of Papua New Guinea
GPG	Global Products Group
GRICS	Governance Research Indicators Country Snapshot
IBRD	International Bank for Reconstruction and Development

ICMM	International Council of Mining and Metals
ICR	Implementation Completion Report
ID	Institutional development
IDA	International Development Association
IDI	Institutional development impact
IFC	International Finance Corporation
IMF	International Monetary Fund
IMR	Interim Management Response
IPAP	Indigenous Peoples Action Plan
IPDP	Indigenous Peoples Development Plan
IPIECA	International Petroleum Industry Environmental Conservation Association
IPP	Indigenous Peoples Plans
LAC	Latin America and the Caribbean Region
MDF	Mineral Development Fund
MIGA	Multilateral Investment Guarantee Agency
MMSD	Mining, Minerals and Sustainable Development Project
MNA	Middle East and North Africa Region
NGO	Nongovernmental organization
NPV	Net present value
OBA	Output-based aid
OD	Operational Directive (World Bank)
OED	Operations Evaluation Department (World Bank)
OEG	Operations Evaluation Group (IFC)
OEU	Operations Evaluation Unit (MIGA)
OGP	International Association of Oil and Gas Producers
OP	Operational Policy (World Bank)
PNG	Papua New Guinea
PPAH	Pollution Prevention and Abatement Handbook
PPAR	Project Performance Assessment Report
PSC	Production-sharing contract
PSD	Private sector development
PSR	Project Supervision Report
QACU	Quality Assurance and Compliance Unit
QAG	Quality Assurance Group
RAP	Resettlement Action Plan
RP	Resettlement Plan
SAL	Structural Adjustment Loan
SAR	Staff Appraisal Report
SAS	South Asia Region
SECAL	Sectoral Adjustment Loan
SIL	Specific Investment Loan
SME	Small- and medium-size enterprise
SSM	Small-scale mining
TA	Technical assistance
TAL	Technical Assistance Loan
TI	Transparency International
UNDP	United Nations Development Programme
UNEP	United Nations Environment Programme
WBG	World Bank Group

Background and Objective

The objective of this study is to evaluate how effectively the WBG has assisted its clients in enhancing the contribution of extractive industries to sustainable development.[5] The WBG's activities in EI have come under increased scrutiny and criticism from several sections of civil society. Some NGO groups have asked the WBG to stop supporting the extractive industries because, in their view, the adverse environmental, social, and governance impacts outweigh whatever economic and social benefits might accrue to the domestic economy and the poor. Others have been concerned with issues of poor governance and the failure to use resource rents effectively in support of sustained economic development. This study responds to these concerns by evaluating the WBG's relevant experience and making recommendations to inform decisions about the WBG's strategy in the sector.

Main Issues for the Sector

Extractive industries can contribute significantly to a country's economic development and often offer the first opportunities for foreign investment and private sector development. They generate government revenues, foreign exchange earnings, and employment, often in depressed and remote areas. However, they also can aggravate or cause serious environmental, health, and social problems, including conflict and war. They provide scope for rent-seeking and opportunities for distorting public expenditure policies. Many resource-rich countries perform worse than resource-poor countries in key aspects of development, including economic, social, and governance.[6] The relationship[7] between EI dependence and economic growth for all WBG borrower countries is shown in Figure 1.1.[8]

Much research, at the WBG and elsewhere, has been done to better understand and address this paradox.[9] The emerging consensus is that the underperformance of resource-rich developing countries is not inevitable, because most of the factors that explain it result from institutional and policy failure.[10] Overall, while the technical requirements for managing volatile and

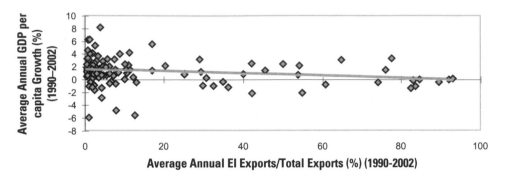

Figure 1.1 — Slower Economic Growth with Greater EI-Dependence: 1990–2002

Source: World Development Indicators; WHO, CONTRADE Database

exhaustible revenue flows and investing them for sustainable development are well understood, they are difficult to implement because of poor governance. Thus, creating good governance is at the heart of the institutional and policy changes needed to sustain sound fiscal management and maximize the benefits from the extraction of mineral resources.

The World Bank Group's Changing Role in the Extractive Industries

The WBG provides only a very small share of the financing for the sector, but its reach—through its access to all stakeholders; the influence of its environmental and social policies, guidelines, and procedures; and the demonstration effects of its projects—is potentially much greater. The WBG's advice on the enabling environment for extractive industries also has a broader effect on the sector than the financing volume would indicate.

The World Bank: The Bank's role has evolved from mainly exploration and production activities support (1960s to the early 1980s), to sector policy reform and commercialization of state-owned enterprises (1980s), to a greater emphasis on capacity-building and private sector development (1990s). Also in the 1990s, the Bank began to help transition economies to maintain production levels, rehabilitate or close uneconomical facilities, and attract foreign investment. Since the mid-1990s, the Bank's approach has evolved toward greater collaboration with civil society, local governments, and private companies. The share of extractive industries in the Bank's overall lending declined from 4 percent in the 1980s to under 2 percent in the 1990s.

The International Finance Corporation: IFC has focused on countries where its value added—as a catalytic agent and neutral third party between governments and private investors—is greatest. Since 1992, investments in oil and gas (but not mining) exploration were discontinued, mainly because of poor results and difficulties associated with assessing exploration risks. The share of EI investment in IFC's total lending portfolio has decreased substantially, from 15 percent in 1990 to 6 percent today. Since the mid- to late 1990s, IFC has focused increasingly on sustainability, especially environmental, health and safety, and social issues, and, most recently, on revenue management and distribution. Many of IFC's sustainability initiatives (such as small- and medium-size enterprise [SME] linkages, IFC Against AIDS) have a particular relevance to, and focus on, the EI sector. IFC's EI portfolio is concentrated in oil and gas (half), gold, and copper (over 10 percent each).

The Multilateral Investment Guarantee Agency: MIGA has supported extractive industries with political risk guarantees and, to a lesser extent, technical assistance and advisory services. MIGA's early involvement was concentrated heavily in the mining sector. Between 1990 and December 2002, MIGA provided guarantees for 31 projects in EI, most of them in mining. Throughout the 1990s, there was high demand for MIGA insurance, with large operations in countries with higher political risk profiles. Learning from its earlier experience, MIGA increasingly has paid more attention to environmental and social aspects of EI projects (and adopted its own environmental assessment and disclosure policies in 1999 and its own interim safeguard policies in 2002). Because of the low volume of new guarantees in extractive industries projects since 2001 and cancellation and expiration of MIGA coverage for some projects, the sector's share in MIGA's portfolio has continued to decrease and is now 11 percent.

Complementary and Coordinated Roles: The different parts of the WBG have coordinated and complementary roles in their approach to extractive industries and resource-rich countries. The Bank has responsibility for country policy dialogue and tends to focus on broader structural and social issues, including sector policy reform and institutional capacity-building, with a focus on poverty reduction. IFC has focused on attracting private sector investment, particularly in "high-risk" countries, where its projects were expected to have a catalytic effect in attracting new investments and demonstrating sound management of environmental and social effects. MIGA specializes in providing political risk guarantees, while at the same time ensuring that the projects it supports comply with applicable environmental and social performance standards. Since the late 1990s, WBG projects and policy work in the extractive industries have been coordinated through joint Bank-IFC Global Product Groups in the oil and gas sector and the mining sector, and joint Bank-IFC-MIGA country assistance strategies (CASs).

From Economic Benefits to Sustainable Development

Project Outcomes

The World Bank: Overall, ex post evaluations show that about 80 percent of the Bank's EI projects[11] have had moderately satisfactory or better outcomes,[12] above the Bank-wide average of 75 percent. The benefits from investment projects included increased production, increased private investment, and improved productivity. Adjustment and technical assistance projects, on the other hand, generated economic benefits through private sector development, improved production levels, institutional capacity-building and policy reform, rehabilitation or closure of uneconomical mines, environmental cleanup, and the integration of artisanal and small-scale mines into the formal sector. However, the Bank's documentation and reporting on the economic benefits of the projects, such as ex post economic analyses and other quantitative indicators, has been limited.[13] Given the questions that have been raised about the justification for the Bank's continued involvement in the sector, improved reporting could inform stakeholders and strengthen accountability.

The main finding that emerges from the review of the Bank's portfolio is that projects with satisfactory outcome ratings tended to be associated with greater government commitment to project objectives and adequate infrastructure, favorable commodity prices, and a high level of stakeholder involvement. The less successful projects appeared to be affected by poor government commitment and unfavorable economic conditions or commodity prices.

The International Finance Corporation: Overall development results in IFC's EI projects[14] were about the same as in other sectors, with 60 percent success. It is noteworthy that IFC's EI investments are concentrated in particularly difficult countries, where many development agencies are struggling to achieve positive results,[15] and are subject to substantial risks (commodity price fluctuations, geological risks, etc.). About three-quarters of EI projects had satisfactory economic returns, with projects in oil and gas performing better than those in other sectors and mining projects performing about the same as those in other sectors. IFC's EI projects often were among the first investment opportunities in the country, frequently followed by other investments, notably in SMEs. Several projects involved privatization and demonstrated that the private sector tends to operate more efficiently and in a more environmentally sound manner than state-owned enterprises. Most projects generated large government revenues, sometimes even where investors lost money. But when little or nothing flowed back to local communities, this created problems—for local people and investors. The distribution of benefits, considered one of the top issues in the sector, was not consistently and sufficiently addressed in IFC projects. Close cooperation within the WBG—in particular between IFC and the Bank's country departments—and between the WBG and the host government will be necessary to address this issue effectively.[16]

IFC's EI projects typically created economic opportunities for people—notably direct and indirect jobs, often in remote areas. Many projects improved local roads, water, and power supply, and the best ones tried to maximize economic opportunities for the local community. Recently, IFC has focused increasingly on enhancing benefits and opportunities for local communities. For example, IFC's "SME linkage" program, which tries to increase supply linkages to large projects, was particularly active in extractive industries, and so was "IFC Against AIDS." IFC also has focused on helping clients improve their community development programs, often using trust funds. The most effective programs, identified through consultations, were community needs, priorities, and aspirations. While overall positive economic effects dominated, there were adverse consequences. For example, economic opportunities often attract a large number of people, and companies and communities found it difficult to deal with this influx, particularly where government capacity was weak. Local people did not always have the requisite skills to take advantage of the opportunities. They sometimes lost agricultural lands, and,

in a few cases, compensation did not restore livelihoods for everyone affected.

The Multilateral Investment Guarantee Agency: All evaluated MIGA projects[17] have been affected adversely by the drop in metal prices since the late 1990s, which reduced their financial and economic returns and sustainability. In most projects, however, economic benefits were above financial rates of return, because of the benefits accruing from creation of jobs and provision of training to the workforce, often in remote and depressed areas. In addition, these projects (several in low-income, resource-rich countries) generated sizable revenues to local and central governments, although governments holding equity shares in return for providing ore reserves were disappointed by lower-than-expected equity returns. Most projects also funded community initiatives, including a few that established exemplary community development programs.

All evaluated MIGA projects were generally consistent with the private sector strategies of their host countries. Most were in countries where international private investors had been reluctant to make large investments because of limited experience with new governments or difficulties faced by previous investments in that country or sector. In these instances, MIGA's political risk insurance was significant in enabling investment flows into the mining sector and, in some cases, has led the way for other investments in the host country.

Linking Project Benefits to Overall Country Assistance

Beyond the generation of project benefits, the WBG's involvement in the transformation of resource riches into sustainable development has been limited.[18] A review of the latest CASs[19] in poorly performing resource-rich countries found that 64 percent recognize the special issues associated with the management of resource rents, but in only a few instances is the discussion linked to specific interventions. The inadequacy of linkages between EI sector activities and sustainable development also was highlighted by 47 percent of the WBG's EI sector staff who responded to a survey; 50 percent attributed it to inadequate support from the relevant country department/country management unit.[20] In addition, the Bank's overall lending to resource-rich countries experiencing negative growth has been lower than average, with no indication of compensating nonlending interventions.[21]

A detailed review in a sample of five resource-rich countries indicates that Bank interventions were only modestly relevant and efficacious in addressing the challenge of improving fiscal policies and public expenditures, with the quality of governance emerging as the key factor. This suggests that good governance is a prerequisite for enhancing the positive linkage between increased fiscal revenue flows and sustainable development.[22] Good governance was also important for development results and IFC's investment results—both were better where country governance was good.[23]

Taken together, these findings suggest that, while the WBG is aware of the underlying causes for the underperformance of many resource-rich countries—primarily unsound revenue management and poor governance—it has yet to formulate and implement viable approaches to address them. If the WBG is to have a more effective role in poorly performing EI-dependent countries, it will require government commitment as well as use of the WBG's full influence to achieve sound fiscal management and build a supportive governance framework. The linkages between resource rents and sustainable development can best be made explicit through CASs, to guide the design of specific projects and the monitoring and evaluation of results.

Mitigating Environmental and Social Impacts and Beyond

Extractive industries tend to have a heavy "footprint"—large, wide-ranging, and long-term environmental and social impacts. Effective implementation of the WBG's safeguard policies is therefore particularly important in this sector for sustaining the rationale for continued WBG involvement in a world concerned with sustainable development.

The World Bank: The assessment of a sample of Bank EI projects found the majority to be substantially consistent with applicable safeguard policies, but the degree of consistency varied depending on the environmental category of the project and the stage of the project cycle.[24] Thus, about 74 percent of the 'A' and 'B' projects were assessed to be substantially (or highly) consistent with safeguards at approval, with the share declining to 67 percent during implementation.[25] The decline may be associated with the finding that safeguards supervision inputs and reporting had been adequate in only 41 percent of the projects. Even so, these findings are more positive than those obtained from the survey of stakeholders, which points to their perception of a need for improved performance in the environmental and social areas.

Most significant shortcomings in the Bank's implementation of safeguards can be traced to inadequacies at the initial project screening, especially for sectoral adjustment and technical assistance projects, where the guidance has been subject to varying interpretations.[26] Inadequate supervision and reporting were other important sources of problems: environmental or social specialists supervised only about 30 percent of the projects in the sample, and fewer than a quarter of the project completion reports had adequate reporting and discussion of this subject.[27]

While the validity of these findings is limited to the sample of 38 EI projects that was reviewed (half of all projects in the EI portfolio), the results make a strong case for strengthening implementation of the Bank's safeguards framework, which is no different for extractive industries than for other types of projects. The findings point, in particular, to the need for clearer and more consistent guidance for the environmental assessment (EA) categorization of sectoral adjustment and technical assistance projects, the identification of applicable safeguards at the initial project screening, the appropriate scope and arrangements for monitoring of safeguards implementation, and the reporting and evaluation of results at project completion. Improvement would be particularly important for extractive industries, given the large share of sectoral adjustment and technical assistance projects, the inadequacies in monitoring and reporting, and the controversy surrounding the sector.

The International Finance Corporation: The evaluation of IFC projects' compliance with safeguard policies and guidelines found oil and gas projects performing significantly better and mining projects significantly worse than those in other sectors. Judging from the desk review of portfolio projects, the performance of mining projects appears to have improved and is now in line with the IFC average.[28] The main problems in mining projects related to the handling of hazardous materials—for which IFC has now developed guidelines—and difficulties in ensuring adequate mine closure. Oil and gas projects featured almost no compliance issues per se, but gas flaring was a concern in many projects, downstream transportation in others.

IFC's supervision of EI projects was significantly better than average better than that of the average IFC project, and IFC's environmental and social specialists spent more time on extractive industries (one-third more in fiscal year 2002) than on any other sector. But gaps remain, in part attributable to insufficient management systems. For example, while project-level supervision was generally strong, no central database identifies which safeguard policies and key issues apply to which project. Clients expressed appreciation for IFC's environmental and social specialists, who helped improve the environmental and social aspects of numerous projects. But they cannot replace local monitoring, particularly because IFC usually exits from projects before project closure. Building local monitoring capacity—either that of local consultants or that of government agencies (through the World Bank)—could help address this issue. Disclosure of environmental monitoring data would likely improve trust and improve performance—possibly even after IFC's exit.

The Multilateral Investment Guarantee Agency: The review of a sample of MIGA EI projects[29] found that 73 percent were consistent[30] with MIGA's (2002) issue-specific interim safeguard policies at the time of MIGA Board approval. The consistency improved during project implementation (while under MIGA guarantee or at the time of cancellation of the MIGA guarantee). Although in at least two cases MIGA played a direct positive role, in other cases these improvements were not clearly attributable to MIGA. The level of consistency was not uniform across all applicable safeguard policies. The project review noted systemic deficiencies in the application of the social aspects of safeguards. OEU found that, in addition to lowering perceived political risks as a guarantee provider, MIGA had the greatest potential to add value with its support to environmental and social aspects of EI projects.

The evaluated projects showed an overall improving trend in the consistency of safeguard policies over time, implying institutional learning from experience and strengthened policies and implementation as MIGA expanded its operations. However, the shortcomings identified point to a lack of a proactive approach with its clients throughout its involvement with the projects to add value by improving their environmental and social impacts.

Need for Continued Updating: The WBG's safeguard policies, guidelines, good practice manuals, and notes have received wide acceptance, even where the WBG is not involved—some other international financial institutions use them, and recently some of the largest private project finance banks have committed to adopt them. But some of them are inconsistent, incomplete, or lacking. For example, while leaders in extractive industries and some governments subscribe to "voluntary principles on security and human rights," the WBG has no comparable guidance. Given that human rights violations frequently have been alleged in connection with the site security of EI projects—including some WBG projects—this is one of the gaps that needs to be filled.[31] Another area is HIV/AIDS, an important issue for the sector, but one not covered by guidelines.[32] Given the wide use of the WBG's guidelines, it is particularly important that they be comprehensive, practical, and updated regularly to reflect lessons and evolving good practice standards. Their standard-setting character points to the potential for the WBG to continue building on its global mandate, public and private sector knowledge, and convening power for catalyzing good practice with respect to environmental, social, and other issues. Besides improving the results of WBG-supported projects, this would also help to define a level playing field among international financial institutions and among different companies.

Beyond Safeguards: The WBG's efforts to "do good" by addressing existing environmental conditions and building capacity for the management of environmental and social impacts have yielded mostly satisfactory results. As part of its sustainability initiative, IFC has started to focus on improving the impacts of its projects "beyond compliance" (for example, by maximizing linkages with local SMEs).[33] These findings point to the continuing potential for the WBG to make a valuable contribution to the development of the host countries and the extractive industries sector, in an area that the private sector alone cannot address.[34]

Addressing the Governance Challenge

High dependence on revenues from extractive industries has been associated with corrosive effects on economic and political life in many countries, including rent-seeking and government ineffectiveness. Indeed, a review of the literature and feedback from NGOs suggests that good governance is central to creating an environment that fosters sustainable and equitable development, and is an essential complement to sound revenue management and safeguard policies. Figure 3.1 shows the negative association between the quality of governance and EI dependence.[35]

Countries such as Botswana and Chile[36] have leveraged their natural resource wealth into sustainable growth through investment-friendly policies, fiscal discipline, and long-term planning. While the highest quality of macro and sectoral governance[37] may not be required for resource extraction to be beneficial to a client country, some minimum conditions should exist to help ensure that the benefits from EI projects are not squandered and the citizens left with costs that can include environmental damage, health risks, and conflict.

At least since the early 1990s, the WBG has been aware of the importance of addressing the governance challenge for ensuring the transformation of resource rents into sustainable development. But there is little discussion of sector-specific governance issues in the country strategies of EI-dependent countries. There are also few cases where a link can be discerned

between a diagnostic assessment of governance, a governance-informed strategic approach to the EI sector set out in the country strategy, and the design of EI projects.[38] Where some links can be observed, such as in Papua New Guinea and Kazakhstan, experience suggests that governance issues take a long time to address, and working to establish good governance in parallel with, or after, supporting increased investment in EI, is a high-risk strategy in countries with poor governance.

This fact points to the need for the WBG to tailor its support for resource extraction on the basis of an assessment of the quality of governance. Important indicators of macro governance include the quality of public financial management[39] and rule of law,[40] as measures of the government's ability to address problems through formal institutional reforms. At present, while the Bank's economic and sector work

Figure 3.1 **Worse Country Governance with Greater EI-Dependence**

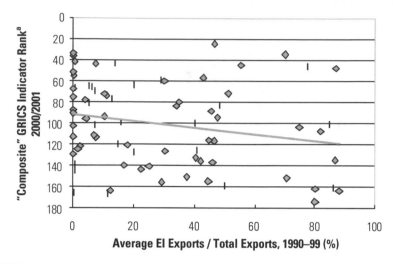

a. "Composite" GRICS ranks are a simple average of individual GRICS rankings for 2000/2001 for Voice and Accountability, Political Stability, Government Effectiveness, Regulatory Quality, Rule of Law, and Control of Corruption.

Source: http://www.worldbank.org/sbi/governance/pdf/2001 kkzcharts.xls

frequently assesses the quality of public financial management, it has no diagnostic instrument to evaluate the rule of law or the quality of sectoral governance. These gaps need to be addressed. This governance analysis then has to inform the risk assessment, structuring, and investment or underwriting decision. Recognizing that fiscal revenues may be misused in countries with poor governance, IFC has developed a position paper outlining possible steps to address this risk.[41] MIGA has not yet addressed the issue of revenue management from extractive industries in a similar way.

Promoting transparency is an essential tool for building good governance, and the WBG has long played a role, mainly in conjunction with its EA policy,[42] but also through institution-building and policy reform efforts aimed at improving the enabling environment for the sector. About 15 percent of Bank EI projects have provisions for disclosure and dissemination of project information beyond the requirements of the EA policy, but with the exception of the recent Bank/IFC Chad-Cameroon Pipeline projects, the WBG has not required disclosure of fiscal revenues from EI, even though it sometimes recommends it. A few companies operating in the sector have started disclosing government revenues, and some global initiatives advocate disclosure.[43] While some governments make such disclosure illegal, and companies are concerned that unilateral disclosure could harm them, industry overall appears to be in favor—if a level playing field can be ensured.

Recommendations

With its global mandate and country development perspective, combined with public and private sector experience, the WBG is well positioned to help countries transform resource riches into sustainable development. The Bank's research has broadened and deepened the understanding of the "paradox of plenty," and the WBG has led or participated in numerous initiatives to address EI issues. In most dimensions, the WBG's EI projects appear to perform at least as well or better than projects in other sectors, but much more needs to be done to improve implementation and monitoring of compliance with existing policies and to address governance, transparency, and revenue management issues. Unless the WBG improves its performance in these areas, it will not be able to maximize the sector's contribution to sustainable development and will face continued—and warranted—criticism. The key recommendations are summarized below. Annexes C, D, and E contain additional specific recommendations for the Bank, IFC, and MIGA.[44]

Recommendation 1: Formulate an Integrated Strategy

The WBG has not devoted enough attention to the developmental needs of the poorly performing resource-abundant countries, many of which experienced negative growth during the 1990s. To address this gap, the WBG needs to formulate and implement integrated sector- and country-level strategies for transforming resource endowments into sustainable development. Such integrated strategies will start with the pre-sumption that successful EI projects—whether financed by the WBG or not—have to provide not only adequate returns to investors but also revenues to governments and benefits to local communities, and mitigate negative environmental and social effects. They will also need to address governance squarely and help to ensure that EI revenues are effectively used to support development priorities. They will also require much better cooperation within the WBG and with other stakeholders.

Formulate a World Bank Group sector strategy: The WBG needs to design and implement a sectoral strategy that closely integrates resource extraction with sustainable development through the effective management of EI revenues in support of developmental priorities and the reliable mitigation of adverse environmental and social impacts. Where macro and sectoral governance are weak, the WBG's assistance should focus on strengthening governance. In such cases, the WBG should carefully assess and report on the risks that EI fiscal revenues may not be used for development priorities. The WBG should not support significant sector expansion unless it can adequately mitigate these risks.[45] Where macro governance is sound but sectoral governance is weak, the WBG should focus on improving sectoral governance and should support the sector only in conjunction with adequate provisions to overcome sectoral governance weaknesses.[46]

Address extractive industries in Country Assistance Strategies: For all resource-rich countries, the WBG should explicitly address extractive industries in the CASs.[47] The CAS should explicitly discuss the sector's current and potential economy-wide linkages (for example, the importance of government revenues, their management, distribution, and use for development priorities) and reference the underlying governance assessment. This approach should guide future project design, facilitate monitoring and evaluation, and provide an agreed framework for WBG-wide coordination and collaboration in the EI sector. The different agencies of the WBG should work together routinely to enhance the development impacts of EI projects; for example, in the form of public-private partnerships with respect to community development programs.

Promote governance improvements: The Bank should compensate for the lower level of lending that may be appropriate for resource-rich countries with weak macro and sectoral governance[48] by devoting greater management attention and an administrative budget for advisory and analytical activities aimed at improving the policy, institutional, and governance framework

for EI. Doing so would enable the Bank to establish and maintain continuity of engagement and facilitate responding quickly to opportunities for assistance when they arise.[49]

Support private sector development and environmental sustainability: In all countries, the WBG should continue its support to close uneconomical mines, reform and privatize state-owned enterprises, and mitigate pre-existing environmental and social problems. Where appropriate, the WBG should help integrate artisanal and small-scale mining (ASM) with the formal sector and internalize their environmental and social impacts, while at the same time creating alternative employment opportunities and supporting the consolidation of ASM activities for greater efficiencies and economies of scale.

Recommendation 2: Strengthen Project Implementation

The WBG needs to strengthen the implementation of projects within its existing policy framework. Given the potential impacts of resource extraction and the controversy surrounding the sector, rigorous implementation of safeguard policies is a minimum requirement for the WBG to operate in a world concerned with sustainable development. In addition, in light of growing concerns about sustainable development, the WBG needs to define, monitor, document, and report on the economic, social, and environmental impacts of its projects more systematically. Specifically, the distribution of benefits, identified by many stakeholders as an important issue for resource extraction, needs to be explicitly monitored and evaluated.

Improve project screening and monitoring: The WBG should provide clearer and more consistent guidance for the categorization of projects,[50] the identification of applicable safeguards at the initial project screening, the appropriate scope and nature of the EA instruments, and the reporting and evaluation of safeguards implementation. This needs to be followed up through the entire implementation framework, from good practice guidelines to appropriate monitoring and training.

Involve specialists throughout: The WBG should provide adequate resources and incentives for the participation of qualified environmental and social specialists in the preparation, appraisal, and supervision of all projects that are likely to have adverse impacts. This will ensure that such impacts are addressed adequately through the upstream design of appropriate mitigation strategies or project alternatives, as well as through the retrofit of timely remediation measures should unexpected impacts materialize during project implementation.

Enhance reporting of results: The Bank should strengthen reporting of its results by ensuring that project completion reports include an ex post economic rate of return or net present value (NPV) or, where that is not feasible, a cost-effectiveness analysis to determine whether the project represented the least-cost solution to attain its objectives. IFC should develop and use a reporting template for environmental and socioeconomic sustainability indicators, building on industry initiatives. MIGA needs to adopt more standardized and timely reporting mechanisms on environmental and social safeguards compliance and ex post development outcomes. The WBG should prepare completion reports for every significant non-lending/guarantee issuance activity.[51]

Evaluate the sharing of benefits: At appraisal and during supervision,[52] the WBG should systematically estimate the distribution of project benefits among different stakeholder groups (government at different levels, private companies, and local communities), evaluate its sensitivity to different scenarios, and discuss the acceptability of benefit-sharing with key stakeholder groups.

Recommendation 3: Engage the Stakeholders

Often in collaboration with other organizations, the WBG has brought together diverse stakeholders in extractive industries to address issues at the local, national, regional, and global levels. The WBG's convening role has been actively sought and has been significant because of its access to all stakeholders, private and public development experience, and ongoing involvement with project investment and technical assistance in the sector. But the WBG has addressed some areas inadequately—notably governance and revenue management. The WBG's performance in these areas can be enhanced by improving consultation with stakeholders, including local communities, and by systematically and transparently reporting on key sustainability indicators. Such an approach also is likely to raise standards and practices of the sector as a whole.

Update policy framework: In consultation with its stakeholders, the WBG should periodically adjust its policy framework for extractive industries to ensure that it remains up-to-date with evolving industry practice. It should resolve remaining inconsistencies, such as those between requirements for different mine types (such as funding for mine closure), onshore versus offshore oil projects, dam safety, and involuntary resettlement. It should address identified gaps, such as those related to consultation and disclosure, community development, social issues of mine closure, security, hazardous materials management, acid rock drainage, gas flaring, and transportation of oil.[53] It should also recognize the expanding awareness of the human rights dimension of WBG policies and projects and explore possible avenues for addressing the issues, especially where it lags industry best practices, such as regarding site security.

Promote disclosure of fiscal revenues from EI: The WBG should vigorously pursue country- and industry-wide disclosure of government revenues from EI and related contractual arrangements (such as production-sharing agreements, concession, and privatization terms).[54] The Bank should work toward and support disclosure of EI revenues and their use in resource-rich countries. IFC and MIGA also should strongly encourage (and consider requiring) their private sector clients to publish their payments to governments.

Develop and monitor sustainability indicators: Together with other stakeholders, the

WBG should develop indicators of economic, social, and environmental sustainability,[55] establish baseline data, provide for adequate monitoring over the life of the project, and report and evaluate the results during supervision and in project completion reports. The WBG also should encourage more independent outside monitoring, ideally using local capacity (which may have to be developed).

Increase local community participation: The WBG should support enhanced community consultation and participation throughout the life cycle of EI projects. The WBG should help countries to increase involvement by local communities in EI decisionmaking processes and ongoing consultation throughout the project life cycle, including closure.

Introduction

This paper presents the response of the Managements of the World Bank, IFC, and MIGA to a four-volume evaluation of the World Bank Group's (WBG's) activities in the extractive industries (EI)—oil, gas, and mining—by their respective independent evaluation units, the Operations Evaluation Department, Operations Evaluation Group, and Operations Evaluation Unit (OED, OEG, and OEU).[56] The evaluation was completed in June 2003, and was considered at a meeting of the Committee on Development Effectiveness (CODE) on July 9, 2003. At that meeting, Executive Directors agreed that Management should delay its response to the evaluation pending the receipt of the report of an independent Extractive Industries Review (EIR) consultation. The EIR report has now been received and a draft Management Response to it has been prepared.

A Thorough and Timely Review. Management welcomes the joint evaluation report. It provides a thoughtful and thorough review of the WBG's activities in EI. A particular contribution of the evaluation was its careful assessment of the impact of WBG activities through a review of a wide range of IBRD/IDA, IFC, and MIGA projects, which included country and project visits in many cases. The report makes an important contribution to understanding the development issues that are key for the WBG's activities in the sector, provides a valuable reference source, and offers a comprehensive set of recommendations that can help guide future WBG activities in EI. It is especially timely because attaining the Millennium Development Goals (MDGs) in the poorest countries is a pressing challenge that will require a substan-

tial commitment of resources by the international community. In many developing countries, especially those in sub-Saharan Africa, well-managed development of natural resource endowments can make a vital contribution toward reducing poverty and attaining the MDGs.

OED/OEG/OEU Findings

The joint evaluation report shows that, on balance, WBG activities in the EI sector have added value and have contributed to the development of the countries concerned. Indeed, EI projects have performed at least as well as projects in other sectors: nearly 80 percent of IBRD/IDA's EI projects have been at least moderately satisfactory. IFC's and MIGA's operations in support of private sector activities in EI were as successful as other operations in their development outcome and financial performance dimensions, despite the fact that EI investments were typically in more difficult country environments. Against this background, OED/OEG/OEU's independent evaluation lays out specific areas for attention and provides important perspectives on key issues for each institution and for the WBG as a whole with regard to its support for EI development.

Summary of Key Messages. Management has noted the following key messages from OED/OEG/OEU's independent evaluation:
- Extractive industries have contributed to sustainable development when projects met appropriate economic and environmental criteria.
- The private sector is usually the most appropriate vehicle for new investment.
- The WBG's support for EI projects has generally been effective.

- The WBG has added value in the environmental and social aspects of its projects.
- The WBG social and environmental policies and experience with their implementation have been useful to others and have helped set industry standards.
- The WBG should remain engaged across the whole of the EI sector, in support both of governments and of private sector investment.
- In a number of important areas the WBG can improve its performance and help ensure that its EI activities make a more effective contribution to sustainable development.

Areas of Overlap with EIR. As was expected, the EIR covered many of the issues raised by OED/OEG/OEU, although with different emphases. Notably, the EIR is more broad-ranging in its coverage of human rights and governance issues and global environmental concerns. The Management Response to the EIR thus complements the Management comments presented below and provides a wider context for the WBG's strategy.

Management Comments

This section sets out Management comments on the WBG's strategy, project implementation issues, and approach to partnerships with sector and project stakeholders—the three broad categories of recommendations in the OED/OEG/OEU evaluation report. Management broadly accepts the recommendations of the report in these areas and has already begun moving to implement them. Complementing the comments in this section, the Annex provides detailed responses to the specific recommendations of the overall report and of the individual OED, OEG, and OEU components.

Other Work Under Way. In some cases, the precise nature of the ultimate WBG response will depend on the outcomes of other processes now under way, such as IFC's revision of its safeguard policies and guidelines, and its review of its disclosure policy. In other areas, such as the recommendation that the WBG should give increased attention to the human rights dimensions of activities benefiting from its support,

Management proposes to wait for the outcomes of ongoing IBRD/IDA and IFC reviews of this issue. However, in the case of EI-specific issues such as, for example, use of security forces to protect private EI project sites, Management proposes to move now to establish appropriate WBG requirements.

World Bank Group's Strategy

The OED/OEG/OEU evaluation, the EIR consultation process and reports, and other recent documents,[57] constitute a major body of work that reviews trends, issues, and the role of the WBG in the EI sector and provides the foundation for the WBG's strategy in the sector. The OED/OEG/OEU evaluation, in particular, emphasizes that the WBG should take a broader, more integrated approach to its activities in EI that should (a) address the ultimate impacts of projects in terms of how the revenues from projects are used for poverty reduction and economic and social development; (b) ensure that Country Assistance Strategies (CASs) for resource-rich countries explicitly address the sector's economywide linkages and focus on policy and institutional capacity development; and (c) continue to support private sector development and environmental sustainability. Across all of these activities, OED/OEG/OEU recommends that WBG involvement should be guided by governance capacity at the sector and national levels.

Sector Contribution to Development Goals and WBG Role. For many developing countries, especially the poorest countries that risk failing to reach the MDGs, the EI are a valuable asset that can and should generate some of the resources that are urgently needed to spur poverty reduction and support economic and social development. Because of the important promise that EIs hold for the economic and social development of many poor countries and because each of the WBG's constituent institutions (IBRD/IDA, IFC, and MIGA) can add substantial value in this process, all of the WBG institutions will aim to remain engaged in EI development by providing financing, technical assistance, and analytic and policy advice in line with their respective mandates and specializations. As developing countries succeed in reducing poverty, their people will increase their consumption of goods and services that are produced with EI inputs, enjoying greater warmth, light, and mobility because of their access to modern sources of energy.

Sector Development Vision Based on Private Sector Financing. In most country circumstances, the appropriate sector development model will continue to be one based mainly on private enterprises, in which all or most investments are financed by private investors and projects operate within an appropriate framework of government oversight to ensure maximum contribution to the sustainable development of affected communities and the country. However, the WBG will support appropriate public sector projects. Overall levels of WBG financing are likely to be broadly in line with those of recent years, that have accounted for less than 5 percent of total WBG financing and 3 percent of investments in EI in developing countries. The WBG can and should help advance improved industrywide approaches to environmental and social practice, making an impact well beyond the modest investments that benefit from the WBG's support. To enhance its effectiveness in this regard, the WBG will leverage its impact by establishing partnerships with stakeholders and supporting demonstration projects that test new standards and approaches.

Emphases in WBG Activities. Because in most countries much of the investment for EI development can be mobilized from the private sector, IBRD/IDA's emphasis will be on helping governments create appropriate policy frameworks and build capacity for improved sector management. Financing of public sector extractive industry investments is likely to remain rare. In IFC and MIGA, support for private sector investment will focus on local, regional, and smaller companies (including service companies), gas, and local energy supply projects. Support for larger projects will be concentrated where WBG involvement can make a significant contribution to sustainability. In all of its operations, the WBG will work with project sponsors

to help encourage and facilitate broader and more sustainable development impacts at the community level.

An Integrated Approach. Management agrees that the WBG needs to take an integrated view of its activities in EI. This will require as a starting point that, in all the projects that the WBG supports, Management will always consider their ultimate impact on communities, the environment, and the macro economy. Management will exercise selectivity in this regard: for each project for which WBG support is proposed, there should be a strong case for WBG involvement and a demonstrable value-added in terms of enhanced sustainable impact. In addition, whenever possible, the WBG will seek to actively engage with countries to help them address their EI issues, even when the WBG is not engaged in EI specifically. Management also agrees that for all its activities, governance issues and risks need to be taken into account during project design and appraisal.

Criteria for Engagement. The overriding objective of WBG engagement in EI is to promote poverty reduction through sustainable development. IBRD/IDA, IFC, and MIGA will refocus on this objective in their work on project design, appraisal, supervision, and reporting. In selecting and implementing projects, the WBG will be guided by its safeguard policies and guidelines, good practice approaches, and its best judgment. While limiting WBG support for EI development would not serve the interests of WBG clients, the design and implementation of projects in EI need to be fully informed by the national, local, and sector governance risks. The assessments of these risks and, where appropriate, measures to address them will be an integral part of the criteria the WBG will use to determine the extent and form of its involvement.

Focus on Governance at the Country Level. As detailed in the Annex, Management will sharpen its focus on governance issues and risks in countries that are heavily dependent on EI. In particular, CASs for such countries should identify and consider how best to address key

EI issues, including related governance issues, and should also provide an overall framework for any WBG activities in the EI sector. Management's proposed approach is to adopt a two-tier classification of countries to recognize differences in terms of resource dependency and focus attention on the most resource-dependent countries where improvement in governance promises to have the largest development impact.[58]

Mitigation of Governance Risks. In large projects, the WBG will require that specific measures be put in place to address the risks that revenues will not be well used. For smaller projects, WBG's appraisal and decision processes will evaluate and report on the governance risks to projects; if they are high and cannot be adequately mitigated, the WBG will not support the project. Governance risks are more likely to be acceptable in EI projects that generate small fiscal revenues. In some instances, WBG support will be warranted even in weak governance environments, if projects are expected to generate real benefits.

Sequencing of WBG Assistance. OED/OEG/OEU raised concerns about the sequencing of governance capacity building and emphasized the importance of addressing capacity weaknesses at the sector and national levels. While Management agrees that governance capacity building, which is a priority for the WBG, can be an uncertain and lengthy process for which the risks need to be weighed and mitigated to the extent possible, the WBG also needs to be able to make judgments based on the specific circumstances of the country and the project, as well as likely development outcomes with and without its engagement. This judgment will be guided by analysis of a country's economic policies and institutions, evaluation of quantitative and qualitative indicators of governance capacity, and assessment of the performance of ongoing WBG and IMF-supported programs. When expectations about project outcomes and decisions about WBG support depend on such a judgment, Management will lay out clearly the rationale for its proposed approach.

Resource Implications. As was stated above, the overall level of WBG activities in EI is not expected to change materially from current levels; new financing commitments in support of projects should remain in line with recent experience and will be concentrated in IFC and MIGA. However, the focus of activities will shift in accordance with the priorities described in para. 11 and in response to changes in country demands reflected in new CASs, which set out the amount of financing commitments to a country in view of competing alternatives and priorities for WBG engagement. As CASs for resource-dependent countries focus increasingly on EI issues, WBG activities in EI could increase—especially analytic and advisory services, economic and sector work, and TA operations to address, for example, management of EI revenues and related governance issues. Such activities will be coordinated with (or often directly integrated into) related initiatives in support of improved economic policymaking and strengthened public financial accountability and management.

Shift Toward Environmental and Social Development Expertise. As IFC and MIGA have increased their focus on environmental and social issues in recent years, there has been a significant increase in staff with skills in those areas. In IBRD/IDA, the number of environmental and social staff working on policy and technical issues has also increased in recent years. The major shifts have largely occurred, but stronger focus on ensuring sustainable impacts will require appropriate resources for the WBG project teams in particular EI projects. Project teams will often require earlier and more extended involvement of environmental and social specialists to ensure implementation of safeguard policies; resources for enhanced disclosure and community consultations; and resources for appraising and supervising value-added activities to increase local benefits and participation in projects. Whether some or all of the additional costs can be recovered from clients will depend on the institution and the project. Management will ensure that project budgets are based on an evaluation of these factors and will make realistic allowances for the costs of staff involved in more detailed preparations and supervision.

Project Implementation Issues

OED/OEG/OEU offer challenging recommendations to enhance the development impact of WBG operations in support of EI development. Because the vast majority of recent and future projects are or will be supported by IFC and MIGA, in line with the WBG's strategic emphasis on supporting private sector development, the following sections are concerned mostly with recent developments and ongoing initiatives in IFC and MIGA.

Screening and Classification of Projects.

Management is aware that the implementation of WBG projects could be improved by carrying out more effective screening and classification of projects, involving environmentalists and social specialists throughout the project life, enhancing the reporting of results from projects, and evaluating the sharing of benefits from projects more explicitly. OED's finding that some IBRD/IDA projects were incorrectly classified and consequently inappropriately supervised reflects, in part, the process of significant change in the WBG's adoption and implementation of safeguard policies and guidelines over the period covered by the evaluation. With the lessons of experience and proposed revision of guidelines, these problems are being addressed. The close involvement of environmental and social specialists in EI projects through the project life cycle is a key part of WBG engagement in these projects. Management's clear objective will be to ensure that the excellent levels of compliance noted by OEG in some areas of the IFC's EI activities become the norm for all WBG activities in the sector.

Growing Contribution from Environmental and Social Specialists in IFC and MIGA. In

IFC and MIGA, which account for most of the new EI investment projects financed by the WBG, the resources devoted to environmental and social due diligence and additional work with clients have increased considerably over the last 10 years. In both IFC and MIGA, Management is taking steps to ensure that environmental and social specialists are more productively integrated with investment staff. While maintaining an independent quality assurance function, IFC has also begun to mainstream environmental and social responsibility so that investment departments see it as a core part of their activities and responsibilities. In May 2004, MIGA added environmental and social staff to its risk management staff, so that a more holistic view will now be possible in assessing projects.

Sustainability Initiatives in IFC. IFC's overall corporate sustainability initiative has increased staff's focus on sustainability issues. Most EI sector staff have now taken part in specialized sustainability training to enhance their awareness of issues and best practice. The contribution that projects can make in the environmental and social arenas, including through enhanced local development, has become a key component of IFC's business in EI. Enhanced analysis of the benefit sharing, which will be part of project design, will further increase this focus and will be applied in IBRD/IDA and MIGA as well. However, the WBG will need to carefully balance attention to social and environmental dimensions against the extra burden such attention imposes on developing country clients and the additional supervision and appraisal costs it entails. IFC's EI activities already account for a disproportionate share of IFC's budget for environmental and social specialists. EI operations are also intensive users of resources for other development impact-enhancing activities, such as small and medium enterprise and corporate governance initiatives.

Recent Changes in MIGA. Management underscores the important changes that have taken place in MIGA since May 1999, when the Board approved MIGA's own specific environmental assessment and disclosure policies and procedures, and May 2002, when MIGA adopted its own interim issue-specific safeguard policies. Although MIGA's clients have found these safeguard policies to be helpful, Management rec-

ognizes that further improvements can be made as WBG views evolve.

Revision and Updating of MIGA Safeguard Policies. Management has made a serious effort in the past five years to address a range of widely acknowledged difficulties in determining how to apply safeguard policies to private sector investors and what is meant by compliance with safeguard policies (see, for example, recent CAO reports on the subject).[59] Differences among experienced professionals in interpreting and implementing safeguard policies can pose a serious challenge, one that is of particular concern to MIGA because of the unique legal and financial implications of denying a claim or canceling a guarantee for noncompliance. MIGA staff will work with IFC staff on updating IFC's safeguard policies, and will take the opportunity to clarify safeguard policy applicability and implementation issues in MIGA-supported operations. Once IFC's updating process is completed, MIGA will revise and update its own safeguard policies in an equivalent manner, in line with the commitment MIGA Management made to the Board in May 2002.

Partnerships for Wider Reach

OED/OEG/OEU recommended a number of ways to enhance the impact of WBG activities on industrywide practice, well beyond the small number of operations that the WBG supports directly. Management agrees with OED/OEG/OEU recommendations in this regard. The WBG will seek to use its international convening power more effectively by making its safeguard policies and guidelines more relevant and accessible, promoting the disclosure of fiscal revenues, developing and monitoring indicators of sustainable development with other stakeholders, and increasing local community participation in projects through meaningful consultation throughout project life.

Setting Industry Standards in Partnership with Others. A number of important initiatives are under way that will help enhance WBG's impact on industry practice. First, IFC has begun the two-year process of revising its safeguard

policies and guidelines, and is giving priority to EI-related issues. For example, revised *Precious Minerals Mining Guidelines* were available in draft for public comment from July 2004. The updated safeguards will be key for sustaining the catalytic role that IFC has assumed in its important partnership with the Equator Banks. Second, IBRD/IDA's proposed revised policy covering Indigenous Peoples (OP 4.10) is expected to be considered by its Board by end 2004, and will contain provisions to help ensure that Indigenous Peoples benefit from development. Finally, the WBG will work in partnerships with governments, industry and civil society to advance best practice and contribute to the sustainable impact of EI development more broadly in initiatives such as the Global Gas Flaring Reduction Partnership, which set voluntary global standards for addressing gas flaring.

Growing Emphasis on Revenue Transparency. Transparency about government revenues and expenditures generally is an important dimension of the macroeconomic policy dialogue between borrowing governments and IBRD/IDA; in this respect, a priority area for IBRD/IDA assistance is to help increase government capacity and accountability. In the area of transparency about EI revenue, the WBG has joined with the UK Department for International Development (DfID) and other partners to support the Extractive Industries Transparency Initiative (EITI), which aims to promote EI revenue transparency at the country level. At the project level, the WBG will now require disclosure of EI revenues and the key terms of relevant contracts for all large projects that benefit from its support; for smaller projects, in two years the WBG will require disclosure of material EI-related payments to governments except when there is a compelling reason to not do so.

Reporting on Outcomes. Management recognizes the need for enhanced reporting on the outcomes of WBG activities in EI and its rationale for engagement. In IFC's ongoing review of its disclosure policy, Management will establish new requirements for investors to make more information about projects available to communities, will enhance the reporting on IFC activities in the sector, and provide for greater disclosure of its rationale for supporting new EI projects. As a part of this process, IBRD/IDA and IFC will continue to work with other stakeholders to develop meaningful, consistent indicators of the contribution of EI to sustainable development.

Focus on Community Involvement. Appropriate consultation with people who will be affected by projects is a core WBG requirement for sustainable development, especially for EI projects that take place in remote areas and may have relatively large effects on local communities. The WBG proposes to adopt use of a process of free, prior and informed consultation with affected communities that leads to broad acceptance by the affected community of the project as a condition for its involvement and will work with investors to promote best practice in this respect, and to generally enhance the involvement of and benefits to communities in the context of EI developments that benefit from WBG support.

Conclusions

Altogether, the WBG has embarked upon a fundamental change in its approach to EI investments. Its past mode of operation presumed that expected overall potential benefits to countries (energy resource development and revenue generation) justified new investments. In its new mode of operation, concerns about the ultimate developmental impacts, including the management of revenues generated by EI projects and the specific, realizable benefits to communities, are regarded as the starting point for discussions of WBG involvement. In moving forward, Management will continue to encourage coordination among activities in IBRD/IDA, IFC, and MIGA, with each institution serving its respective clients, pursuing objectives in line with its mandate, and using its own business models and processes. Coordination among the three institutions has already benefited from preparation of this joint Management Response and will continue to be facilitated by the joint IBRD/IDA/IFC Oil, Gas, Mining and Chemicals

Department which ensures strong links between IBRD/IDA and IFC, and by the Energy and Mining Sector Board, which ensures links to Regional and country programs and MIGA. At the country level, enhanced attention to EI issues in the CAS will serve to strengthen coordination with the WBG's country assistance programs.

Tracking Progress in Implementation of the New Approach. Management expects to measure implementation of the comprehensive set of reforms implied by the new approach as follows:

Short-Term Indicators – within one year

a. New guidance and processes that address EI-specific safeguard issues such as mine closure/decommissioning; use of security forces; monitoring and disclosure of environmental, social, and economic impacts; transparency requirements for new investments; gas flaring; acid rock drainage; and HIV/AIDS.

b. New guidelines and processes for disclosure of information about WBG-supported EI projects and about activities in EI, including development of sustainability indicators.

c. Development of a database for all IFC projects that indicates position regarding all key sustainability indicators (including mine closure/decommissioning plans, safeguard compliance, gas flaring, and use of security forces).

d. Clearer guidelines for WBG environmental categorization of projects.

e. CASs for resource-rich countries and countries with significant resources start to address relevant EI-related issues.

Three-Year Indicators

f. The extent to which new CASs have dealt with extractive industry issues in resource-rich countries and countries with significant resources.

g. Effective implementation of partnership initiatives (including GGFR, CASM, and EITI) involving civil society, industry, and governments, and outcomes of these partnerships in terms of contributing to the development of sector best practice.

h. Revenue transparency improvement through effective implementation of programs in participating countries under the EITI.

i. Support for sustainable new private sector EI investment at average levels broadly comparable to those of the recent past.

j. Continuing levels of IBRD/IDA financing in line with recent average with a focus on:

    i. Oil and gas: environmental management, TA (especially for transparency, revenue management), and gas industry development.

    ii. Mining: coal sector restructuring, TA, and mining sector policy reform.

    iii. Capacity building for social and environmental monitoring in both sectors

Management proposes to report on progress on its activities in EI every year. It also proposes to set up a working level advisory group with representative of governments, industry, civil society, and other parts of the WBG to provide inputs and perspectives on the WBG's activities in EI.

Annex	Recommendations of the Joint OED/OEG/OEU Evaluation and Management Response Matrix

A. Recommendations of the Main Report

Recommendation of the Main Report of the Joint OED/OEG/OEU Evaluation	Management Response

1 Formulate a Sector Strategy

1a The WBG needs to design and implement a sectoral strategy that closely integrates resource extraction with sustainable development through the effective management of EI revenues in support of developmental priorities and the reliable mitigation of adverse environmental and social impacts. Where macro and sectoral governance are weak, the WBG's assistance should focus on strengthening governance. In such cases, the WBG should carefully assess and report on the risks that EI fiscal revenues may not be used for development priorities. The WBG should not support significant sector expansion unless it can adequately mitigate these risks. Where macro governance is sound but sectoral governance is weak, the WBG should focus on improving sectoral governance, and should only support the sector in conjunction with adequate provisions to overcome sectoral governance weaknesses.

Management accepts this recommendation. The overall approach to EI activities, as set out in this Management Response and in responses to individual recommendations, provides a framework for the WBG's activities in EI that gives a central place to promotion of good governance and increased transparency. Management has identified indicators of implementation progress for its strategy, and it will monitor them. Management will strengthen its efforts to promote use of fiscal revenues for development priorities and to mitigate risks due to poor governance. The ultimate objectives are sustainable impacts at the local, national and global levels. The appraisal reports for new EI projects in countries with weak governance will clearly assess the risks that EI fiscal revenues may not be used for development priorities. See also responses to OED 1a and OEG 1b. Overall, the level of activities of the three institutions in EI is not expected to increase materially and will not demand additional resources. Resources are expected to continue to be allocated to EI activities through the country and regional resource allocation processes on the basis of country and regional priorities. Trust funds and partnerships will continue to be an important source of additional resources for EI activities, especially for programs outside the scope of single-country programs and specific projects.

Address EI Issues in CASs

1b For all resource-rich countries the WBG should explicitly address extractive industries in the CASs. The CAS should explicitly discuss the sector's current and potential contribution to sustainable development (for example, the importance of government revenues, their management, distribution, and use for development priorities) and reference the underlying governance assessment. This should guide future project design, facilitate monitoring and evalua-

Management accepts this recommendation and has developed a two-tiered approach to improving the focus of CASs on relevant EI issues. This approach uses a higher cut off for resource-rich countries (more than 50 percent of government revenues derived from EI) than that used by the Evaluation (15% of exports) so as to exclude relatively less EI-dependent but to include non-exporting countries. With limited staff and country resources and competing priorities, the WBG will thus focus on the most resource-dependent countries and on countries where it can have the most impact. The proposed approach already targets more than 50 countries (with sub-

(continued)
**Recommendation of the Main Report
of the Joint OED/OEG/OEU Evaluation**

Management Response

tion, and provide an agreed framework for WBG-wide coordination and collaboration in the EI sector. The different agencies of the WBG should routinely work together to enhance the development impacts of EI projects, for example in the form of public-private partnerships with respect to community development programs.

stantial overlap with the evaluation list). CASs for resource-rich countries will be expected to address relevant EI issues and related governance issues. In countries with substantial resources (where 30-50 percent of government revenues or exports are from EI), the CAS will be expected to identify key EI sector issues and whether and how IBRD/IDA will be involved in addressing them. This does not rule out CAS discussion on EI issues in other countries where they are important, and the thresholds and guidelines will be reviewed in the light of experience. Where possible, IBRD/IDA, IFC, and MIGA will work together as recommended by OED/OEG/OEU. Moreover, IBRD/IDA will encourage resource-rich countries and countries with substantial resources to address relevant EI issues in their own overall development strategies, such as PRSPs. The WBG institutions will work pro-actively in the EI sector to identify opportunities for cooperation. COC will continue effective implementation of major partnership initiatives such as the Gas Flaring Reduction Partnership, CASM, and the EITI, and report on their progress.

Governance

1c Promote Governance Improvements: The Bank should compensate for the lower level of lending that may be appropriate for resource-rich countries with weak macro and sectoral governance, by devoting greater management attention and administrative budget for advisory and analytical activities aimed at improving the policy, institutional, and governance framework for EI. This would enable the Bank to establish and maintain continuity of engagement and facilitate responding quickly to opportunities for assistance when they arise.

Management accepts this recommendation. Where the WBG is not involved in financing operations but where EI issues are important and where governance is weak, the WBG will aim to devote greater resources to technical assistance and analytic and advisory activities that can, for example, help countries manage their resource industries more effectively, including addressing relevant broader policy, institutional, and governance issues. The CAS for resource-rich countries with weak macro and sectoral performance will identify the needs for TA in this area, and will discuss whether and how IBRD/IDA should be involved in meeting these needs. Implementation of this recommendation may require additional IBRD/IDA administrative budget resources for certain countries. Including its activities relating to transparency, over the next three years, Management will aim to increase the level of nonlending activities aimed at policy improvements compared to the past three.

Recommendation of the Main Report of the Joint OED/OEG/OEU Evaluation	Management Response

Support Private Sector Development and Environmental Sustainability

1d In all countries, the World Bank Group should continue its support to close uneconomic mines, reform and privatize state-owned enterprises, and mitigate pre-existing environmental and social problems.

Management accepts this recommendation. There remains an important role for IBRD/IDA to assist governments to restructure their mining and coal industries, including helping to close uneconomic coal mines and to mitigate social and environmental problems. Much of the world's oil industry is government-owned and, where appropriate, IBRD/IDA will consider supporting government efforts to improve the effectiveness of these operations, where governments have ruled out privatization for the foreseeable future.

1e Where appropriate, the World Bank Group should help integrate artisanal and small-scale mining (ASM) with the formal sector and internalize their environmental and social impacts, while at the same time creating alternative employment opportunities and supporting the consolidation of ASM activities for greater efficiencies and economies of scale.

IBRD/IDA will continue to work with others, particularly through CASM, to develop effective approaches and best practices. Given country differences, the CAS for countries where ASM is important will be expected to consider approaches that are integrated effectively into overall country and poverty reduction strategies. Clearly an important component of any overall approach is to create better opportunities for those involved in other parts of the economy. COC will aim over a three-year period to develop three or more operations that aim to integrate ASM into the broader economy and/or improve its social, environmental, or economic outcomes.

2 Improve Project Screening and Monitoring

2a The World Bank Group should provide clearer and more consistent guidance for the categorization of projects, the identification of applicable safeguards at the initial project screening, the appropriate scope and nature of the EA instruments, and the reporting and evaluation of safeguards implementation. This needs to be followed up through the entire implementation framework, from good practice guidelines to appropriate monitoring and training.

WBG will provide updated guidance for the categorization of projects concerned with EI. This guidance will address project screening and the use of appropriate assessment instruments. Sectoral approaches will be used for periodic reporting and evaluation of safeguard aspects of EI projects. This information will be disseminated through periodic training activities for staff from the WBG, clients, and other parties.

(continued)
**Recommendation of the Main Report
of the Joint OED/OEG/OEU Evaluation**

Management Response

Involve Specialists Throughout

2b The World Bank Group should provide adequate resources and incentives for the participation of qualified environmental and social specialists at the preparation, appraisal and supervision of all projects that are likely to have adverse impacts. This will ensure that such impacts are adequately addressed through the upstream design of appropriate mitigation strategies or project alternatives, as well as through the retrofit of timely remediation measures should unexpected impacts materialize during project implementation.

This is agreed and is dealt with more specifically in the responses to recommendations of OED (2b), OEG (2a, 2b) and OEU (1b, 2a, and 3c) below.

Enhance Reporting of Results

2c The Bank should strengthen reporting of its results by ensuring that project completion reports include an ex post economic rate of return or net present value or, where that is not feasible, a cost effectiveness analysis to determine whether the project represented the least-cost solution to attain its objectives. IFC should develop and use a reporting template for environmental and socio-economic sustainability indicators, building on industry initiatives. MIGA needs to adopt more standardized and timely reporting mechanisms on environmental and social safeguards compliance and ex post development outcomes. The WBG should prepare completion reports for every significant non-lending/guarantee issuance activity.

Management accepts this recommendation, as is detailed in the response to the recommendations of OED (2c) and OEG (2c). As noted in responses to the OEU recommendations (see 1a, 2a, and 2d below), MIGA is taking steps to implement more standardized and timely reporting mechanisms on safeguard compliance and development outcomes, especially of Category A projects. Management will ensure that an "activity completion summary" or equivalent for all significant nonlending EI activities in IBRD/IDA, IFC, and MIGA is prepared.

Evaluate the Sharing of Benefits

2d Evaluate the sharing of benefit: At appraisal and during supervision, the WBG should systematically estimate the distribution of project benefits among different stakeholder groups (government at different levels, private companies, and local communities), evaluate its sensitivity to different scenarios, and discuss the acceptability of benefit-sharing with key stakeholder groups.

Management agrees that an analysis of the distribution of the benefits of extractive industries developments should be part of the WBG's project evaluation and supervision work. The appraisal report for EI projects will be expected to assess the sensitivity of distribution to different assumptions about key project variables. The extent of discussions of benefit-sharing with key stakeholder groups will need to be considered carefully in the project and country context, given the role of governments (and sometimes constitutions) in setting the distribution of EI revenues.

Recommendation of the Main Report of the Joint OED/OEG/OEU Evaluation	Management Response

3 Update Policy Framework

3a In consultation with its stakeholders, the WBG should periodically adjust its policy framework for extractive industries to ensure that it remains up-to-date with evolving industry practice. It should resolve remaining inconsistencies such as those between requirements for different mine types (such as funding for mine closure), onshore versus offshore oil projects, safety of dams, and involuntary resettlement. It should address identified gaps such as those related to consultation and disclosure, community development, social issues of mine closure, security, hazardous materials management, acid rock drainage, gas flaring, and transportation of oil. It should also recognize the expanding awareness of the human rights dimension of WBG policies and projects, and explore possible avenues for addressing the issues, especially where it lags industry best practice such as, for example, regarding site security.

Agreed. See responses to recommendations of OED (3a), OEG (3a), and OEU (3c) below.

Promote Disclosure of Revenues from EI

3b The WBG should vigorously pursue country- and industry wide disclosure of government revenues from EI and related contractual arrangements (such as production sharing agreements, concession and privatization terms). The Bank should work toward and support disclosure of EI revenues and their use in resource-rich countries. IFC and MIGA should also strongly encourage (and consider requiring) their private sector clients to publish their payments to governments.

Management accepts this recommendation because increased transparency about resource revenues is an important step toward better governance and the use of resources in resource-rich countries. IBRD/IDA is now actively supporting the EITI led by DfID, and in this context, is working in a number of pilot countries. In addition, the WBG will support other initiatives as appropriate, and will work for greater transparency of revenues and expenditures within its country programs. In the context of new EI investment operations, WBG support will be conditional on transparency commitments by investors. Disclosure of payments to governments will be required effective immediately for major projects and will be expected for all projects in two years, when appropriate implementation modalities are expected to have been developed and tested under the EITI and similar activities. Over the next three years, IBRD/IDA will aim to complete five or more EITI pilots with countries and will aim to mainstream the approach to revenue transparency more broadly in the WBG.

(continued)
**Recommendation of the Main Report
of the Joint OED/OEG/OEU Evaluation**

Management Response

Develop and Monitor Sustainability Indicators

3c Together with other stakeholders, the World Bank Group should develop indicators of economic, social and environmental sustainability, establish baseline data, provide for adequate monitoring over the life of the project, and report and evaluate the results during supervision and in project completion reports. The World Bank Group should also encourage more independent outside monitoring, ideally using local capacity (that may have to be developed).

Management accepts this recommendation. The WBG will work with stakeholders to define appropriate sustainability indicators that can be used to monitor and report on outcomes. OP 4.01 requires the collection of baseline data. IFC has recently produced a good practice note *(Addressing the Social Dimensions of Private Sector Projects)* that provides guidance on collection of baseline data; a similar exercise is planned for environmental data. These notes can also serve to guide IBRD/IDA and MIGA. The development of independent local capacity for monitoring the impact of EI projects is important. Capacity building within governments is already a key objective of IBRD/IDA activities in the sector. Development of community/civil society capacity can help with project monitoring and can often be considered in the project context. In the case of very large projects (such as in the Chad-Cameroon pipeline or BTC pipeline projects), the creation of independent monitoring groups may be practical and effective, and will be considered. In some cases it may be appropriate to develop local capacity to play a role in such forms of oversight. In addition, see the responses to the recommendations of OEG (2a) and (3c) below.

Increase Local Community Participation

3d The WBG should support enhanced community consultation and participation throughout the life cycle of EI-projects. The WBG should assist countries to increase involvement by local communities in EI decision-making processes, and ongoing consultation throughout the project life cycle, including closure.

Management agrees with this recommendation. Enhanced community consultation and participation in EI projects is a key area of evolving best practice for the WBG. See the response to recommendation of OEG (3d) for details.

B. Recommendations of the OED Evaluation Report

Recommendation of the OED Evaluation   **Management Response**

1   Formulate a Sector Strategy

1a The Bank, together with other members of the WBG needs to design and implement a sector strategy that closely integrates resource extraction with sustainable development through the effective management of EI revenues in support of developmental priorities and the reliable mitigation of adverse environmental and social impacts. Where macro and sectoral governance are weak, the Bank's assistance should focus on strengthening macro and sectoral governance. In such cases, the Bank should carefully assess and report on the risks that fiscal revenues may not be used for development priorities. The Bank should not support significant sector expansion unless it can adequately mitigate these risks. Where macro governance is sound but sectoral governance is weak, the Bank should focus on improving sectoral governance.

Management accepts this recommendation. The overall approach to EI activities, as set out in this Management Response and in responses to individual recommendations, provides a framework for the WBG's activities in EI that gives a central place to promotion of good governance and increased transparency. Management has identified indicators of implementation progress for its strategy, and it will monitor them. Management will strengthen its efforts to promote use of fiscal revenues for development priorities and to mitigate risks due to poor governance. The ultimate objectives are sustainable impacts at the local, national, and global levels. The appraisal reports for new EI projects and relevant sector reforms in countries with weak governance will clearly assess the risks that EI fiscal revenues may not be used for development priorities. See also OEG 1b.

Address EI issues in CASs

1b For all resource-rich countries the Bank should explicitly address extractive industries in the CASs. The CAS should discuss the sector's economy wide linkages (such as the importance of government revenues, their management, and distribution) and reference the underlying governance assessment. This should guide future project design, facilitate monitoring and evaluation, and provide an agreed framework for WBG-wide coordination and collaboration in the EI sector.

Management accepts this recommendation and has developed a two-tiered approach to improving the focus of CASs on relevant EI issues. This approach uses a higher cut off for resource-rich countries(more than 50 percent of government revenues derived from EI) than that used by the evaluation (15% of exports) so as to exclude relatively less EI-dependent but to include non-exporting countries. With limited staff and country resources and competing priorities, the WBG will thus focus on the most resource-dependent countries and on countries where it can have the most impact. The proposed approach already targets more than 50 countries (with substantial overlap with the evaluation list). CASs for resource-rich countries will be expected to address relevant EI issues and related governance issues. In *countries with substantial resources* (where 30-50 percent of government revenues or exports are from EI), the CAS will be expected to identify key EI sector issues and to discuss whether and how IBRD/IDA will be involved in addressing them. This does not rule out CAS discussion of EI issues in other countries where they are important, and the thresholds and guidelines will be reviewed in the light of experience. Where possible, IBRD/IDA, IFC, and MIGA will work together as recommended by

(continued)
Recommendation of the OED Evaluation   **Management Response**

OED/OEG/OEU. Moreover, IBRD/IDA will encourage resource-rich countries to address relevant EI issues in their own overall development strategies, such as PRSPs. The WBG institutions will work proactively in the EI sector to identify opportunities for cooperation, and to develop private-public partnerships. A good-practice note on EI issues will be prepared and disseminated as part of the guidelines for CASs and engagement in LICUS.

Governance

1c Promote Governance Improvements: The Bank should compensate for the lower level of lending that may be appropriate for resource-rich countries with weak macro and sectoral governance by devoting greater management attention and administrative budget for advisory and analytical activities aimed at improving the policy, institutional, and governance framework for EI. This would enable the Bank to establish and maintain continuity of engagement and facilitate a quick response to opportunities for assistance when they arise.

Management accepts this recommendation. Where the WBG is not involved in financing operations but where EI issues are important and where governance is weak, the WBG will aim to devote greater resources to technical assistance and analytical and advisory activities that can, for example, help countries manage their resource industries more effectively, including addressing relevant broader policy, institutional, and governance issues. The CAS for resource-rich countries with weak macro and sectoral performance will identify the needs for TA in this area, and will discuss whether and how the WBG should be involved in meeting these needs. Implementation of this recommendation may require additional administrative budget resources for certain countries. Over the next three years, Management will aim to increase the level of nonlending activities aimed at policy improvements (including those related to revenue transparency) compared to the past three.

Support Private Sector Development and Environmental Sustainability

1d In all countries, the Bank should be ready to support the closure of uneconomic mines, privatization of state-owned enterprises, and mitigation of pre-existing environmental and social problems.

Management accepts this recommendation, as there remains an important role for IBRD/IDA to assist governments to restructure their mining and coal industries, including helping to close uneconomic coal mines, and mitigating social and environmental problems. Much of the world's oil industry is in state hands and, where appropriate, the Management will consider whether IBRD/IDA should become involved, for example, to help governments improve the effectiveness of these operations, where governments have ruled out privatization for the foreseeable future.

Recommendation of the OED Evaluation	Management Response
1e Where appropriate, the Bank should help integrate artisanal and small-scale mining (ASM) with the formal sector and internalize their environmental and social impacts, while at the same time creating alternative employment opportunities and supporting the consolidation of ASM activities for greater efficiencies and economies of scale.	IBRD/IDA will continue to work with others, particularly through CASM, to develop effective approaches and best practices. Given country differences, the CAS for countries where ASM is important will be expected to consider approaches that are integrated effectively into overall country and poverty reduction strategies. Clearly an important component of any overall approach is to create better opportunities for those involved in other parts of the economy. COC will aim over a three-year period to develop three or more operations that aim to integrate ASM into the broader economy and/or improve its social, environmental, or economic outcomes.

2 Improve Upstream Project Screening

2a The Bank should provide clearer and more consistent guidance for the categorization of sectoral adjustment and technical assistance projects, the identification of applicable safeguards at the initial project screening, the appropriate scope and nature of the EA instruments, and the reporting and evaluation of safeguards implementation. This needs to be followed up through the entire implementation framework, from good practice guidelines to appropriate monitoring and training.	IBRD/IDA will provide updated guidance for the categorization of sectoral adjustment and technical assistance projects concerned with EI. This guidance will address project screening and the use of appropriate assessment instruments. Sectoral approaches will be used for periodic reporting and evaluation of safeguard aspects of EI projects. This information will be disseminated through periodic training activities for staff from the Bank, clients, and other parties.

Provide for Adequate Specialist Involvement

2b The Bank should strengthen the implementation of its safeguard policies by providing adequate resources for the participation of qualified environmental and social specialists at the preparation, appraisal, and supervision of all projects that are likely to have adverse impacts. This will ensure that such impacts are adequately addressed through the upstream design of appropriate mitigation strategies or project alternatives, as well as through the retrofit of timely remediation measures should unexpected impacts materialize during project implementation.	Is it agreed that project teams should have effective participation of environmental and social specialists at all stages of the project process, particularly for projects likely to have adverse impacts. Project budgets will need to be set adequately to ensure this.

(continued)
Recommendation of the OED Evaluation   **Management Response**

Enhance Reporting of Results

2c   The Bank should strengthen the implementation of its completion reporting requirements by (i) ensuring that project completion reports include the calculation of an ex-post economic rate of return or net present value or, where that is not feasible, a cost-effectiveness analysis to determine whether the project represented the least-cost solution to attain its objectives; and (ii) preparing an activity completion summary for every significant non-lending activity.

It is agreed that project completion reports should provide these quantitative estimates of impacts wherever possible, and should state the reasons where this is not possible. An activity completion summary should be prepared for every significant non-lending activity.

Evaluate the Sharing of Benefits

2d   At appraisal and project completion, the Bank should systematically estimate the distribution of project benefits among different stakeholder groups—government at different levels, private companies, and local communities—evaluate its sensitivity to different scenarios, and discuss its acceptability with key stakeholder groups.

Management agrees that distribution of the benefits of extractive industries developments is important. The appraisal and project completion reports for EI projects will be expected to assess the sensitivity of distribution to different project scenarios. The extent of discussions of benefit-sharing with key stakeholder groups will need to be considered carefully in the project and country context, given the role of governments (and sometimes constitutions) in setting the distribution of EI revenues. See also the response to OEG recommendation 2d below.

3   Update Policy Framework

3a   In consultation with its stakeholders, the Bank should periodically adjust its policy framework for extractive industries to ensure that they remain up-to-date with evolving industry practice. It should resolve remaining inconsistencies within the WBG and address identified gaps. It should also recognize the expanding awareness of the human rights dimension of Bank policies and projects, and explore possible avenues for addressing the issues, especially where it lags industry best practice.

In the context of the overall WBG approach to these issues, Management will evaluate and help develop best practice approaches to EI-specific issues. Current opportunities include the ongoing review of IFC safeguard policies, the revision of the IBRD/IDA Indigenous Peoples policy, and the consideration of approaches to human rights by IFC and IBRD/IDA (where a Senior Adviser on human rights has been appointed).

Recommendation of the OED Evaluation	Management Response

Promote Disclosure of Revenues from EI

3b   The Bank should vigorously pursue country- and industry wide disclosure of government revenues from EI and related contractual arrangements (such as production sharing agreements, concession and privatization terms). It should work toward and support disclosure of EI revenues and their use in resource-rich countries.

Management accepts this recommendation because increased transparency about resource revenues is an important step toward better governance and the use of resources in resource-rich countries. IBRD/IDA is now actively supporting the EITI led by DfID, and in this context, is working in a number of pilot countries. In addition, the WBG will support other initiatives as appropriate, and will work for greater transparency of revenues, expenditures, and contracts (where feasible and appropriate), within its country and sector programs. Notably, AAA such as public expenditure reviews and country financial accountability assessments, and related policy dialogue, will be the main vehicles for promoting transparency. In the context of new EI investment operations, WBG support will be conditional on transparency commitments by investors. Disclosure of payments to governments will be required effective immediately for major projects and will be expected for all projects in two years, when appropriate implementation modalities are expected to have been developed and tested under the EITI and similar activities. Over the next three years, Management will aim to complete five or more EITI pilots with countries and will aim to mainstream the approach to revenue transparency more broadly in the WBG.

Define and Monitor Sustainability Indicators

3c   Together with other stakeholders, the Bank should define indicators of economic, social, and environmental sustainability, establish baseline data, provide for adequate monitoring over the life of the project, and report and evaluate on the results during supervision and in project completion reports. The Bank should also encourage more independent outside monitoring, ideally using local capacity (that may have to be developed).

Management accepts this recommendation. The WBG will work with stakeholders to define appropriate sustainability indicators that can be used to monitor and report on outcomes. OP 4.01 requires the collection of baseline data. IFC has recently produced a good practice note (*Addressing the Social Dimensions of Private Sector Projects*) that provides guidance on collection of baseline data; a similar exercise is planned for environmental data. These notes can also serve to guide IBRD/IDA and MIGA. The development of independent local capacity for monitoring the impact of EI projects is important. Capacity building within governments is already a key objective of IBRD/IDA activities in the sector. Development of community/civil society capacity can help with project monitoring and can often be considered in the project context. In the case of very large projects (such as in the Chad-Cameroon pipeline or BTC pipeline projects), the creation of independent monitoring groups may be practical and effective, and will be considered. In some cases it may be appropriate to develop local capacity to play a role in such forms of oversight. In addition, see the responses to the recommendations of OEG (2a) and (3c) below.

(continued)

Recommendation of the OED Evaluation	Management Response

Increase local community participation	
3d The Bank should support enhanced community consultation and participation throughout the life cycle of EI-projects. The Bank should assist countries to increase involvement by local communities in EI decision-making processes, and ongoing consultation throughout the project life cycle, including closure.	Management agrees with this recommendation. Enhanced community consultation and participation in EI projects is a key area of evolving best practice for IBRD/IDA, in line with evolving experience in IFC. See the response to recommendation of OEG (3d) for details.

C. Recommendations of the OEG Evaluation Report

Recommendation of the OEG Evaluation	Management Response

1 **Formulate an Integrated Strategy**	*See response to the Main Report, 1a above.*
1a IFC should work closely with other parts of the WBG to ensure that CASs for resource-rich countries explicitly discuss the EI sector's contribution to sustainable development (e.g., importance of fiscal revenues, their management, distribution, and use for development priorities) and obstacles for enhancing its contribution. The CAS should provide an agreed framework for WBG-wide cooperation, with a particular focus on close interaction between IFC and the World Bank's country departments. IFC and the World Bank should routinely work together to enhance the development impacts of EI projects, for example in the form of public-private partnerships with respect to community development programs. IFC and the WBG should build on existing initiatives such as Business Partners for Development and the Comprehensive Development Framework to enlist the help of other stakeholders, such as the IMF, other bilateral and multilateral institutions, industry and civil society.	IFC Management supports this recommendation, and proposals in this respect are set out in the detailed responses to recommendations of the Main Report and OED reports and in the overall Management Response. IFC will work proactively in the EI sector to identify opportunities for cooperation with IBRD/IDA and MIGA, and to develop private-public partnerships as appropriate in the context of individual projects.

Recommendation of the OEG Evaluation	Management Response
1b Where country governance is weak, increase transparency and address the weaknesses: Together with the World Bank and other stakeholders, IFC should analyze all aspects of country governance quality and the risks that poor governance may detract from sustainable development. In particular, IFC should encourage enhanced transparency and disclosure concerning contractual agreements between investors and governments, the amount of fiscal revenues generated and their distribution. IFC — together with the World Bank and other stakeholders — should encourage such transparency sector wide in the country.	Weak governance can lead to poor oversight of the EI sector and poor management of, and use of revenues from, resource projects. The IFC approach to this issue will be to work with IBRD/IDA to ensure that EI issues are addressed in the CAS (see response to recommendation of the Main Report 1b above) and to generally support IBRD/IDA efforts on transparency initiatives, such as the EITI.

1b *(cont.)* When financing projects whose major expected development contribution is the generation of revenues to governments, IFC should carefully review and discuss the governance risk that these revenues will not be used productively. Where such governance risk is high, and the project's revenues are significant, IFC should work with the government (in partnership with the World Bank and IMF) to put in place mechanisms to reduce this risk, including possibly ring-fencing of project revenue management. For all proposed EI investments, IFC should address these issues in Board Reports.

For significant new projects (typically, those large enough to generate 10 percent or more of host government revenues), IFC will require adequate mitigation measures to be put in place to reduce the risks that revenues will be wasted, and it will require transparency about EI-related payments to governments and the terms of key contracts with governments that are of public interest (such as Host Government Agreements, IGAs). For smaller projects, the IFC will evaluate carefully the risks that revenues will not be used properly, and compare these and other risks against expected benefits, and evaluate the value of its involvement. Where risks are too high, it will not proceed. As a part of its Summary of Project Information that is usually published 30 days before a project goes to its Board for approval, IFC will summarize this risk review. Within two years IFC will expect EI payments to governments to be disclosed for all EI projects with which IFC is involved. In some areas that are not essential for the public interest, companies may need to maintain confidentiality to protect their legitimate commercial interests, and IFC will work with them to ensure this.

(continued)

Recommendation of the OEG Evaluation	Management Response
1c IFC should focus on projects that can serve as role models for environmental and social performance, transparency, and disclosure. Where laws and regulations—or their enforcement—are weak, IFC should insist on special measures to ensure a project's sound environmental and social performance. Such measures could include building local monitoring capacity, and disclosure of independently audited and publicly disclosed monitoring reports. They could also include an explicit assessment of the risk of conflicts, and measures to deal with them.	IFC will continue to support only projects that, at a minimum, meet the requirements of its evolving social and environmental policies and guidelines. In addition, it will aim to make an added contribution to the sustainable impact of such projects and, where possible, help make the projects role models for activities in the sector and country. Where local capacity outside of the project is weak, IFC will work with sponsors to mitigate this with project design and operation/supervision processes, etc. When appropriate, it will work with other stakeholders (including IBRD/IDA) to increase capacity outside of the project in local and national government and otherwise (see response to recommendation 2a below). Annual monitoring reports are independently audited and disclosed now in some large projects. Independent auditing is not feasible for small projects; but in the context of IFC's review of its disclosure policy (now under way), IFC plans to require for all new EI projects regular disclosure to local communities by investors of appropriate information about the environmental, social, and economic impacts of projects. When it is appropriate, IFC will assess the potential for conflict.

2 Focus on Implementation

2a IFC should continue to require high-quality environmental impact assessments that establish baseline data for relevant environmental and socio-economic impact indicators. These indicators—compared to the baseline—should be consistently tracked and aggregated for IFC's management. Appropriate requirements to allow IFC to adequately mitigate risks and monitor all its projects should be included for all investments, particularly equity. Where IFC finds poor environmental and social systems or performance, it should address them proactively and vigorously.	Management agrees with the need for high-quality environmental impact assessments that establish appropriate baseline indicators. OP 4.01, Environmental Assessment, the principal safeguard policy for project environmental impact assessments, requires the establishment of baseline data. In Dec. 2003, the staff of the IFC Environmental and Social Department (CES) published a good practice note to improve the social component of the environmental impact assessment. Since 2000, IFC has used an Environmental and Social Risk Rating (ESRR) system to prioritize supervision, and rate project performance. A rating of 4 (substandard) requires a site visit by CES staff/investment officers. IFC has improved the effectiveness of its environmental and social functions by mainstreaming the work within operational departments, as well as by adopting a policy of active portfolio management. Management will work with CES and COC to develop an appropriate database for all projects, including portfolio projects, to help monitor key indicators. When issues are discovered, corrective action plans to remedy problems are prepared and agreed with the sponsor. Ultimately IFC can use loan agreements to try to ensure cooperation. Performance indicators are being developed in the review of IFC's safeguard policies and the sustainability framework. The issue of requirements for equity investments is one that applies to all sectors; IFC will address this issue in the context of the current revision of safeguard policies and guidelines.

Recommendation of the OEG Evaluation	**Management Response**
2a *(cont.)* IFC's investment officers and nominees to company boards should be co-responsible with technical specialists for the environmental and social performance of their projects. Where possible, IFC should also develop and use local monitoring capacity.	In the broadest sense, responsibility for project outcomes lies with the Investment Department Management. However, the different responsibilities of the investment officer, who is the overall "task manager" for the project, and the environmental and social specialists, who provide technical input and ensure compliance with IFC guidelines (with reporting relationships to IFC CES), are important ones. The latter's own reporting lines and budget provide a valuable degree of independence. IFC is now mainstreaming environmental and social responsibilities are "mainstreamed" to Investment Departments, but with CES retaining responsibility for quality assurance. The outcome of this experience will guide future arrangements (see response to recommendation 2b below). It is agreed that when possible, IFC should promote the development and use of local capacity to monitor projects. The IFC nominees to company boards can support Investment Department Management in ensuring IFC requirements are met and its views understood, and that company issues and concerns in this respect are brought to Management's attention.
2b IFC needs to ensure that its environmental and social specialists are consulted throughout the project life and as early as possible and that investment officers fully share relevant information. To that end, investment officers need to be better trained to identify risks and opportunities. Also, changing the incentive structure by making the investment officer and department explicitly accountable for environmental performance would likely provide better incentives for calling in the experts as early as possible, not after a problem has materialized.	It is agreed that the early involvement of environmental and social specialists is warranted. Beginning with its first environmental review procedure in March 1990 and continuing through subsequent procedures (1992-1993 and 1998), IFC has developed a culture of ensuring that its environmental and social specialists are involved as early as possible in the project cycle and throughout appraisal and supervision. Following the adoption of the 1998 "Procedure for Environmental and Social Review of Projects" a corporate-wide training program was conducted to apprise investment officers of project environmental and social requirements, as well as risks and opportunities. Sustainability training began in the spring of 2002 on a departmental basis, and it covers issues of governance, environment, and social matters. For about two years, environmental and social specialists have been co-located in the Oil, Gas, Mining, and Chemical Department's mining and oil and gas divisions; this has fostered coordination and early involvement in projects. As mentioned in response to recommendation 2a above, the environmental and social mainstreaming initiative at IFC explicitly places accountability and responsibility for environmental and social inquiry, decision making, and performance on line management. CES will retain an independent quality assurance role. IFC has also pioneered "Departmental Scorecards" that set departmental targets across a range of indicators, including development impact and the volume of investments. IFC also recognizes outstanding environmental and social work in its performance awards system.

Recommendation of the OEG Evaluation	**Management Response**
2c IFC should develop a reporting template that specifies for each portfolio project which safeguard policies and guidelines apply, whether the company is in compliance with them, and how it performs with respect to key sustainability indicators for the industry. Where relevant, IFC should also include "beyond the fence line" issues, such as transportation and project-related security issues.	The recently introduced iDesk system for IFC project information includes such a provision for each new project on which safeguard policies and guidelines apply. Compliance with these policies and guidelines for portfolio projects are tracked by the ESRRs (see response to recommendation 2a above). IFC will supplement this with a consistent internal management database for all IFC projects that indicates the status of all key sustainability indicators (including mine closure/decommissioning plans, safeguard compliance, gas flaring, use of security forces, etc.). Work is underway to improve key sustainability indicators and enhance their usefulness (see responses to recommendations 1c, 2a, and 3c). COC, in conjunction with CES, will also review iDesk to ensure that it can provide Management with appropriate information and indicators for all projects (see response to recommendation 2a). IFC will review "beyond the fence" issues where it is appropriate to do so and will make this explicit. All future IFC-supported projects will require that investors meet a set of requirements relating to the use of security forces along the lines of the Voluntary Principles on Security and Human Rights that were developed through a process of dialogue between the Governments of the U.K and the U.S., EI companies, and NGOs.
2d IFC should develop global comparators for the distribution of benefits from EI—among investors, governments at different levels and local communities. For its projects, IFC should analyze the distribution and compare it to other EI projects. At appraisal, IFC should include the distribution effects in its sensitivity and risk analysis (e.g., distribution of benefits at different levels of output and prices), track actual distribution during the project life, and aggregate the data at the country and sector level.	IFC already reviews the split of resource project net benefits between investors and government. It also reviews the ways investors obtained access to resources. Management will follow the recommendation to review more explicitly and to test the distribution of benefits to different stakeholders, including levels of government. Wherever feasible it will compare the distribution of benefits to government and others with international comparators using established reference sources, evaluated against different assumptions about key variables such as oil prices and production. IFC's annual project supervision reports now track key development outcomes, and where revenue distributions are an important expected outcome, it will track these also.

Recommendation of the OEG Evaluation	Management Response

3   Engage Stakeholders

3a   In consultation with stakeholders, IFC should continuously update its environmental and social safeguard policies, guidelines, and processes in line with evolving good practice in the industry. The WBG should use its convening power and the help of its member governments to promote their use by governments, industry, and other financiers. IFC should develop, update or clarify policies and guidelines on Indigenous Peoples (or "vulnerable people"), safety of dams, natural habitats (or biodiversity), security and human rights, HIV/AIDS prevention, mining (closure—funding and social issues, acid rock drainage, precious metal mining), and oil and gas (gas flaring, downstream transportation of oil).

Management has taken its response to the recently completed CAO Safeguard Policies Review to CODE, and IFC has embarked on a program to revise its safeguards. This revision will take into account CAO and OEG views on EI and recommendations such as those for safety of dams, mine closure, acid rock drainage, etc. Within the WBG, there is agreement that IFC will take the lead in the updating of the 1998 PPAH. One objective of the updating is to eliminate the inconsistencies in the PPAH. Ongoing collaborations between the WBG and MFIs, as well as the adoption of the "Equator Principles" by a growing number of commercial banks that will use IFC safeguards for their project finance lending in developing countries, demonstrate that other financiers find the safeguards useful and relevant. Industry and governments also often refer to the safeguard policies and guidelines, and the updating of the safeguards and the PPAH will make them more attractive to these stakeholders.

3b   IFC should encourage—and consider requiring—its clients to publish information in 3a above. Where client confidentiality undertakings initially restrict disclosure, IFC could report results on an aggregate country, regional or sectoral level and participate in initiatives advocating such disclosure. IFC needs to balance client confidentiality with its own accountability as a public institution and the public's desire to know more. On balance, increased communication and transparency is likely to help IFC and its clients and reduce misconceptions, distrust, and criticism.

See responses to recommendation 1b above concerning transparency of EI revenue payments and recommendation 1c concerning regular publication of information about projects by investors. IFC is currently reviewing its disclosure policy; it is likely that this review will to lead to changes in its general approach. In the case of EI projects IFC proposes to require new investors to provide information on a regular basis concerning the environmental, social, and economic impacts of IFC-financed projects. This will include, for example, appropriate information that is now contained in Annual Monitoring Reports. IFC will work with investors to agree on an effective and meaningful approach to such information provision. As a part of the review of its disclosure policy, IFC will consider how it can better provide information about its aggregate activities in EI.

3c   In consultation with other stakeholders, IFC should develop and track key sustainability indicators and consider disclosing them to demonstrate the economic, social and environmental impacts of its EI projects. Reporting on credible sustainable development indicators will help overcome the current inability to systematically demonstrate results achieved.

See responses to recommendations 1b, 1c, 2a, 2c, and 3b above. IFC is developing an improved process to collect relevant baseline socioeconomic data for its projects, and it will collaborate with IBRD/IDA in this work and with external stakeholders. The size of projects (including their ability to bear the cost of such analysis) and their range of potential impacts will inform the choice of indicators and baseline data. IFC already monitors key development outcomes expected from projects and reports on these in its internal annual project monitoring reports. It will discuss its approach with others and take note of best practice in the sector, as appropriate, given the nature of IFC's portfolio and its objectives. It will consider whether and in what form relevant information from these can be disclosed.

3d This evaluation found strong evidence that improved community consultation is in the best long-term interest of our clients. IFC should thus make community development programs with ongoing consultations the norm for EI projects. Such programs should start with a participatory assessment of the community's situation and long-term development needs. They should include ongoing consultations, focus on sustainable solutions to meet these needs, and prepare communities for the time after the extractive operations cease. Good communication is also likely to improve results—by listening to people and being exposed to public scrutiny and challenge.

It is agreed that good, ongoing consultation with communities is important and should be the norm, and this approach will be applied to new EI projects within two years. In 2000, IFC prepared a community development resource guide for companies ("Investing in People: Sustaining Communities through Improved Business Practice"). This guide provides IFC clients and private investors with practical advice on establishing community development programs. IFC will encourage existing clients to engage in ongoing consultations and will disseminate its community development resource guide to clients. In parallel, the practice of CES for high impact EI projects is to focus on community development opportunities. For example, the requirement for resettlement action plans in OD 4.12 is normally complemented with actions for broader community development plans. Also, vulnerable groups under OD 4.20, Indigenous Peoples, and OD 4.30, etc., are now the focus of community development plans. IFC's Corporate Citizenship Facility works with IFC clients and other stakeholders to develop capacity at the community level. In cooperation with IBRD, as appropriate, IFC will aim to work with investors to develop as a pilot a "sustainable community development plan" that would involve all stakeholders, including communities, local governments, and investors as envisaged in the MMSD report, Breaking New Ground. COC is currently developing proposals for a sustainable EI development facility that will aim, through project interventions and partnerships with stakeholders, to broaden the practical application of best practice to EI projects.

3e IFC should routinely share best practice among clients and encourage them to apply it. IFC should communicate its information needs better to its clients, for example by tailoring reporting to their own requirements. Clients very much appreciated assistance they had received from IFC staff, but were eager for more. IFC should build on its various initiatives to add value and further facilitate exchange of ideas among its clients, for example by organizing conferences and further developing toolkits on how to best address environmental and social issues.

IFC will institute a more systematic approach to advising clients of updates/changing best practices and encourage them to apply these even when they are not obliged to. The new relationship with the "Equator Banks" provides an important additional way for IFC to communicate beyond its direct client base. IFC needs to ensure that client reports cover at least its minimum requirements in terms of safeguards. It will work with sponsors to ensure reporting is as effective as possible for both IFC and the client, given specific project needs. As noted (see response to recommendation 3a above), IFC is now responding to the CAO review of its safeguards, and updating and revising safeguards may offer the opportunity to make these more "customer friendly" without diluting their key objectives. Management agrees that it can (often as a WBG approach) use its convening power and range of clients to promote the exchange of ideas and best practices and it will do this selectively. A schedule for best practice notes, lessons learned, and good practice notes is under preparation for FY05; this will cover areas relevant to EI.

D. Recommendations of the OEU Evaluation Report

Recommendation of the OEU Evaluation

Management Response

1   **Strategy and Rules of Engagement:** MIGA needs to recognize and promote the potential benefits it brings to EI projects through its internationally recognized and comprehensive set of safeguard policies and its environmental and social impact mitigation services. MIGA's engagement with EI projects should move beyond compliance with its environmental and social safeguard policies toward the promotion and achievement of the development effectiveness of these projects.

MIGA Management is committed to implement this recommendation and will look for such opportunities to promote the potential benefits it brings to insured projects through its internationally recognized and comprehensive set of safeguard policies and its environmental and social impact mitigation services. Management is committed to promoting projects with the greatest development impact and that are economically, environmentally, and socially sustainable. MIGA's new organizational structure will facilitate this. Management reviews will focus on development effectiveness, and these reviews now will be done early in the project process cycle. See responses below concerning specific recommendations in this subject area.

1a   Recognizing that MIGA has the opportunity to add value to EI projects by adopting an explicit business strategy focused on providing proactive environmental and social advice to its guarantee clients that brings EI projects closer to best practices in the industry, with the goal of achieving sustainable development. This requires strengthening the economic and social components in MIGA's work in addition to the environmental component. This calls for a more proactive, forward looking approach to servicing clients that goes beyond the current practice of intervening only when events warrant it.

Management fully recognizes that MIGA should be more proactively involved in the social and economic aspects of EI projects. MIGA this year has hired a senior social specialist as part of MIGA's Environment group. A senior manager, whose responsibilities include reviewing the economic, environmental, and social aspects of MIGA projects, has also joined the MIGA Management team as Director and Chief Economist in the newly formed Economics and Policy Group. This expansion of MIGA's in-house capacity and additional economic, social, and development impact training of staff will enable MIGA to take a more proactive approach to EI clients. Moreover, MIGA has just undergone a major reorganization of its functional groups, to better integrate environmental, social, and economic analysis, to offer a more holistic approach to assessment of developmental impact of prospective projects, and to integrate the guarantees program and technical advisory services to better serve clients. MIGA will adopt a more proactive approach to offer advice and support to EI projects, especially sensitive or complex projects. The budgetary implications of providing proactive support subsequent to issuing coverage will need to be analyzed further, and MIGA will seek to secure support of a Trust Fund to enable a more intensive focus on such work.

1b Strengthening the upstream involvement of environmental and social issues in MIGA's underwriting decision-making process. This entails consistently identifying applicable safeguard policies to clients as early as possible in the underwriting process, and using risk assessments early on to identify where failures in the safeguard system may occur to avoid adverse impacts on the environment and local communities.

Management concurs that it is advantageous to strengthen the upstream involvement and consideration of these issues. Management will notify clients as early as possible about applicable MIGA safeguard policies. Management notes that in recent years experienced EI investors tend to be well aware of these policies before coming to MIGA. It should be noted that a large majority of guarantee applications arrive at MIGA with the environmental assessment process already completed and the environmental impact assessment approved in the host country.

MIGA needs to make a greater effort to work with clients to ensure compliance with its environmental and social safeguard policies and guidelines at the time of Board approval.

Management concurs with the thrust of this recommendation, and the recent hiring of a social specialist will facilitate this. Management notes that its business model (and the Operational Regulations) provides scope for including as conditions of guarantee, the completion of proposed or ongoing critical safeguard tasks, subject to Board approval. As has been done since MIGA adopted its own environmental policies and procedures in 1999, Management's commitment is to notify the Board of any outstanding, significant concerns that will need to be addressed as part of contractual requirements in the guarantee(s) for the project. The expansion of MIGA's in-house environmental and social expertise will lead to greater effort in monitoring subsequent compliance for projects that have high risk during implementation.

In addition, MIGA needs to consider how its work in assessing, underwriting, and supervising its guarantee projects can go beyond the monitoring of compliance with safeguards toward promoting development effectiveness in its projects.

Management will offer prospective clients advisory support to enhance the developmental impacts of projects, to go beyond compliance with safeguards and promote sustainable development. A model of this might be work done over the past four years by MIGA's environmental specialist in the context of the Antamina Mine in Peru. The budgetary implications of this proactive support will need to be analyzed further as Management gains additional experience in this effort to add value to clients.

1c Associating with investors committed to sustainable development and avoiding those who are unable to provide MIGA with timely environmental and social monitoring reports during implementation.

Management associates with investors that are committed to sustainable development, but also notes that this recommendation poses some challenges for lenders or minority partners. The majority of MIGA guarantees that have been issued have been held by lenders or minority partners, clearly demonstrating the value of MIGA's products to this type of investor. The implications for these investors will need to be carefully assessed in the context of how their investments contribute to outcomes of sustainable economic and social development. Proactive measures (e.g., working through the best

Recommendation of the OEU Evaluation	Management Response
	efforts of the investor or lender to implement best practices, distribution of best practices, etc.) can be taken. In this respect, MIGA will take comfort in those lenders that have committed to the "Equator Principles." Management also notes that great care will be needed to ensure that "South-South" investments are not discriminated against.
MIGA should satisfy itself before engaging in new EI projects that the investor understands its environmental and social responsibilities and demonstrates ownership at the top management level to community development and mitigating environmental and social impacts. The project enterprise's organizational structure, policies, and stated mission should be consistent with these goals.	Management agrees with this recommendation and has put in place an upstream review process for all projects, to address this and other issues. Management takes into account client reputation, and assesses indicators of the likely risk for noncompliance during implementation and the associated risks of faulty implementation.

2 Policies, Procedures, and Enforcement Mechanisms

MIGA should strengthen its internal policies and support them by appropriate procedures and guidelines to staff to ensure accountability.	See responses 2a, 2b, 2c, and 2d below.
2a Establishing internal requirements for MIGA's timely engagement and systematic monitoring to maximize environmental and social benefits.	See response to recommendation 4a. Management accepts that it could do more in this area (see response to recommendation 1a). In particular, MIGA will encourage investors in EI projects to approach MIGA at a very early stage. Management has had internal guidance with respect to the selection and prioritizing of site monitoring over the past four-five years. In July 2003, Management implemented a more standardized approach to monitoring compliance and performance of all new EI projects.
This will entail avoiding projects where MIGA can not address environmental or social issues to improve the outcome due to its late participation.	Management will avoid projects whose net outcomes are not anticipated to be positive.
Site visits by MIGA's environmental and social experts should be required as early as possible in its involvement in category 'A' and other high-risk projects to assess which policies are applicable. MIGA should not rely exclusively on assessments and reports of non-WBG institutions.	Under the newly reorganized structure of the Agency, project teams will normally visit the project site prior to any decision to recommend approval of the project to the Board. MIGA's Environmental and Social Review Procedures call for a site visit as part of the environmental and social review and due diligence during the underwriting of Category A projects; these also will be carried out as early as possible. The procedures allow for the site visit to be carried out by qualified MIGA or IFC experts or by a qualified consultant (whose work will be reviewed by qualified staff).

2b   Incorporating standards recognizing the rights of individuals relating to security arrangements at EI projects into its policies and Operational Regulations.

In the context of the overall WBG approach to these issues, Management will evaluate and help develop best practice approaches to EI-specific issues.

2c   Making better use of MIGA's Contracts of Guarantee to enable the Agency to facilitate compliance with its policies and standards. In addition to the current requirement to comply with safeguard policies and environmental and health and safety guidelines, for future projects MIGA should ensure that the contracts clearly and explicitly state which environmental and social safeguard policies and guidelines apply to the project under guarantee and establish thresholds and conditions for timely and effective compliance.

With respect to environmental guidelines, MIGA's practice for the past five years has been to attach the appropriate guidelines to the contract as conditions of coverage. With respect to safeguard policies, see response to the next part of this recommendation.

When applicable, contracts should also specify requirements for implementation of Environmental Management Plans (EMPs), Resettlement Plans (RPs), Community Development Programs (CDPs), and Indigenous Peoples Plans (IPPs).

Management agrees with this recommendation. Management sees this approach as the mechanism by which project-specific requirements of the safeguard policies can be addressed by binding and legally sound contract requirements. Management takes care that any contractual requirements are clearly defined in a way that failure to comply can be reasonably assessed in the event of arbitration arising over the decision by MIGA to deny a claim or unilaterally cancel coverage due to noncompliance.

As required by the involuntary resettlement and Indigenous Peoples policies, MIGA should ensure that investors prepare RPs, CDPs, and IPPs before project approval rather than leaving them to implementation.

Management agrees that these plans should be prepared before project approval. However, these are not static plans and require adaptation to evolving circumstances. Also, Management believes its business model provides scope for including, as conditions of guarantee, the completion of proposed or ongoing critical tasks, subject to Board approval. In such cases, MIGA conducts necessary follow-up and monitoring to ensure compliance.

2d   Establishing necessary mechanisms to ensure systematic, timely, and regular monitoring and supervision of safeguard compliance of MIGA EI guarantee projects (e.g., MIGA should require in its Contracts of Guarantee timely environmental and social monitoring reports from its guarantee holders during the project implementation phase).

Management believes it is obtaining information in timely and cost-effective ways for sensitive projects (e.g., Category A), and not levying excessive demands on guarantee holders for Category B projects. Management believes these judgments are important contributions to the Agency's efficiency and effectiveness, as noted in paras. 49-51 of the OEU report. Nevertheless, in response to this recommendation, Management has implemented a more standardized approach to monitoring compliance and performance of all new EI projects.

Recommendation of the OEU Evaluation	Management Response
MIGA should also require sponsors to set up environmental and social project management systems at a sufficiently early stage to effectively monitor impacts, including during the construction stage.	Management identified this matter in 2000 as a lesson learned from its experience with Antamina project in Peru. Management now considers this in all prospective EI projects where it has been identified as a potentially significant concern and risk.

3 Internal Organization

MIGA should update its business model by clearly assigning the locus of responsibility for better integration of economic, environmental, and social issues in MIGA operations. This is needed in order to support other departments in the achievement of these objectives and to provide guidance to operational staff, as well as, for the analysis and monitoring of economic, environmental, and social issues in an integrated manner.	See responses below to specific recommendations in this subject area. MIGA has just undergone a major reorganization that created a unit to integrate the assessment of economic, environmental, and social issues in MIGA operations, and to approach developmental impact assessment in a more holistic fashion.
3a Scaling up the analysis of developmental impacts of prospective projects integrating new concepts in harmony with the rest of the WBG. In so doing, MIGA should closely cooperate with the other members of the WBG to benefit from synergies, complementarities, and expert knowledge, with the objective of promoting a holistic approach to EI projects.	MIGA Management supports the recommendation and has made significant steps over the past few years to more closely cooperate with other members of the WBG (e.g., work on CASs, sector strategy papers, the Extractive Industries Review, etc.) to benefit from synergies, complementarities, experience, and expert knowledge. Efforts will continue to be made to scale up these actions.
This will also require building internal capacity by both recruiting needed economic skills and appropriate training to current staff.	MIGA Management has built and intends to further build its internal capacity in these areas. Initial training of underwriters has already been conducted by an IFC economist, who has subsequently joined MIGA's staff as senior manager (Director and Chief Economist) for country assessment, policy, economics and strategy (Economics and Policy Group).
3b Establishing an internal system that allows a more integrated and timely monitoring of developmental impacts of guaranteed projects.	The recent reorganization of functional groups, and the intent to increase site visits to prospective projects, will offer opportunities to increase timely monitoring of guaranteed projects in MIGA's portfolio. The planned closer collaboration with OEU will enhance this.

3c Upgrading and expanding the role of environmental and social specialists and, at the same time, building internal social skills capacity to effectively enable the application of social safeguards in MIGA projects.

As previously noted, an experienced social specialist has been hired as part of MIGA's Environment group (which has now been incorporated into the newly formed Economics and Policy Group) to augment and build internal capacity.

3d Formalizing the practice of ensuring that MIGA environmental staff are involved in projects beyond the submission of clearance memos, and requiring that MIGA environmental and social staff to provide inputs to guarantee and legal documentation to incorporate any environmental and social concerns. In addition, MIGA underwriting staff should be required to keep environmental and social specialists appraised of all relevant changes beyond Board approval and contract signing.

Management agrees with this recommendation and is making changes in its internal procedures to enhance the timeliness and extent of its environmental and social specialists involvement in these and other operational areas.

4	Active Projects

MIGA needs to review its portfolio of active EI projects to identify potential or actual deficiencies in the application of safeguard policies and to swiftly take appropriate remedial actions.

See responses below to specific recommendations in this subject area. MIGA has taken and will take appropriate remedial actions to address deficiencies that are identified.

4a Identifying projects that may not be consistent with safeguard policies. In particular, where resettlement and land acquisition has taken place without follow-up audits to determine compliance with WBG policies regarding resettlement, third-party audits should be required. Similarly, where Indigenous Peoples have been affected without the provision for Indigenous Peoples Plans to mitigate the impacts, sponsors should be asked to prepare and implement such plans. Providing briefings on potential problems with sensitive projects, a system currently used by MIGA, is useful but not sufficient. MIGA should take appropriate remedial actions to address existing safeguard deficiencies in extractive industry projects that are still active in MIGA's portfolio.

Management notes that since late 1997 MIGA has extensively and regularly identified "higher risk" projects vis-à-vis safeguard policies. This identification has been used to develop a monitoring program of site visits, which has included eight EI projects in the course of a three-year period. MIGA plans to expand this effort. Also, soon after the Office of the CAO was established in 2000, MIGA provided a list of all projects in MIGA's portfolio that involved involuntary resettlement or Indigenous Peoples, discussed the risks of each project with the CAO, and described the monitoring that MIGA directly had been carrying out or had been relying on to track the projects' compliance issues. Briefings of the CAO on sensitive projects in the pipeline and the portfolio have been regularly provided (approximately quarterly) since then, as have exchanges of information with the IFC on common projects. MIGA continues to review regularly the project portfolio and identify priority projects for monitoring visits, focusing particularly on projects with higher risk. Management will consider on a case-by-case basis the need for a third-party audit of compliance with MIGA's poli-

Recommendation of the OEU Evaluation

Management Response

4b Making every effort to encourage consistency with MIGA's safeguard policies in active extractive industries projects with reinsurance agreements pre-dating the new MIGA practice. New agreements require that environmental and social standards applied by partners are consistent with MIGA's own safeguard policies and guidelines.

cies. Management believes that it has taken care to ensure that, when Indigenous Peoples are at risk for significant adverse impacts, plans have been established and implemented to effectively mitigate those impacts.

There are no longer any remaining active reinsurance contracts of this type. As noted by OEU, this matter has been addressed in new contracts.

Background

This joint evaluation was one of the major sector evaluations in OED's FY03 work program. It was undertaken in parallel with the EIR, an independent, multi-stakeholder consultative exercise, headed by Mr. Emil Salim, former Minister of Environment of Indonesia. The EIR focuses on the future role of the WBG in extractive industries (comprising oil, gas, and minerals and metals mining). The EIR was launched by Bank Management following the 2000 Annual Meetings in Prague, where a group of NGOs approached the Management of the World Bank with a proposal that the WBG should cease its support for EI projects, on the grounds that these projects did more harm than good in developing countries. Management decided to undertake a review of the WBG's involvement in this sector, and the EIR is its response to this commitment.

Main Findings and Recommendations

Conducted in parallel with the EIR, the joint evaluation by the three WBG-independent operations evaluation units assesses the effectiveness of WBG assistance to clients in enhancing the contribution of EI to sustainable development. The evaluation report's main message is that—while there are differences in performance between WB, IFC, and MIGA projects—EI projects have produced positive economic and financial results and have contributed to sustainable development where projects meet appropriate social, environmental, and economic criteria. While the majority of WBG projects were in compliance with its environmental and social safeguards, the degree of compliance has been uneven. The WBG is well positioned to assist countries in overcoming the policy, institutional, and tech-

nical challenges to transforming resource endowments into sustainable benefits for their people. The OED/OEG/OEU evaluation reports include recommendations directed at the Bank, IFC, and MIGA, respectively.

The key recommendations for the WBG are that it remain engaged in EI and that it should (i) formulate integrated strategies for the sector and resource-abundant countries that address the risk that EI contributions to fiscal revenues may not be used effectively for development priorities; (ii) not support significant sector expansion where the risk that EI fiscal revenues may not be used for development priorities cannot be adequately mitigated; (iii) strengthen the implementation of the existing policy framework; adapt the safeguard policies and guidance to be in line with evolving best practice; rigorously apply safeguard policies; and monitor, document, and report on the social, economic, and environmental/safety impacts of its EI projects and specifically monitor the distributional benefits; and (iv) proactively engage stakeholders with a focus on governance, revenue management, and community development; define and report on key sustainability indicators; and work toward and support disclosure of fiscal revenues from EI. In its comments on the joint evaluation, the External Advisory Panel supports the recommendations but believes they should be made more comprehensive and binding.

Conclusions and Next Steps

The Committee welcomed the report's findings, including the positive performance of the WBG portfolio in EI. It was generally satisfied with the scope and analysis presented in the OED/OEG/OEU evaluation. The Committee believed that the Interim Management Response (IMR) was appropriate and also agreed with Management's proposal to formulate a comprehensive Final Management Response (FMR) following completion of the external EIR (expected in December 2003). The Committee will have a more extensive second-round discussion, focusing on the recommendations and their policy implications, at the time it discusses the FMR and the findings of the EIR. The Committee agreed with OED's recommendation that the joint evaluation, the IMR, CODE Chairman's Report, and the report of the External Advisory Panel be disclosed following this first-round CODE discussion.

Governance

The Committee emphasized the importance of the Bank addressing governance and revenue management issues both in resource-abundant and resource-poor countries in a proactive and transparent way. Members supported the evaluation's recommendation to develop a WBG strategy for sequencing its EI interventions taking governance issues into account. They also recognized the difficulty of implementing this and cautioned against a one-size-fits-all approach. Members considered that there are questions about how issues of governance, including human rights, should be addressed in EI projects. These questions require further attention by all parties. The WBG's involvement in such issues should be consistent with its mandate and comparative advantage. At the same time, the approach adopted in each country needs to have local ownership. Management noted the importance of governance issues and agreed to address them, as well as the question of CAS treatment of EI issues, in its FMR.

Revenue Generation from EI Projects

The Committee noted that revenue generation from EI projects constitutes a particular challenge. Some members noted that when assessing the impact of EI, the focus on revenues was too narrow, and some underlined the importance of assessing the full impact of EI projects on poverty, employment, and the environment. The Committee underlined the need for the WBG to be even more forthright in its dialogue with clients in addressing the issue of disclosure of revenues

and noted that good models existed from the Botswana and Chad-Cameroon projects. Some members noted that they were not convinced by the "resource curse" arguments presented in the joint review and cautioned that resource-poor countries and non-EI sectors also have governance issues. The performance of resource-rich countries, however, could be adversely affected by the so-called Dutch-disease problem. They recommended including examples from successful countries to provide a more nuanced understanding of the relationship between the EI sector and macroeconomic performance and were of the opinion that revenue management should be addressed primarily within the context of overall public finance management. Management agreed that it would be key to address transparency and distribution issues related to EI revenue management in its FMR.

Safeguards and Performance of the Portfolio

Members asked for clarification of the recommendation that safeguard policies in extractive industries projects be rigorously applied and, in particular, whether there would be a different standard for EI projects. The DGO responded that the recommendation was that existing policies be implemented and that this recommendation should apply to all sectors, not just EI. Some members noted that the report suggested that there were still gaps and overlaps in safeguard policies, and that further consideration needs to be given to human rights issues. Management noted that considerable progress had been made by public and private entities in improving environmental management of EI resources.

Report of the External Advisory Panel

Members would have liked to have seen more substantiation of the conclusions of the OED/OEG/OEU's external advisory panel report. They did not agree with the advisory panel's assessment regarding the limited value of a "rear-view approach" and reemphasized the importance of evaluation to the Bank's operations. The DGO clarified that the advisory panel has been used for several major evaluations and that the role of the panel was to advise OED/OEG/OEU in the development of the review but stressed that panel comments were conveyed to CODE as written by the panel.

Scope of the Final Management Response

Committee members provided their expectations regarding the scope of the FMR. They asked that it provide a framework for WBG involvement in the EI sector and a clear assessment of the recommendations in both the evaluation and the EIR reports. Members also noted that the WBG should forge partnerships to address recommendations that touched on areas outside of the WBG's mandate.

Communication

The Committee suggested that Management consider a communication to the public explaining the background and process for the two-stage response by Management to the OED/OEU/OEG evaluation. It also suggested that WBG Management consider a workshop on the results of the OED/OEG/OEU study, perhaps in connection with the EIR process. It was agreed that the Committee chair would inform the Board concerning the discussion of the OED/OEG/OEU review and the two-stage process by which Management will respond to it.

Finn Jonck, *Chairman*

Operations Evaluation Department:
Evaluation of World Bank Experience

ANNEX C: WORLD BANK EXPERIENCE

1. Introduction

Background and Context

In resource-abundant countries, the extractive industries should be expected to play a major role in support of sustainable development. They can be an important source of government revenues and foreign exchange and generate employment in otherwise economically neglected areas. They can attract investment for local and national infrastructure, and provide countries with opportunities to strengthen their institutional and administrative capacities. But these industries also provide opportunities for rent-seeking that can hinder the conversion of EI revenues into sustainable development. Paradoxically, over the past three decades, resource-abundant developing countries have experienced poor economic performance in higher proportion than resource-poor developing countries. The factors that lead to underperformance have been studied extensively but are not fully understood, nor is the design of appropriate strategies for dealing with them (see Box C1).

The World Bank helps its client countries develop their mineral resources through a variety of lending and nonlending activities in the extractive industries. Lending assistance is provided through specific investment loans, technical assistance, and structural adjustment loans. Nonlending activities consist of a variety of advisory and analytical activities, including sector-related economic and other studies, workshops and conferences, and training. The focus of the Bank's involvement has evolved over four decades, beginning with an emphasis on production and exploration in the 1960s and 1970s, proceeding to commercialization of state enterprises in the 1980s and private sector develop-

ment in the 1990s, and to a more inclusive approach involving civil society, local governments, and the private sector in recent years.

The involvement of the Bank and the WBG in the extractive industries has come under increased scrutiny in recent years from several sections of civil society. Some are concerned that the extractive industries exact a heavy toll on the environment, with the poorest citizens paying the highest price, and they have put the spotlight on the treatment of local populations, especially where a project involves involuntary resettlement.[60] Others have been concerned with issues of poor governance and failure to use rents effectively to support sustained economic development.[61] At the Annual Meetings in 2000, some NGOs asked the WBG to stop supporting the extractive industries, because, in their view, the adverse environmental, social, and governance impacts outweigh whatever economic and social benefits may accrue to the domestic economy and the poor from the extractive industries.[62]

In response to these concerns, the independent evaluation units of the World Bank Group[63] have prepared evaluations of the extractive industries activities supported by the WBG. Concurrently, WBG management launched the Extractive Industries Review[64] to better understand stakeholder views and advise the Bank on its role in the sector. While the evaluations have consulted with the EIR, they constitute a separate exercise that has been conducted independently. This annex reports on the Operations Evaluation Department evaluation of the World Bank's experience.

Study Objective and Process

This evaluation assesses the effectiveness of the World Bank in enhancing the sustainable devel-

Box C1   The "Paradox of Plenty"

In recent decades, many resource-abundant developing countries have experienced significantly lower rates of growth than resource-poor developing economies.[a] This phenomenon is accompanied by poor governance and lack of transparency in managing EI revenues, and significant negative environmental and social impacts. This phenomenon is referred to as the "paradox of plenty."

Figure C1: Slower Economic Growth with Greater EI Dependence[a]

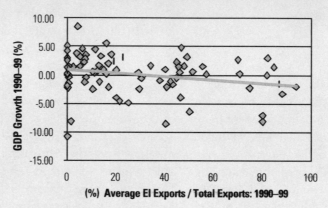

Source: World Bank, World Development Indicators.

Economists and social scientists (among them, Auty 2000, Gelb 1988, Isham 2002, and Sachs and Warner 1995) have proposed several explanations for the phenomenon and strategies to deal with it, but no single model yet synthesizes the interplay of institutional, social, and political factors that is behind the observed paradox.[b] The emerging consensus is that the underperformance of resource-abundant developing countries, to the extent that it is the result of institutional and policy failure, is not inevitable. Overall, while the technical requirements for managing volatile and exhaustible revenue flows and other impacts such as the so-called Dutch disease, and devoting them to sustainable development are well understood, creating good governance appears to be at the heart of the institutional and policy changes needed to improve fiscal management, mitigate negative environmental and social impacts, and maximize benefits from the development of extractive industries.

Another perspective on this debate is that "the appropriate public policy question is not should we or should we not promote mining in the developing countries, but rather where should we encourage it and how can we ensure that it contributes as much as possible to economic development and poverty alleviation" (Davis and Tilton 2001).

a. This relationship, which is statistically significant at the 95 percent confidence level (t-statistic = −2.39), illustrates a conclusion that is widely accepted in the literature. No claim is made that EI dependence is the sole determinant of a country's economic growth. When non-borrower countries are included in the regression, the slope is statistically significant (t-statistic = −2.82) and steeper (−0.038 vs. −0.032).

b. Analysis in the 1960s focused on how to manage the macroeconomic impacts of resource export income, which raised domestic prices and made other exports less competitive internationally (so-called Dutch disease). More recent analysis emphasizes poor use of fiscal revenues from resources.

opment contribution of the extractive industries and distills lessons from experience to inform the Bank's future role in the sector. The evaluation design is based on the widely supported view that the main elements of a strategy to address the underperformance of many resource-abundant countries will be sound fiscal policies, rigorous mitigation of negative environmental and social impacts, and good governance.[65] Thus, the evaluation focuses on assessing economic effects, environmental and social effects, and governance issues associated with the Bank's interventions in the sector.

Economic Effects

- Improving the generation of fiscal revenues from the development of extractive industries
- Promoting the distribution and expenditure of the revenues in support of sustainable development and poverty reduction
- Strengthening the framework for managing the volatility and exhaustibility of fiscal revenues from extractive industries
- Ensuring the adequacy of provisions for legal entitlements and compensation for negative impacts

Environmental and Social Effects

- Mitigating the adverse environmental impacts and enhancing positive impacts
- Mitigating the adverse social impacts, including those associated with resettlement and closure of existing facilities, and contributing to social objectives

Governance

- Improving the institutional and policy framework
- Strengthening governance processes

Evaluation Criteria

At the project level, this study evaluates the effectiveness of Bank-supported EI projects based on an assessment of their outcome, sustainability, and institutional development impact.[66] At the country level, the Bank's effectiveness is evaluated based on an assessment of the overall coherence, level of effort, and results of its assistance to resource-abundant countries for enhancing the contribution of the extractive industries to sustainable development.

Evaluation Process

The evaluation has been carried out in two phases: Phase I consisted of a review of the portfolio of World Bank extractive industry projects (referred to as the Portfolio Review hereafter), supplemented by a review of CASs and a literature survey.[67] The Portfolio Review covered all 76 Bank-supported projects in the EI sectors that were approved since fiscal year 1993—48 "closed" or completed projects and 28 "active" or ongoing projects.[68] The list of projects reviewed is in Attachment 1.

Phase II built upon the findings from Phase I and consisted of the following:[69]

- Three Thematic Studies of the Bank's EI portfolio: (i) revenue management, (ii) safeguards implementation, and (iii) governance (referred to hereafter as the Revenue Study, Safeguards Study, and Governance Study, respectively)
- Five Country Case Studies for Ecuador, Equatorial Guinea, Ghana, Kazakhstan, and Papua New Guinea (PNG)[70]
- Seven recent PPARs
- Two Surveys: (i) of task managers of active EI and EI-related projects and country economists of resource-abundant countries[71] and (ii) of participants of the EIR's Regional Stakeholder Workshops.[72]

Structure of the Report

Following the Introduction, Chapter 2 outlines the evolution of Bank involvement in the EI sectors and characterizes the EI portfolio and its performance. Chapter 3 reviews the economic benefits of Bank projects. Chapter 4 assesses the extent to which the Bank's portfolio implemented its environmental and social safeguard policies and addressed issues of environmental capacity-building and mine closure. Chapter 5 discusses the Bank's efforts to improve the generation, management, and utilization of fiscal revenues from resource extraction. Chapter 6 reviews the Bank's approach to governance issues in EI-dependent countries. Chapter 7 presents the recommendations.

2. The World Bank's Extractive Industries Role and Portfolio

The World Bank's role in extractive industries has evolved from mainly supporting exploration and production activities (1960s to the early 1980s), to sector policy reform and commercialization of state-owned enterprises (1980s), to a greater emphasis on capacity-building and private sector development (1990s). Also in the 1990s, the Bank began to help transition economies maintain production levels, rehabilitate or close uneconomical facilities, and attract foreign equity to their extractive industries sectors. Since the mid-1990s, the Bank's approach to extractive industries has been evolving toward addressing social, environmental, mine closure, revenue management, and sustainable development issues in a more holistic manner. It also has increased its collaboration with civil society, local governments, and the private sector.

The Bank's EI portfolio from the 1980s to the present illustrates the most recent shifts in its role. Between the 1980s and the 1990s, the Bank's overall lending to the EI sector decreased marginally in absolute terms and significantly relative to the Bank's overall lending. Lending for oil and gas fell considerably, while lending for mining rose sharply. Over the same period, the quality of EI project outcomes has been better than that of the Bank's projects as a whole, while the mining sector improved over the oil and gas sector during the 1990s.

The Bank's Evolving Policy and Role in the Extractive Industries

1960s to the early 1980s: The Bank assisted public sector investment efforts to enhance productive capacity in both the oil and gas sector and the mining sector. This trend accelerated in the oil and gas sector when the Bank established an Energy Department, in part to support lending for oil and gas operations after the second oil shock of 1979. The Bank established a program to attract private financing for oil and gas exploration in countries that lacked resources to develop national petroleum industries.

1980s: The Bank shifted its focus toward supporting sector policy reform and the commercialization of state-owned enterprises. Later in the decade, the Bank pursued sector reform and liberalization and developed a framework for private investment, leading to active promotion of private investment, such as for developing exploration data. In 1984, the Bank issued policy guidelines for oil and gas (Operational Manual Statement 3.82).[73]

The guidelines under OMS 3.82 provided for the Bank to assist borrower countries to (1) design and implement effective energy policies; (2) design and implement effective investment plans and sound policies for exploration, development, and use of petroleum; (3) mobilize the domestic and external financial resources required; and (4) develop local capacity to conduct petroleum operations and to provide petroleum service efficiently and competitively. The guidelines also suggested that the Bank promote exploration only where no significant exploration was taking place.

Early 1990s: In keeping with OMS 3.82, the Bank supported private provision of services in the extractive industries and encouraged new direct private investment. This trend was strengthened as Central and Eastern European countries began their transition to a market economy in the early 1990s. The Bank supported this shift by providing technical assistance and advisory services for the modification of legislative, institutional, and taxation regimes to accommodate and attract foreign equity investment in the extractive industries. The Bank's attention shifted more explicitly to creating an enabling environment for the private sector (thus changing the role of the government from owner-operator to regulator), privatization, mine closure, and industry restructuring as outlined in the 1992 Africa Technical Department Paper, *Strategy for African Mining*.[73] Thus, as countries moved from public to private ownership and extractive resource exploitation, the Bank moved from direct lending for production-related projects to supporting initiatives that would bolster private sector growth.

The late 1980s and early 1990s also witnessed rising public concern about environmental degradation and social inequity. A Bank Operational Directive (OD) on environmental assessment (OD 4.01) was issued in 1989 and, revised as a more comprehensive policy for environmental and social impacts, adopted in 1991. In 1999, it was converted to Operational Policy (OP) 4.01, which covers all projects except for structural adjustment loans.

OP 4.01 is particularly important for the EI sectors because of their potential for negative environmental and social impacts. The objective of the policy is to ensure that projects are environmentally and socially sustainable by preventing, mitigating, or compensating for potential adverse impacts. Under the policy, the environmental assessment of projects should take into account the natural environment (air, water, and land), human health and safety, social aspects (involuntary settlement, indigenous peoples, and cultural property), and transboundary and global environmental impacts.

The formulation and implementation of safeguard policies, which have been widely accepted and emulated outside the Bank, illustrate how the Bank can play a convening role and have influence beyond the implementation of projects (see Box C2).

Mid- and Late 1990s: The mid-1990s saw the Bank take a more inclusive approach to its developmental operations and begin to emphasize the need for external partnerships connecting government, the private sector, and civil society in the design and implementation of socially and environmentally sensitive projects. In the latter part of the 1990s, there was an increased focus on reform and deregulation programs in an effort to further good governance as a central element in the improvement of country economic performance. In 1998, growing management concern about environmental and social impacts led to the creation of the Bank's safeguards policy framework, which combined the environmental assessment policy with nine other "do no harm" policies.[74] This was followed by the establishment

---

Box C2	Channeling the Bank's Convening Power for Sustainable Development of the Extractive Industries Sectors

The Bank, often in collaboration with other organizations, has helped bring together various stakeholders in the extractive industries sectors to address issues at the national, regional, and global levels. This convening power is prized because the Bank has access to all stakeholders, broad development experience, and ongoing involvement with project investments and technical assistance in the sector.

In the oil and gas sector, the Bank has collaborated with the government of Norway in a major Global Gas Flaring Reduction Initiative,[a] which was the subject of a 2002 conference in Oslo that hosted representatives of industry, government, the research community, and NGOs. In September 2002, an international training program, Good Governance in a Global Economy—Oil and Gas Policy and Regulation, held in Calgary, Canada, in collaboration with the Canadian Petroleum Institute and the IFC, again brought together senior government and industry representatives.

In the mining sector, the Bank and the government of Papua New Guinea co-sponsored the September 2002 Conference on Mining and the Community for Asian and Pacific Nations in Madang. The event, in which other Asian mining countries took part, is widely seen as having had an important impact on the awareness of social and community issues in Papua New Guinea and in the region. A similar event, Mining and the Community, was held for Latin American nations in Quito, Ecuador, in 1998. In May 1995, in Washington, D.C., the Bank hosted an International Roundtable on Artisanal Mining that brought together representatives from different parts of the world. In March 2001, the Bank, along with other multilateral institutions, launched the Communities and Small-Scale Mining Initiative[b] to improve coordination among miners, communities, donors, governments, and other stakeholders. Another significant event was a roundtable focused on foreign investment and mining development in western China. The October 2000 conference, Attracting Private Mining Investment, was held in Urumqi, China, and was organized jointly with the Association of South East Asian Nations (ASEAN) Federation of Mining Associations, the Malaysian Chamber of Mines, and the Metal Mining Agency of Japan.

a. For details, see http://www.worldbank.org/ogmc/global_gas.htm.
b. For details, see www.casmsite.org.
Source: World Bank.

of an enhanced safeguards compliance system in 1999, a concerted effort to implement the policies, which previously had been more flexibly interpreted as "guidelines."

New priorities began to emerge for sustainable mining and regional and local economic development through private investment in mining, and community development. The evolution in the Bank's mining strategy was presented in two World Bank Technical Papers: *World Bank Group Assistance for Minerals Sector Development and Reform in Member Countries*[75] and *A Mining Strategy for Latin America and the Caribbean.*[76] The new priorities were documented in various partnerships, publications, conferences, and workshops on community issues, mine closure, revenue management, and sustainable development supported by the World Bank Mining Division between 1997 and 2002.

In the late 1990s, it became clear that despite efforts to coordinate over the years, IFC and the Bank had not capitalized enough on synergies between transactions and policy work. To integrate WBG activities and advisory work in the extractive industries more closely, the oil and gas unit and the mining unit of the Bank and IFC were reconstituted as joint Bank-IFC Global Product Groups.

Energy Business Renewal Strategy, 2001: The most recent rethinking of the Bank's role in the energy sector is reflected in the Energy Business Renewal Strategy (EBRS), which was presented to the Board in 2001. The EBRS recognizes a declining demand for traditional IBRD/IDA products in the energy sector and shifts the focus to the WBG's priorities—including poverty alleviation—and comparative advantages: addressing poverty, macro-governance, and the environment; supporting reform and regulation to help support competitive energy markets; facilitating the transfer of knowledge among developing countries; and catalyzing investment in noninvestment-rated countries. The EBRS aims to facilitate access to modern fuels, create objective and transparent regulatory mechanisms, and catalyze private investments. It continues the Bank's emphasis on closing loss-making mines and oil refineries; promoting clean transport fuels and switching from coal to gas; and facilitating environmentally sustainable exploration, production, and distribution of oil, gas, and coal. Reducing gas flaring and facilitating carbon trading and joint investments to reduce greenhouse gas (GHG) emissions are also priorities under the new strategy (see Box C3).

Box C3 **Climate Change: The WBG's Approach**

It is increasingly recognized that the adverse effects of climate change, especially through burning of fossil fuels, can produce changes in precipitation patterns and rise in sea levels that can pose major developmental challenges for developing nations. Hence, the WBG supports its client countries in (a) mitigating the adverse impacts of climate change, (b) reducing vulnerability and improving adaptation, and (c) building capacity for both a and b. Successful support requires policy dialogue, integrated planning and generation, and dissemination of knowledge backed by investment lending.

The WBG's approach to mitigating the effects of and vulnerability to climate change is laid out in *Fuel for Thought* (World Bank 2000), which highlights appropriate policy for improving energy efficiency and the use of clean technologies and fuels. Further, the WBG seeks to leverage external resources, particularly the Global Environment Facility (GEF), as well as new instruments, such as the Prototype Carbon Fund, Community Development Carbon Fund, Bio-Carbon Fund, and private sector resources within the framework of the Kyoto Protocol. In terms of capacity-building, the WBG helps clients through methodological, technical, and investment work to develop market mechanisms, sectoral and national plans, and international cooperation.

Source: World Bank.

Overview of the 1980s and 1990s Projects

Lending for oil and gas decreased while mining increased: Between the 1980s and 1990s, the overall amount of Bank lending to the EI sectors declined by 6 percent (Figure C2). However, this overall decline masks a difference between the two sectors: lending for the oil and gas sector fell by 34 percent, while for the mining sector it rose by 63 percent. During the same period, the EI sectors' share of the Bank's entire portfolio declined from 4 percent of lending to 2 percent.

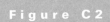

Figure C2	Increased Lending to Mining Has Been More Than Offset by Decreased Lending to Oil and Gas

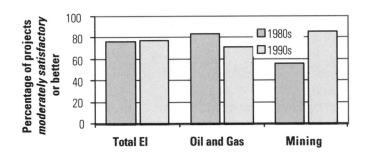

Figure C3	Quality of WB Lending for EI Projects

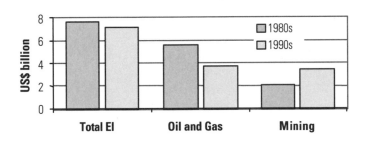

Figure C4	Institutional Development Impact of EI Projects

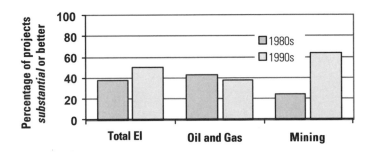

Figure C5 **Sustainability of EI Project Outcomes**

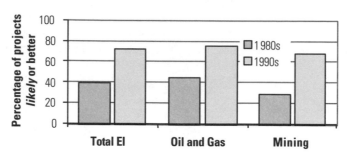

Outcome: Overall EI project outcome[77] ratings were higher than the Bank-wide average during the 1980s and 1990s, though they fell somewhat for oil and gas and rose sharply for mining projects. EI projects with outcomes rated "moderately satisfactory" or better rose slightly (77 percent to 78 percent). The percentage dropped for oil and gas projects (84 percent to 71 percent) and rose significantly for mining projects (55 percent to 86 percent). Taken together, these outcomes are better than for the Bank as a whole, for which the comparable ratios rose from 65 percent in the 1980s to 75 percent in the 1990s.

Institutional Development Impact: The institutional development impact[78] for all EI projects improved between the 1980s and 1990s, declined somewhat for oil and gas, and rose appreciably for mining projects. The institutional development impact of all EI projects—in terms of percentage of projects that were rated "substantial" or better—rose from 38 percent to 50 percent between the 1980s[79] and 1990s. The oil and gas sector saw moderate decline (43 percent to 38 percent), while the mining sector showed considerable improvement (24 percent to 64 percent) over the same period. Taken together, these ratings are higher than the average for all Bank projects, which rose from 30 percent in the 1980s to 43 percent in the 1990s.

Sustainability: The sustainability[80] of project benefits saw very large gains in both the oil and gas sector and the mining sector. The sustainability of outcomes—in terms of the percentage

of projects for which the rating was "likely" or better—improved from 39 percent to 72 percent for all EI projects between the 1980s and 1990s with gains in both oil and gas (44 percent to 75 percent) and mining (28 percent to 68 percent). Overall, these ratings improved much faster than the Bank-wide average, which rose from 44 percent in the 1980s to 56 percent in the 1990s.

Highlights of the Portfolio of Projects under Review: FY93–FY02

The Portfolio Review covered all 76 EI projects[81] approved during the fiscal period 1993–2002. This portfolio consists of 48 completed projects (oil and gas: 24; mining: 24) and 28 *active* projects (oil and gas: 15; mining: 13). This section describes the main characteristics of this portfolio.[82]

The transitional economies of the Europe and Central Asia Region accounted for the largest share of lending: For completed projects in both the oil and gas sector and the mining sector, the Europe and Central Asia (ECA) Region received the major share of lending (Figure C6). The East Asia and Pacific (EAP) Region accounted for the next largest share of oil and gas lending, and Latin America and the Caribbean (LAC) had the next largest share of mining lending.

The most common project objectives reflected some of the similarities between the two sectors: Analysis of the project objectives (each project could have more than one)

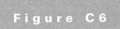

Figure C6 — The Europe and Central Asia Region Accounted for the Largest Share of Lending in Both Sectors

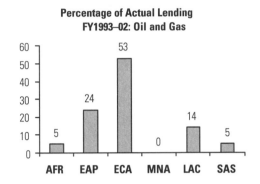

Percentage of Actual Lending
FY1993–02: Oil and Gas

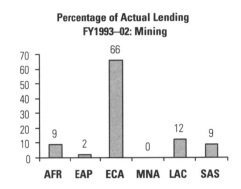

Percentage of Actual Lending
FY1993–02: Mining

identified a few similarities and many differences between the two sectors. Among the similarities, for both oil and gas projects and mining projects, institutional development, private sector development (PSD), and environmental management were among the leading objectives.

But the remaining objectives tended to differ across the two sectors and between completed (older) and ongoing (more recent) projects. For completed oil and gas projects, the next most frequent objectives included pipeline construction, policy reform, production, and social objectives, in descending order. For active projects, the other objectives were production, pipeline construction, and social issues, in descending order. For completed mining projects, other objectives were rehabilitation/closure of mines, social issues, production, and ASM. For active mining projects, the other objectives were social issues and policy reform—production did not figure at all.

The importance of the environmental assessment policy is apparent in the high percentage of projects in categories A and B: Among oil and gas projects, approximately 33 percent of all active and completed projects came under Category 'A'[83] of the Bank's environmental assessment policy (OD/OP 4.01). For Category 'B,' the corresponding percentages

were 25 and 13. For mining projects, only 20 percent of the completed projects and none of the active projects came under Category 'A.' In addition, 50 percent of completed and 30 percent of active mining projects came under Category 'B.'

Project performance ratings have been better than average: The Bank's portfolio of completed EI projects generally has performed well in all three categories used by OED: outcome, sustainability, and institutional development impact.[84] Of the completed oil and gas projects, outcome was rated "moderately satisfactory" or better for 71 percent, sustainability was rated "likely" or better for 73 percent, and institutional development impact was rated "substantial" or better for 37 percent. Of the completed mining projects, outcome was rated "moderately satisfactory" or better for 86 percent, sustainability was rated "likely" or better for 68 percent, and institutional development impact was rated "substantial" or better for 64 percent.

The portfolio of active projects also has been performing well according to supervision reports. All active oil and gas projects had development outcome ratings of "satisfactory" or better, and no adverse issues were reported regarding compliance with the Bank's safeguard policies. All active mining projects had ongoing development outcome ratings of "satisfactory" or better, and only one project reported less than satisfactory compliance with a provision under the Bank's safeguards policies. It should be noted, however, that OED has not validated these self-assessments of active projects.

3. Economic Benefits from Bank Projects

Extractive industries have the potential to make a major contribution to the development of resource-abundant countries by transforming their mineral wealth into sustainable development. The rationale for Bank projects is based on the expectation that they will support the country's development goals, and this expectation is underpinned by an economic appraisal intended to ensure that the objectives have been chosen appropriately and that the project is the least-cost way of attaining the stated objectives.[85] The discounted present value (NPV) of the net benefits, the economic rate of return (ERR), or, where the benefits cannot be measured in monetary terms, a cost-effectiveness criterion are the indicators of choice for making this determination. Following completion of the project, an ex-post recalculation of the economic rate of return or the cost-effectiveness criterion is used to determine whether the project produced the expected benefits in an efficient manner.[86] This chapter discusses the available information on the extent and sources of the economic benefits drawing from the Portfolio Review of the Bank's extractive industries projects.

Reporting of Economic Benefits

The Implementation Completion Reports (ICRs) are an integral part of the Bank's knowledge management and accountability reporting system and are intended to document and evaluate the outcomes and impacts of the project, including their economic benefits. As summarized in Table C1, the Portfolio Review found that, out of the 44 completed projects, ICRs of 17 (mostly investment loans) had re-estimates of ERRs and NPVs, and an additional 13 ICRs (mostly of technical assistance and sectoral adjustment loans) featured at least some ex-post quantification and valuation of the benefits.[87] This finding is consistent with the relative simplicity of attributing and quantifying the costs and benefits of investment projects compared with other types of projects. Nevertheless, given the issues that have been raised about the economic contribution of extractive industries projects, a greater effort to document and analyze economic benefits would be desirable, including a cost-effectiveness assessment where an ERR is not feasible, in line with the *Guidelines for Preparing ICRs*.[88]

For the Specific Investment Loans (SILs), the benefits derived mainly from increased production, increased private investment, and improved productivity. Out of 20 SILs[89] in the portfolio, 18 had an ERR or NPV estimated at appraisal, of which 16 were re-estimated at com-

Table C1		Economic Evaluation in Implementation Completion Reports					
Instrument (number)[a]	ERR/NPV/ least-cost analysis conducted at appraisal	ERR/NPV/ least-cost analysis reported in ICR	Quantification of benefits feasible?	Quantification done in ICR?	Monetary value of benefits feasible?	Monetary value provided in ICR?
			Yes/No/Partly	Yes/No/Partly	Yes/No/Partly	Yes/No/Partly
SILs (20)	18	16	20/–/–	17/–/3	20/–/–	15/2/3
TALs (15)	3[b]	1	4/4/7	3/9/3	6/2/7	3/8/4
SECALs (9)	–	–	7/1/1	5/3/1	6/1/2	6/3/–
Total (44)	21	17	31/5/8	25/13/7	32/3/9	24/13/7

a. SILs include one emergency rehabilitation loan (ERL); technical assistance loans (TALs) include one GEF project; Sectoral Adjustment Loans (SECALs) include one rehabilitation investment loan.

b. The Equatorial Guinea Petroleum technical assistance (TA) project estimated a financial rate of return (FRR) and the Azerbaijan Petroleum TA.

pletion. While it is comforting to note that, in 15 out of these 16 cases, the returns were greater than 10 percent,[90] it would have been feasible to have reported ex-post analyses for three of the remaining SILs.[91]

The 15 Technical Assistance Loans (TALs)[92] in the portfolio were associated with quantifiable and valuable benefits, such as increased private investment, increased gas sales, increased oil and minerals production, increased fiscal revenues, improved environmental conditions, and improved sector efficiency, as well as benefits that are more difficult to quantify, such as improved legal and regulatory frameworks and institutions, and preparatory studies for future projects. Of the 15 TALs, one had a re-estimated ERR[93] and 7 ICRs provided at least some indication of the monetary value of the benefits. Because some benefits were amenable to monetary valuation in 12 of these projects, more could have been done to document their cost-effectiveness and highlight their economic contributions.

All nine completed Sectoral Adjustment Loans (SECALs)[94] were in the mining sector and were associated with increased or decreased production of minerals (coal, in most cases), reduced government subsidies, cleaner environment, increased operational efficiency, improved profitability, and increased private investment. Six of the ICRs provide some data on these achievements, from which a judgment can be made about the efficiency of the projects. The other three ICRs did not provide any quantitative information on results.

Economic Benefits from Private Sector Development

World Bank efforts to promote privatization and boost private investment had largely positive outcomes. Eleven out of 16 completed projects with PSD components yielded or promised to yield significant benefits by laying the groundwork for improving the efficiency of public enterprises through commercialization and privatization, and increasing EI activity by attracting private investment.

Privatization was politically complex in all cases. Wherever progress was made, it was largely due to strong government commitment, supplemented by flexibility on part of the Bank. This is evident in Bolivia's Regulatory Reform and Capitalization and Hydrocarbon Sector Reform projects, as well as in Peru's Privatization Adjustment Loan and Energy/Mining projects. Privatization of coal mines in Russia was a highly complex task carried out in a difficult political and industrial relations environment, and it might not have been possible without strong government commitment and efforts at consulting important stakeholders, together with Bank flexibility in the design and implementation of the projects. On the other hand, inadequate government commitment and political consensus, apart from issues of evolving sector strategy and commercial viability, appear to be behind the limited progress of privatization in Poland's Hard Coal SECAL I and II projects. The slow progress in privatizing Zambia Consolidated Copper Mines can be attributed largely to unfavorable market conditions for copper and political interference in the process.

A particularly effective form of PSD intervention was attracting increased private investment—such as in the mining sectors of Guinea and Tanzania—through relatively low-cost TA interventions (see Box C4).

Economic Benefits from Mine Closure or Rehabilitation

More than 60 percent of completed mining projects, including six completed SECALs in Poland, Russia, and Ukraine, involved large-scale rehabilitation or closure of uneconomical coal mines. On a smaller scale, 15 small copper mines and 66 chrome mines were closed or privatized in Albania. The economic benefits from such projects derive mainly from the reduced burden on government budgets (see Box C5).

Rehabilitation and closure of coal mines in Russia were major tasks, as already noted, but government commitment, stakeholder consultation, and Bank flexibility contributed to the positive results. In Ukraine, favorable results were obtained under less difficult conditions. The strategy of approaching Ukraine's rehabilitation/closure process cautiously, starting with the smaller-scale Ukraine Coal Pilot project and

Box C4	Experience with Private Sector Development in the Extractive Industries Sectors

The Bank's efforts at commercialization and privatization and at improving the climate for private investment yielded largely positive returns in terms of increased investments and exports and reduced burden on state budgets. These efforts generally involved TALs that were smaller than investment and adjustment loans. The positive results were associated with strong government commitment, the prior establishment of an appropriate legal and regulatory framework, and flexibility on the part of the Bank. However, even where earnest efforts were made, volatile commodity prices and macroeconomic crises affected some of the outcomes adversely.

Armed with a strong mandate for privatization, Bolivia moved ahead quickly with the sale of three state-owned hydrocarbon enterprises that yielded US$828 million and improved prospects for investment of up to US$2 billion during 1998–2000. Strong government commitment also was evident in Peru, where the hydrocarbon sector was opened to private investment. Despite strong political and labor opposition, Russia achieved a major feat by privatizing 77 percent of coal assets by 2001, helping decrease subsidies by 40 percent.

Tanzania's and Guinea's success in attracting high levels of private investment to their mining sectors was aided by a relatively integrated approach to developing an enabling legal, regulatory, and fiscal framework. Tanzania's mineral exports grew from US$15 million to US$312 million during 1992–2001, while in Guinea, mineral exports rose from US$400 million to US$500 during 1996–2001.

Argentina's Mining Development TALs made a good beginning in improving the institutional framework for privatization, but the economic crisis in 2002 has diminished their immediate impact. Little headway was made in Zambia on privatizing the dominant Zambia Consolidated Copper Mines because of a volatile market for copper and stakeholder disagreements. The overall efficacy of the World Bank's interventions in Ghana's mining sector during the 1990s is judged to be substantial because of the success in attracting private capital and strengthening sector management capabilities, particularly of the Minerals Commission.

In Ecuador, a new Mining Law passed in 1991 and amended in 2000 included much-improved provisions to attract private sector investment and helped develop a regulatory framework close to best practice. But the country's political instability and unreliable judicial system acted as disincentives, which were compounded by the negative effect of falling international commodity prices.

Finally, Kazakhstan's Petroleum TA project was successful in improving the capacity of key petroleum sector agencies to attract foreign investment. It financed the continuation of technical, financial, and legal advisory services that were critical to the conclusion of two major Caspian Sea projects. On the negative side, the effort to privatize Uzenmunaigas, the country's largest state-owned petroleum enterprise and a centerpiece of the Bank-funded TA program, did not make much headway. On the other hand, the Bank also helped reform in a broad range of sector policy issues covering petroleum legislation and taxation, pricing, and privatization of retail petroleum trade.

Source: World Bank.

leveraging its success for the larger Ukraine SECAL, appears to have worked well. A notable feature of Poland's Hard Coal SECALs I and II was that they succeeded in reducing uneconomical production levels and excess employment while keeping a tense situation from exploding.

However, in all three countries, attempts to generate alternative employment in other sectors for laid-off workers remained an important issue, although there was progress in resolving the employment problem in Russia as the economy began to recover from the crisis of 1998. This may imply that adequate attention to the demanding task of generating alternative employment should be the focus of projects outside of the extractive industries sectors.

Box C5	Economic Benefits of Rehabilitation or Closure of Uneconomical Mines

The economic benefits of closing uneconomical mines derive mainly from reducing the burden on government budgets through lowered or eliminated subsidies, reduced waste of resources, the freeing up of labor that can be used more productively elsewhere, and improved climate for privatization and competition contributing to overall efficiency.

The experience was positive in Poland, Russia, and Ukraine. The Poland Hard Coal SECAL I and II projects reduced excess coal production capacity by 23 percent to 105 million tons per year and employment by 36 percent to 155,000 between 1997/98 and year-end 2001. In Poland, the coal industry's financial performance improved from a loss of US$1.0 billion in 1998 to a profit of US$43.3 million by 2001 (at an exchange rate of US$1 = 0.2545 PLN). Under Ukraine's Coal Pilot and Coal SECAL projects, more than 25 percent of Ukraine's coal mines were closed, and the efficiency of the remaining mines was increased 85 percent between 1998 and 2000. The coal production workforce was reduced by 24 percent between 1995 and 1999, while production dropped by only 3 percent. Subsidies for loss-making coal mines were halved, from US$500 million in 1996 to US$250 million in 1999.

As of 2001, Russia's Coal SECAL I and II led to the closure of the 183 most uneconomical mines, of which 158 completed substantive closure works. As a result of these projects, budgetary subsidies for the coal sector were reduced from 1.05 percent of gross domestic product (GDP) in 1993 to 0.07 percent of GDP by 2001.

In both Russia and Ukraine, Bank support not only helped reduce subsidies, but also shifted the composition of subsidies away from operating expenses toward social mitigation, mine closure, and environmental cleanup.

Source: World Bank.

Economic Benefits from Environmental Cleanup and Mitigation

Most of the projects in the EI portfolio had environmental components of varying magnitude and importance. Some dealt with cleanup of existing environmental conditions, and others were concerned with mitigating the environmental effects of new operations under the project or related projects. Only a few projects—five completed and three active—focused mainly on dealing with existing or ongoing environmental problems. These projects were expected to yield economic benefits through healthier living conditions, greater resources for productive activities, and improved productivity of resources, through reclamation of land and improvement to air, water, and soil quality.

Five completed projects, in Brazil, Ecuador, India, Russia, and Thailand, focused on technical assistance for addressing environmental impacts of past or ongoing extractive industries activities. While the outcome was broadly satisfactory in India (strategy for managing coal mine fires in Jharia coalfields), Brazil (reclaiming degraded mining areas and constructing tailings ponds through the Environmental Conservation and Rehabilitation project), and Thailand (converting to unleaded fuel production in a Bangchak refinery), in the case of the recently completed Coal Sector Environmental and Social Mitigation project in India, an Inspection Panel investigation found it to be out of compliance with some safeguards provisions.

Notwithstanding the lack of compliance, the project resulted in considerable improvement in Coal India's approach to social and environmental mitigation. The Oil Spill Contingency project for the western Indian Ocean islands of Comoros, Madagascar, Mauritius, and Seychelles seeks to build their capacity to comply with related international conventions and protocols.

Among the projects that were not focused exclusively on environmental issues but contained significant environmental components, the Bolivia-Brazil Gas Pipeline project contained provisions for stakeholder consultation and community participation that gave credibility to environmental initiatives and improved their chances of success. Bolivia-Brazil's experience stood in contrast to the Ecuador and India projects in this respect. Another feature worth noting is that while many projects in the portfolio contained significant environmental components, almost none of them explicitly factored the environmental benefits into their economic cost-benefit analysis. A notable exception was Bolivia-Brazil's pipeline project, which applied an environmental premium for the displacement of more polluting fuels by natural gas in its economic analysis.

Economic Benefits of Artisanal and Small-Scale Mining

The rationale for promoting ASM needs to rest on its potential for alleviating poverty by creating and maintaining employment in a socially and environmentally acceptable manner. Among the Bank projects reviewed in this study, ASM issues were a significant component in three completed projects in Ecuador, Ghana, and Tanzania and four active projects in Burkina Faso, Madagascar, Mozambique, and Zambia. The main approaches involve improving the legal framework/formalization of ASM activities, increasing tax revenues (Ecuador, Madagascar, Mozambique, Tanzania), improving production methods and technology and providing extension services (Burkina Faso, Ecuador, Ghana, Mozambique, Tanzania), improving environmental awareness and management (Burkina Faso, Ecuador, Ghana, Madagascar, Tanzania), and improving the capacity of government to deal with ASM (Burkina Faso, Ecuador, Ghana, Madagascar, Tanzania, Zambia). Based on results to date, the main lesson is to recognize ASM as a poverty-driven issue and to move from using a narrow technical approach to a more integrated approach—ensuring an appropriate legal and fiscal framework, involving ASM communities in decisionmaking, and considering environmental and social aspects of ASM at the project design stage (see Box C6).

Conclusions

Overall, 73 percent of the ICRs of completed extractive industries projects contained at least some ex-post quantification and valuation of the benefits, but only 39 percent had a re-estimated ERR or NPV, and the rest do not discuss the cost effectiveness of achieving the objectives.[95] Based on an evaluation of the feasibility of additional economic analysis, this share could have been raised to about 89 percent. While the project's economic returns constitute only an intermediate outcome in the transformation of mineral wealth into sustainable development, adequate reporting and validation of project benefits, in line with Bank policy, constitutes the basis for most further evaluation and should be an essential component in the Bank's accountability reporting. Some improvement in this area also would help the Bank address the perception that the economic benefits of the projects may have been outweighed by adverse environmental and social impacts.

Aside from the reporting issue, the main lesson that emerges is that projects with satisfactory outcome ratings tended to be associated with greater government commitment to project objectives and adequate infrastructure (India Coal Sector Rehabilitation, Russia I and II Oil Sector Rehabilitation, and Thailand Gas Transmission I and II), favorable commodity prices (Russia I and II Oil Sector Rehabilitation), and a high level of stakeholder involvement (Bolivia-Brazil pipeline and Bosnia-Herzegovina's Natural Gas System Reconstruction projects). The less successful projects appeared to be affected by poor government commitment (Ethiopia's Calub Gas Development project) and unfavorable economic conditions or commodity prices (Korea's Petroleum Distribution and Sector Improvement project and Mongolia's Coal project). These lessons are broadly consistent with the Bank's experience in other sectors.

4. Environmental and Social Impacts and Their Mitigation

Addressing Environmental and Social Impacts

The potential benefits from the extractive industries often have been undermined by adverse environmental and social impacts. Negative environmental impacts from oil and gas activities can result from leakages and spills, flaring of excess gas, and the opening of access to new areas where settlement and deforestation can occur. Mining activities can be associated with defor-

---

Box C6	Artisanal and Small-Scale Mining

Nearly 13 million people are involved in ASM worldwide, with a high proportion of women (10 to 45 percent) and children (5 to 30 percent) in several countries. ASM production accounts for 15 to 20 percent of the value of the world's nonfuel mineral production—and as much as 90 to 100 percent in some countries. The majority of earnings from ASM, especially artisanal mining, are used for subsistence. Being largely in the informal sector (50 percent), artisanal and small-scale miners often have no legal rights to mine, do not pay taxes, and are prone to exploitation by middlemen. In general, ASM is characterized by poor standards of safety and health and greater environmental cost per unit of output than large-scale mining activities.

Developmental priorities for ASM are improving the legal and regulatory framework, investing revenues for sustained benefits, avoiding or mitigating negative environmental and social impacts, encouraging alternative economic activities, adopting a gender-sensitive approach, ending child labor, and ensuring good relationships between miners and other stakeholders.

In Ghana, upon advice from the Bank, gold production by small-scale artisanal miners was legalized in 1989 by passage of the Small-Scale Mining Law. The establishment of a legal purchasing arrangement, initially by a public and later by private buying agents offering world prices for gold and diamonds to artisanal miners, was the result of active policy dialogue with the Bank.

Ecuador's Mining Development and Environmental Control project helped to formalize most of the country's ASM activities by granting title to 166 of 169 ASM associations that existed before 1995. This may have contributed to the absence of land invasions by informal miners in the country in recent years. Currently, 99 percent of ASM enterprises in the country have presented environmental impact assessments (EIAs) or environmental management plans (EMPs) either individually or through associations. The project helped demonstrate the feasibility of reducing ASM-related contamination, succeeded in promoting change to less polluting processing technologies, and increased environmental health and safety awareness among miners and other stakeholders.

Sources: Mines and Minerals for Sustainable Development (MMSD) 2002; Country Case Studies; World Bank.

---

estation, soil erosion, contamination of surface and groundwater from toxic wastes, and mine tailings and coal mine fires. In addition to the damage from ongoing projects, closed and abandoned projects have often left a legacy of cleanup costs that no one may be willing or able to pay.[96]

Negative social impacts can arise from resettling local populations, including indigenous peoples, or from disrupting traditional lifestyles to make way for extractive industries. Other social impacts can follow after resources are exhausted or have become uneconomical to extract, resulting in unemployment and scaled-down or abandoned infrastructure. On the whole, social impacts tend to be more prominent for mining than oil and gas activities, given the higher employment generated at the local level and greater exposure to environmental, health, and safety hazards.

To mitigate the adverse environmental and social impacts of the projects it supports, the World Bank, over the past two decades, has developed a comprehensive framework of safeguard policies (see Chapter 2). Its main objective is to ensure that projects "do no harm"; that is, that they are environmentally and socially sustainable by ensuring that potentially adverse impacts on the natural environment (air, water, and land), human health and safety, and social aspects (involuntary settlement, indigenous peoples, and cultural property), and transboundary and global environmental impacts are prevented, mitigated, or compensated. These policies define explicit requirements for the Bank to follow. In light of the potential adverse impacts associated with oil, gas, and mining activities, the evaluation included a review of the degree to which the Bank's appraisal and implementation of extractive industries projects have been consistent with these requirements (the Safeguards Review), whose findings are summarized in the first section of this chapter.

Beyond achieving the objectives of the safeguards, an important aspect of the Bank's approach to development assistance involves the pursuit of positive environmental and social goods, such as the remediation of pre-existing conditions resulting from past mining and petroleum activities (legacy issues), and the strengthening of the policy and institutional framework to promote the implementation of safeguards across the entire economy. Many extractive industries projects have such components to "do good," and their experience is also discussed.

Consistency with Objectives of the Safeguards: "Do No Harm"

The Safeguards Review focused on assessing the projects' consistency with the objectives of the safeguard policies in three areas: at approval, during implementation, and in the adequacy of Bank supervision inputs and reporting. Desk reviews were carried out on a sample of 38 projects drawn from the portfolio of 76 closed and active extractive industries projects approved during or after fiscal year 1993.[97] The sample was purposely chosen to include projects that were likely to have adverse environmental or social impacts and included 19 oil and gas and 19 mining projects.[98] In terms of the categorization of projects under the Bank's Environmental Assessment Policy, the sample included 15 'A' projects, 17 'B' projects, 5 'C' projects, and 1 uncategorized project.[99]

The Bank's safeguard policies contain a long list of requirements that have been subject to differing interpretation, and no independent and generally agreed criteria have been established to determine if a project is in substantial compliance.[100] In the absence of an established approach, the Safeguards Review has synthesized the policy requirements into a set of basic criteria and applied them for sample projects. While there have been minor changes in some of the policies since 1993, each project was evaluated based on the specific version of the policy in force at the time the project was approved.[101]

Overall, most projects were found to be substantially consistent with the applicable safeguards at approval and during implementation. About 74 percent of the sample of 'A' and 'B' projects were substantially consistent with safeguards at approval, 67 percent during implementation, and only 41 percent were rated to have had adequate supervision inputs and reporting. The 'A' projects' performance was higher than the 'B' projects' performance in all three areas, but the difference was greatest at the approval stage. While the degree of consistency was lower than the WBG aims to achieve, there is no implication that the performance pattern of these projects is different from that in other sectors, as they are all subject to the same policies, procedures, and constraints.[102]

The degree of consistency appears to have improved modestly over time. A comparison of the findings for the 'A' and 'B' projects in the sample approved before and after year-end 1995 indicates that, at the approval stage, there has been no overall trend. At the implementation stage, however, there has been some improvement in the more recent projects.[103]

The findings of the Safeguards Review fall between those of the external and internal surveys. The survey of participants of the EIR's Regional Stakeholder Workshops[104] found that, with regard to the promotion of sustainable environmental performance and mitigation of negative environmental effects, the WBG's effort was rated "mostly effective" or better by 60 percent of respondents and its success as "mostly effective" or better by 46 percent. With regard to the promotion of sound social development and the identification and mitigation of negative social impacts on local communities and indigenous peoples, the WBG's effort was rated "mostly effective" or better by 40 percent of respondents and its success as "mostly effective" by 28 percent. Bank staff involved in EI projects feel more positive about the adequacy with which EI projects have mitigated negative environmental impacts (83 percent) and social impacts (75 percent). While the survey findings corroborate that the EI portfolio faces a gap in fully achieving the objectives of the safeguards, the difference from the Safeguards Review points to the possibility of both internal and external perception gaps.

The review also identified a number of promising practices that have established new benchmarks for safeguard policy implementation performance and "value added." Such practices were found in the Bolivia-Brazil Gas Pipeline project, Chad-Cameroon Petroleum Development and Pipeline project, Poland Coal SECAL II, and Thailand Clean Fuels and Environmental Improvement project. These projects have achieved international recognition for the comprehensiveness of their environmental and social mitigation measures and stand as examples of what compliance with safeguards can achieve.

Issues During Safeguards Implementation

The most important inadequacies in the implementation of safeguards are associated with shortcomings at the initial project screening. Another important source of problems, and a possible explanation for the decline in safeguards implementation from approval to implementation, is inadequacies in supervision and reporting.[105]

Initial Project Screening

A major finding of the Safeguards Review is that the initial screening of projects[106] has important implications for the subsequent preparation, appraisal, and supervision of the project. In some cases, screening decisions resulted in assignment of a lower environmental category than may have been warranted.[107] This is important because less attention and fewer resources tend to be devoted to the assessment and mitigation of environmental impacts in lower EA categories.

On the other hand, not all difficulties in achieving the objectives of the safeguards can be traced to shortcomings in the initial project screening process. In fact, while 69 percent of the projects that were not substantially consistent with safeguards had been incorrectly screened, over half of the projects that had been incorrectly screened were substantially consistent with policy requirements at the approval stage in terms of the adequacy of provisions for mitigation of potential adverse impacts (see Figure C7). These findings suggest that, while shortcomings at the initial project screening are an important source of concern, these upstream

Figure C7   Initial Project Screening and Consistency with Safeguards

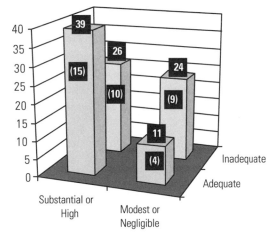

errors often can be overcome by appropriate efforts during subsequent project preparation and appraisal.

EA Categorization

The Safeguards Study concluded that, of the sample of 38 projects, 6 out of the 17 Category 'B' projects should have been classified as Category 'A,' and all 5 of the 'C' projects should have been 'B.' The definitions of EA categories were developed mainly for application to "investment" projects and before the social and legal safeguard policies assumed as much importance as they have in the past decade. Since the late 1980s, the Bank has been diversifying and expanding its array of lending instruments,[108] while EA categorization definitions and guidance on application of appropriate EA instruments[109] have not kept pace. The study found two major areas where greater clarity is needed:

Sectoral Adjustment Projects: Five of the six 'B' projects that should have been categorized as 'A's were SECALs involving the closure of mines.[110] While the OP 4.01 can be interpreted to allow categorizing them as 'B's, it would have been more appropriate to categorize them as 'A's, given the significant, diverse, and unprecedented cumulative impact of the mining sector on the environment and communities in the mining areas and to ensure a level of attention, normally associated with a full EA, commensurate with the degree of environmental and social impacts and risks.[111] Thus, the guidance set out in the 1993 *EA Source Book Update on Environmental Screening* recommends that Sectoral EAs be carried out for SECALs, and the 1991 *EA Source Book*[112] recommends that EIAs be carried out on each individual mine closure plan.[113] While these guidelines are not mandatory, they support the objectives of the safeguards policies, and OED has used them to underpin its assessment.

Among mining SECALs, the Poland Coal SECAL II illustrates the potential usefulness of a Sectoral EA, which, for this project, found that the damage costs of saline water discharge were not as serious as previously estimated[114] and identified land subsidence as a potential problem. It also found several shortcomings in clar-

ity and prioritization of recommended actions in the mine-specific EIAs. Other mine-restructuring SECALs did not follow this model and therefore may have missed the opportunity for considerably more appropriate and cost-effective actions for mitigating negative environmental and social impacts.

Technical Assistance Projects: While six of the Technical Assistance projects in the sample were correctly categorized as 'A' or 'B' projects, five were incorrectly categorized as 'C.' As noted in the 1993 *EA Source Book Update on Environmental Screening*, *"while most technical assistance (TA) projects should fall into Category 'C'... certain TA operations are designed to pave the way for major investments or privatization.... In such cases, it is appropriate to undertake a limited review of the environmental institutional and regulatory framework for the sector and recommend improvements (as needed). Category 'B' is normally the correct classification for such projects."*[115]

The Colombia Energy TA project, a 'B,' illustrates the importance of early attention to the environmental and institutional and regulatory framework, which allowed for the preparation of a well-designed set of components to operationalize the application of the Bank's safeguard policies. On the other hand, in line with the objectives of the safeguard policies, TA projects in Cameroon, Kazakhstan, Papua New Guinea, Russia, and Zambia all should have been categorized as 'B's rather than 'C's, which resulted in less attention being given to reviewing substantial issues of environmental and social impacts that can emerge in the process of attracting major investments and preparing for privatization.

Identification of Applicable Safeguards

An important function of the initial project screening is to identify the safeguard policies that should apply to a particular project. Aside from the EA policy, the most frequently triggered safeguards in the sample of extractive industries projects relate to involuntary resettlement, indigenous peoples, natural habitats, dam safety, and cultural properties. There is a natural inclination to downplay the relevance of individual safeguards in order to simplify processing of projects. Moreover, in the case of TA projects, such issues as protection of natural habitats, cultural property, and indigenous peoples, and so forth, while possibly relevant to the sector, had not been triggered when needed, as the policies have been worded to apply when "investment" projects are undertaken. This is unfortunate, as often the TA projects are helping governments to improve the regulatory system for private investments in extractive industries, for which such issues are highly relevant.

Involuntary Resettlement: Of the seven projects that should have triggered the Involuntary Resettlement policy, four had prepared comprehensive Resettlement Action Plans (RAPs), while for three of the projects the RAPs were either not prepared or inadequate. The risks associated with inadequate safeguard identification at the screening stage are illustrated by the Second Gas Transmission project in Thailand,[116] where the issue of resettlement arose very late in project preparation—so late, in fact, that it had to be dealt with at loan negotiations. At this stage it was not even certain how many people had to be relocated and how many had to be compensated for loss of income during pipeline construction or for loss of structures. While the completion document reports that the resettlement of the few families was in line with the guidelines and carried out without a problem, it also reports that problems with land acquisition were compounded by difficulties in purchasing the right-of way because of landowner lock-outs. There were also problems with squatters moving onto the pipeline route in an attempt to obtain compensation.[117] It is quite possible that problems, which happened before in earlier projects, could have been reduced through earlier identification of resettlement issues and the earlier involvement of resettlement specialists in planning for their mitigation, as would have been appropriate.

Indigenous Peoples: Three out of the seven projects for which the indigenous peoples policy applied met the requirement for preparation of an Indigenous Peoples Development Plan (IPDP). A good example of an IPDP was prepared for the Bolivian section of the Bolivia-Brazil Gas Pipeline project. Under this plan, indigenous peoples' land rights were established through land titling, and communities were supported in developing sustainable resource management practices. A trust fund of US$1 million was also established for protection and management of the Kaa-Iya National Park, which is co-managed by an indigenous NGO and Bolivia's National Protected Areas Agency.

Natural Habitats: Three of the five projects in which the Natural Habitats policy applied met the requirements of this policy. For the Chad-Cameroon Pipeline project,[118] alternative corridors for the pipeline were assessed and alignment of the pipeline within the preferred corridor was optimized from cost, technical, safety, environment, and social perspectives. In addition to aligning the pipeline to follow existing infrastructure and/or traverse degraded land to the extent possible, because of the proximity of the right-of-way to areas of important natural habitat in Cameroon, biodiversity impact mitigation measures included two environmental offsets—one for the semi-deciduous forest and one for the Atlantic Littoral forest.

Supervision, Monitoring, and Consultation

Other issues that emerged from the Safeguards Review relate to the (a) adequacy of supervision inputs and reporting, (b) management and/or action plans that were prepared, (c) adequacy of provisions for monitoring and evaluating environmental and social impacts, and (d) provisions for disclosure and stakeholder consultation.

Supervision Inputs and Reporting: The study found that in only 41 percent of the sample projects, the task teams had adequately supervised and reported the implementation of safeguard policies. About 30 percent of the projects (all of which were likely to have adverse impacts) included environmental or social specialists in at least one supervision mission, which is about half the level projected in the supervision plans prepared at appraisal.[119] Frequent changes in task teams, especially task leaders, and the lower managerial attention and resources devoted to safeguards supervision in incorrectly screened and categorized projects also contributed to the modest intensity of safeguards supervision, as reflected in infrequent and inadequate reporting on safeguard policy matters in aide-memoires, supervision reports, and completion reports.

These issues are important because they account for the entire slippage in the projects' consistency with safeguards from the approval to the implementation stage. Thus, for about a quarter of the 23 projects for which supervision inputs and reporting were inadequate, the consistency with safeguards deteriorated during implementation. On the other hand, of the 14 projects that were supervised adequately, not a single one failed to meet the safeguard objectives, and two previously inconsistent projects (14 percent) became substantially consistent with safeguards during implementation (see Figure C8).

The oversight and reporting of safeguards compliance and EMP implementation can be only as effective as the environmental and social monitoring reporting system provided for under the projects. Since these were found to be deficient in nearly half of the projects reviewed, the same can be said for the oversight system. Supervision reports generally record safeguards compliance positively without any discussion or evidence provided in the text, and only a single reported violation of safeguard policies was reported.[120] Finally, less than a quarter of the ICRs reviewed discuss the implementation of safeguards, even though the Bank's ICR policy requires such a discussion for all Category 'A' projects and those that triggered any other safeguards and could reasonably be expected for all Category 'B' projects. The paucity of monitoring, documentation, and reporting of the projects' implementation of safeguards is a serious weakness in the oversight system

Environmental and Social Management and Action Plans: The basic instruments that the Bank safeguard policies rely on for implementation of environmental and social mitigation measures are the EMPs, RAPs, and Indigenous Peoples Action Plans (IPAPs). The review found that EMPs are being prepared to an appropriate standard for 93 percent of the 'A' projects but only 60 percent of the 'B' projects. Because the EA policy leaves the decision on the scope of EMPs to the judgment of Bank staff, this would likely have been less of a compliance problem if the projects had been assigned to their proper

Figure C8 — **Adequacy of Project Supervision and Change in Consistency with Safeguard Objectives**

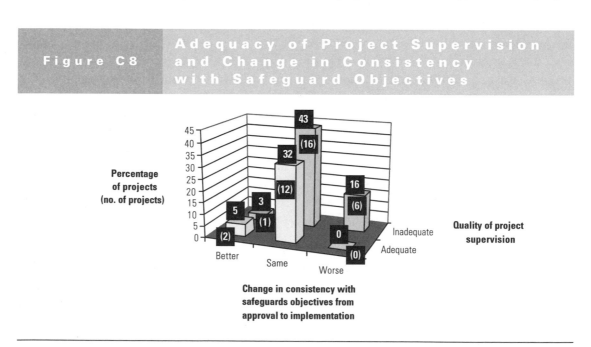

Percentage of projects (no. of projects)

Quality of project supervision

Change in consistency with safeguards objectives from approval to implementation

EA category at the screening stage, with attendant availability of more resources for specialist staff to help define and supervise the EMP. Similarly, about half of the sample projects that involved involuntary resettlement and affected indigenous peoples did not have comprehensive and implementable RAPs and IPAPs, largely because the relevant safeguards had not been triggered at the initial project screening.

Monitoring and Baseline Surveys: An important requirement, often overlooked, is that of monitoring and evaluating safeguard compliance "on-site," which was implemented effectively in only about 33 percent of the projects reviewed. This weakness in the compliance oversight and supervision system, if allowed to persist, can lead to substantial and costly failures for the borrower as well as the Bank. Moreover, it is rare that a monitoring plan, no matter how well prepared, will cover all the potential environmental and social impacts in any new project completely. Some impacts become evident only during implementation. Such impacts can be documented most quickly and effectively if comprehensive environmental and social baseline surveys have been prepared before project implementation, as was done for about half of the 'A' projects in the sample.[121]

Public Disclosure, Consultation, and Participation: Bank policy expects the borrower to consult affected groups and local NGOs for all Category 'A' and 'B' projects, to disclose relevant EA materials, and to incorporate their legitimate concerns into project designs. The requirements are somewhat more rigorous for 'A' than for 'B' projects. The Safeguards Review found that public consultation in the EA preparation process had been substantially addressed in 73 percent of the 'A' projects in the sample and 38 percent of the 'B' projects. Stakeholder participation, in terms of opportunities to influence and share control over development initiatives, decisions, and resources, is not required under Bank policy and has been attempted in only a few projects.

Here again, the 'B' projects appear to have had fewer resources than necessary to devote to

this area. The ICRs of several 'B' projects where consultation took place noted the importance of stakeholder consultation. OED's assessment of a 'B' project in Ecuador, in which full public consultation only started five years into implementation, concludes that the projects and programs involving natural resources extraction need to be managed carefully and proactively. Effective communication, consultation, and stakeholder participation strategies need to be designed early during preparation and maintained throughout implementation.

Beyond consultation, the Bolivia-Brazil Gas Pipeline project offers an excellent model for establishing a participatory safeguards compliance monitoring, evaluation, and reporting framework. The completion report notes that continuous dialogue and exchange of information between the local communities and civil society representatives and the environmental inspectors, environmental auditor, and ombudsperson was an important feature of the on-site supervision of environmental and social concerns. This process allowed a growing understanding of the concerns of each of the stakeholders, the identification of new issues, better monitoring of the performance of social compensation programs in the field, and, more important, an improvement of the environmental inspection/monitoring system, which resulted in a better definition of roles and functions for the contractor environmental field inspectors, the environmental inspection team and management unit independent from the contractor, and the independent environmental auditor and ombudsperson.

Beyond Safeguards: "Doing Good"
An important aspect of the Bank's approach to development assistance involves the pursuit of positive environmental and social impacts beyond strict compliance with safeguards, such as the remediation of pre-existing conditions resulting from past mining and petroleum activities and the strengthening of the policy and institutional framework to promote the implementation of safeguards across the entire economy. Many extractive industries projects have such objectives and components.

Box C7	World Bank Projects and Pre-existing Environmental Impacts

In the oil and gas sector, the efforts included controlling drilling wastes and reducing environmental impacts from oil and gas operations (Russia); controlling and mitigating pollution from refinery activities (Thailand); controlling pollution from leaking pipes and storage facilities (Tanzania); and addressing the impact of petroleum development in an area of extreme environmental sensitivity near the Caspian Sea (Azerbaijan).

In the mining subsector, pre-existing pollution issues included water and air pollution from mine tailings and airborne particles (Guinea, Peru, Poland, and Mongolia); environmental impacts on surrounding communities (Ghana, Russia); contamination from activities of artisanal and informal miners (Ecuador, Peru); a strategy to control widespread mine fires that were affecting local infrastructure, farmland, and habitation and could potentially dislocate hundreds of thousands of people in the Jharia coalfields (India); and passage of a new environmental code for mining to ensure cleanup of existing pollution and rigorous guidelines for new foreign investors (Peru).

The efforts in Tanzania and Thailand yielded positive results, and good progress was made in Peru, where contamination levels were reduced by 15 to 20 percent, and in Poland, where saline water and solid discharge from coal mines were reduced by 21 percent and 29 percent, respectively. Under the Mongolia Coal project, a beginning was made by establishing an Environmental Management Unit. In Guinea, environmental audits of all mining operations were carried out. Ghana's project made some headway in reclaiming three pilot areas reclaimed and launched a "green communities" plan.

Source: Portfolio Review.

Addressing Pre-existing Environmental Conditions

Environmental Rehabilitation: Nine completed projects (oil and gas: 5; mining: 4) provided assistance for addressing environmental impacts from past or ongoing extractive industries activities, while other completed projects approached them as part of larger efforts in economic transition. Based on the generally limited information provided in the ICRs, pre-existing environmental conditions appear to have been addressed in a moderately satisfactory or better manner, in all but two cases (see Box C7).

Pre-existing environmental impacts tended to be given less priority in countries where the sector faced poor economic and financial conditions, where the priority was to restore production levels and earn import revenues, and where the mitigation components were a relatively small part of the project. All these factors were evident in Russia's Oil Sector Rehabilitation I and II projects as well as in Coal SECAL I and II projects. In countries where the economic and financial situation was better (Poland's Hard Coal SECAL I and II) and in cases where environmental components were larger relative to the entire project (Mongolia Coal project) and where stakeholder participation was higher (Tanzania Mineral Sector Development TA), there was greater progress in dealing with pre-existing environmental impacts.

Social Rehabilitation: Important coal mine rehabilitation projects in Poland, Russia, and Ukraine substantially achieved their mine closure objectives, but the results on the social front have been mixed. The greatest difficulties were in generating alternative employment for workers who lost their jobs in the rehabilitation and mine closure process. The difficult economic transition in Russia and Ukraine made it very hard to generate alternative employment, and it is not clear if these issues were addressed through projects in sectors other than the extractive industries. Another area of concern was finding alternative funding sources for social services that previously had been provided by the state mining enterprises. These issues are important because the process by which employment reduction is handled is crucial for the acceptance by the mining communities of economically necessary mine closure programs.

Capacity-Building and Reform for Environmental and Social Management

Components in support of capacity-building, institutional development, and policy reform for environmental management were part of 16 completed and 9 active projects. Most of the activities were completed satisfactorily. For many of these efforts the impacts are not evident from the ICRs, perhaps because results may be realized only in the long term. Projects in three countries—Burkina Faso, Madagascar, and Mauritania—aim to improve capacity for environmental management in their mining sectors. Burkina Faso's Mining Capacity-Building project seeks to establish capacity for environmental management. The Madagascar Mining Sector Reform project will establish capacity in the country by means of pilot projects to identify and address environmental as well as social impacts from mining. The Mauritania Mining Sector Capacity project has an Environmental Management System to include capacity-building at the Ministry of Mining and Industry, for monitoring and enforcing environmental regulations.

Capacity-building for environmental and social management represents a valuable contribution by the Bank to client countries at a relatively low cost. While it is too early to judge the impacts of these project components in many cases, indications are that most of the changes are sustainable, especially in countries that already had a reasonable level of institutions and human resources in these areas. The Bank's cross-country experience also helped client countries to learn from other countries facing similar environmental situations. The number of efforts to build capacity for environmental management in extractive industries projects appears to be increasing.

Other Environmental Benefits from Extractive Industries Projects

In the portfolio of 48 completed projects, 5 projects produced other miscellaneous environmental benefits. Under Brazil's Gas Sector Development project, the creation or improvement of 13 national parks was initiated. This project, as well as Thailand's Gas Transmission I and II projects, made available larger amounts of environmentally acceptable fuel—natural gas—and, along with Thailand's Clean Fuels and Environmental Improvement, had consequent benefits for air quality and health. Bosnia-Herzegovina's Natural Gas System Reconstruction project helped reduce environmental pollution through rehabilitating war-damaged gas distribution systems.

Missed Opportunities in Addressing Adverse Impacts

The survey of Bank staff followed up on a recent Quality Assurance Group (QAG) Quality-at-Entry Assessment, which noted, "in numerous interviews with task teams, panelists detected an aversion to including project components that may trigger safeguard policies, …[and]…that it was too risky to design operations with significant social safeguard issues."[122] Thus, the survey asked if the WBG has avoided good projects in the EI sectors due to concerns related to safeguards policies. The majority of respondents agreed that this has been the case, particularly in response to concerns originating from WBG management (86 percent) and WBG task managers (56 percent), rather than client countries (22 percent) or private investors (40 percent). This response suggests that the WBG is missing opportunities to help its clients address adverse impacts in the sector mainly because of an internally generated aversion based on the significant costs and risks associated with its safeguard policies.

Conclusions

The Safeguards Review of a sample of extractive industries projects most likely to face environmental and social challenges found the majority to be substantially consistent with applicable safeguard policies, but the degree of consistency is below the expectation that Board-approved policies will be implemented as a matter of routine.[123] The degree of consistency varied greatly depending on the phase of project cycle and the environmental category of the projects. The degree of consistency appears to have improved modestly over time. The review also found that supervision inputs for and reporting of safeguards compliance had been adequate for less than half of the projects.

The most important shortcomings with regard to the implementation of safeguards can be traced to inadequacies in the initial project screening. Another important source of problems was inadequacies in supervision inputs and reporting. Inadequate attention to compliance during project implementation also is reflected in the fact that environmental and social specialists were involved in supervision in only about 30 percent of the sample and that fewer than a quarter of the project completion reports discuss this subject.

While the validity of these findings is limited to the sample of projects that was reviewed, some of them may be helpful for strengthening the Bank's safeguards framework, which is no different for extractive industries than for other types of projects.[124] In particular, the findings point to the need for clearer and more consistent guidance for the categorization of sectoral adjustment and technical assistance projects; the identification of applicable safeguards at the initial project screening; the appropriate scope and arrangements for monitoring of safeguards compliance during project implementation, including the preparation of comprehensive baseline surveys at the start of the project; and the reporting and evaluation of results at project completion. Improvement would be of particular importance to the extractive industries portfolio, given its large share of sectoral adjustment and technical assistance projects, the inadequacies in monitoring and reporting, and the controversy surrounding the sector's environmental and social impacts.

On the other hand, the Bank's safeguards policies have received wide acceptance, even for projects where the Bank is not involved, which points to the potential for the Bank to continue building on its global mandate and convening power for catalyzing good practice in respect to safeguards and other issues. Beyond compliance with safeguards, the Bank's efforts at "doing good" by addressing environmental legacy issues and building capacity for the management of environmental and social impacts have yielded mostly satisfactory results. These appear to be areas where the Bank should continue to make a valuable contribution to the development of resource-abundant countries.

5. From Resource Revenues to Sustainable Development

From a country development perspective, the most important component of the economic benefits from extractive industries is usually the flow of revenues that can be used for growth-promoting public expenditures.[125] This chapter assesses the Bank's efforts to integrate the incremental revenues from resource extraction into the countries' overall development strategy through improved fiscal management and expenditure policies.[126] While the potential for major fiscal revenues is generally greater from the petroleum than the mining sector, it is useful to discuss them together in light of their shared characteristics of volatility and exhaustibility.

Linking Extractive Industries Sector Development to Overall Country Assistance

The management of EI revenues cannot be isolated from the larger context of economic management. In a resource-rich country, EI revenues deserve special attention because of their importance to the economy and their concentration in a few sources, which affords greater scope for rent-seeking. Hence, an assistance strategy for a resource-abundant country must not only recognize the specific issues involved in managing EI revenues but also chart their linkages with the broader management of the country's development.

A review of the World Bank's most recent CASs[127] found that 64 percent of those for poorly performing EI-dependent countries[128] recognized one or more issues related to the management of EI revenues (see Figure C9).[129] The issues spanned a wide range, including managing of volatility and exhaustibility of EI revenues (Azerbaijan, Mongolia), achieving macroeconomic stability (Gabon, Trinidad, and Tobago), public

Figure C9 — Percentage of Countries Whose CAS Refers to EI Issues

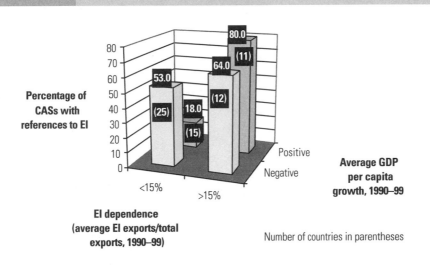

Percentage of CASs with references to EI

EI dependence (average EI exports/total exports, 1990–99)

Average GDP per capita growth, 1990–99

Number of countries in parentheses

expenditure policies for EI revenues (Bolivia, Chad), transparency in handling EI revenues (Kazakhstan, Papua New Guinea), diversifying of economic activity (Nigeria, Zambia), and reducing subsidies to the EI sectors (Russia).

In general, the mention of EI revenue issues in a CAS does not appear to translate readily into developmental interventions by the Bank. The dearth of follow-up interventions could be related to the relatively low level of Bank involvement in poorly performing EI-dependent countries. World Bank lending per capita over 1990–99 was significantly lower (at US$47) for poorly performing EI-dependent countries than for better-performing EI-dependent countries (US$80) or poorly performing non-EI-dependent countries (US$61; see Figure C10). While this is a consequence of the Bank's country policy and institutional performance-based allocation of IDA credits, there is no indication

Figure C10 — IBRD/IDA Lending per Capita (number of countries)

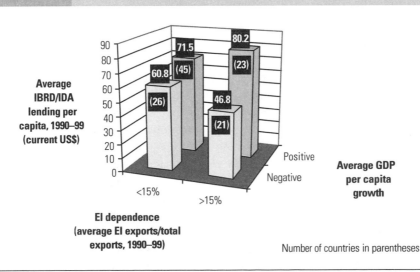

Average IBRD/IDA lending per capita, 1990–99 (current US$)

EI dependence (average EI exports/total exports, 1990–99)

Average GDP per capita growth

Number of countries in parentheses

Box C8	Analytical and Advisory Activities in the EI Sectors

The Bank has engaged in a variety of analytical and advisory activities (AAA) in the EI sectors, including economic and sector work (ESW), as well as sponsoring meetings, conferences, and workshops for stakeholders.

None of the AAA in the EI sectors has been evaluated through either self-evaluative Activity Completion Summaries[a] or the annual reviews of ESW by the QAG from 1998 to 2001. However, some reporting in the ICRs, as well as in country case studies prepared for this evaluation, gives an idea of the integration of representative AAA with project preparation.[b]

In Papua New Guinea, the Bank has provided a range of ESW on many occasions since the 1980s in the mining sector, and it undertook reviews of environmental issues in 1992 and again in 2000 that provided input into the mining TA project. The Argentina Mining Sector Review (1993) helped improve the quality of project preparation for the country's Mining TA and Mining Sector Development TA projects. In Ecuador, the Bank assisted the government in the preparation of a Mining Sector Policy and Strategy Paper in 1990 (updated in 1993) stressing the need for legal and institutional reform to attract private sector investment in the sector and to address environmental impacts of artisanal and small-scale mining.

Other illustrative publications from the oil and gas sector on institutional development and policy issues include *Legislative Frameworks Used to Foster Petroleum Development* (1995), *Management of Oil Windfalls in Mexico: Historical Experience and Policy Options for the Future* (2001), and *Does Mother Nature Corrupt?—Natural Resources, Corruption and Economic Growth* (1999).

In the mining sector, several country-level sectoral reviews have been prepared, among them the *Kyrgyz Republic: Mining Sector Review* (World Bank 1994a), *Russian Federation: Restructuring the Coal Industry: Putting the People First* (World Bank 1994b), *Kazakhstan: National Gas Investment Strategy Study* (ESMAP 1997), and *Ecuador—Public Sector Reforms for Growth in the Era of Declining Oil Output* (1991). *A Mining Strategy for Latin America and the Caribbean* (Van de Veen et al. 1996) and *Strategy for African Mining* (World Bank 1992) spell out strategies for boosting private investment in the regions.

a. At least since 1998, the Bank has required Activity Completion Summaries to be prepared for all ESW with a budget of $50,000 or above, within six months after "delivery to client." In AFR, there is no threshold, and in ECA it is $15,000.

b. A detailed list of ESW by the Bank in both the oil and gas sector and the mining sector is included in the Bibliography annexed to the Portfolio Review.

Sources: Country Case Studies; World Bank.

---

that the shortfall in lending has been mitigated by nonlending interventions, such as economic and sector work, as would seem desirable in light of these countries' needs[130] (see Box C8).

For a more in-depth assessment of the Bank's involvement in the revenue management issues of EI-dependent countries, the Revenue Study reviewed CASs, Country Assistance Evaluations (CAEs), project documents for EI and other sectors, and adjustment lending and Public Expenditure Reviews and other documents for five EI-dependent countries: Bolivia, Ecuador, Ghana, Kazakhstan, and Papua New Guinea.[131]

The study found that in all five countries, governance was the key to successful management of EI revenues and fed into the quality of revenue distribution and utilization, as well as attempts at economic stabilization and diversification. Ecuador and Ghana lacked the political will and the fiscal discipline to maintain macroeconomic stability, putting other reforms in jeopardy. Kazakhstan and Papua New Guinea showed little institutional development or commitment to governing openly or fairly. Only in Bolivia did the government show a commitment to managing its revenues within the context of overall public finance management, but even Bolivia is having difficulty maintaining fiscal discipline. The Revenue Study also found that desirable structural reforms were slowed in the face of large resource flows from resource extraction (see Box C9).

Box C9	EI Revenue Management and Macroeconomic Performance: Some World Bank Country Experiences

The World Bank has assisted several EI-dependent countries in reconciling EI revenue management with broader macroeconomic management. In most cases the outcomes have been less than satisfactory.

In Ecuador, in the 1990s, the Bank identified constraints to macroeconomic performance as the major negative effect of the decline in oil revenues and their mismanagement, but it failed to develop a more comprehensive strategy to isolate the economy from volatility and exhaustibility of the resources and to share oil benefits. Though the Bank provided financial assistance to sectoral rehabilitation and macroeconomic stabilization, the expected reforms were not implemented, and export and fiscal revenues went to finance highly inefficient public expenditures. Overall, the Bank had a very limited influence on how oil revenues were managed to promote macroeconomic stability and social equity.

In Ghana, during the 1990s, the Bank supported efforts for better financial management and civil service reform, but OED's CAE of 2000 found these efforts were only partly successful. Many shortcomings remain in the overall quality of Ghana's public governance, as illustrated by politically motivated spending on public sector wage increases and consumer subsidies before each election in 1992, 1996, and 2000. These increases led to persistent macroeconomic instability with negative consequences for investment and growth.

In Kazakhstan, an inflow of petroleum revenues created prosperity that began to produce symptoms of the Dutch disease and reduced commitment to overall reform, to the point that the country has forgone sound advice from the World Bank regarding the management of EI revenues.

In Papua New Guinea, private investment in the EI sectors created some prosperity in the early 1990s, after which the government discontinued reforms, which precipitated a financial crisis. Subsequently, the WBG supported a new government effort to restore macroeconomic stability and initiate structural reform, with emphasis on governance and economic diversification. But macroeconomic mismanagement continued, compounded by political uncertainty and poor transparency and accountability, forcing the Bank to suspend the second tranche of a structural adjustment loan.

In Bolivia, WBG strategy in both hydrocarbons and minerals had great success in generating revenues, helped in large measure by the country's own "capitalization" program. However, public expenditure management in the country is still weak, and Bolivia has not responded well to several WBG technical assistance and structural adjustment operations targeted at public finance management, civil service reform, customs administration, and judicial reform.

Sources: Revenue Study; Country Case Studies.

The Revenue Study also found that while economic diversification through directing public expenditure toward socially profitable investments is necessary for the sustainable development of EI-dependent countries, this approach is difficult to promote in the face of poor governance. Bolivia successfully developed agriculture in the lowlands but at the cost of additional environmental damages that are difficult to control. The Bank and the government showed clear commitment to develop agriculture in Papua New Guinea, but after 10 years of assistance the strategic options for stimulating agriculture have yet to be developed. Ghana had difficulties in developing agriculture and streamlining cocoa production management, and competition between mining and agriculture for arable land continues to be an important issue. The Bank advised Kazakhstan that efficient management of the National Oil Stabilization Fund and better management of public finances in general were preconditions for promoting economic growth in the nonextractive industries sectors, but governance of the oil fund and of public finance continue to be difficult problems. Ecuador's poor management of public expenditures is the core cause of the continuous financial crises the country faced in the 1990s, and it is still excessively dependent on oil exports. In general, while the World Bank supported diversification in all these countries, it has not been able to address these diversification issues with any clarity, and the efficacy of its interventions has been low.

Overall, the Revenue Study concluded that the relevance of the World Bank's interventions for revenue management in the EI sectors had been modest for Ecuador and Kazakhstan, substantial for Papua New Guinea, and high for Bolivia and Ghana. The study rated the efficacy of interventions as negligible for Ecuador, Kazakhstan, and Papua New Guinea, modest for Ghana, and substantial for Bolivia.

Managing Volatility and Exhaustibility of Revenues

Fewer than half the CASs for EI-dependent countries (12 out of 26) recognized the importance of dealing with volatility and exhaustibility of revenues from the EI sectors. These CASs identified broad approaches to dealing with the issues: creating a windfall fund and encouraging growth outside the oil sector (Gabon); offshore funds (Kazakhstan); longer-term strategy of fiscal management of copper revenues and diversifying

exports (Mongolia); developing a strong private sector in industries other than oil (Azerbaijan); creating an oil stabilization fund (Colombia); and keeping a sizable reserve cushion (Chile).

In two CASs a clear link was found among issues relating to volatility and exhaustibility of EI revenues, appropriate policy dialogue, and a lending/nonlending program to address them: The Papua New Guinea CAS addresses the country's vulnerability to external shocks and suggests enhancing macroeconomic stability through appropriate policy dialogue and a structural adjustment loan. The Kazakhstan CAS addresses the volatility inherent in commodity-led growth by proposing careful management of oil revenues, reflected in lending for public sector resource management and structural adjustment, as well as nonlending initiatives.

A general review of experiences with savings and stabilization funds, with or without Bank intervention, as well as recent analytical work, suggests that the experience with such funds has been mixed, with the few important successes coming from countries with a strong history of fiscal prudence (Botswana, Chile). Without such

---

Box C10   **How Effective Are Resource Funds?**

A number of EI-dependent countries have responded to the prospect of volatility and exhaustibility of EI revenues by setting up petroleum, resource, or future generations funds, with the objectives of maintaining fiscal discipline, achieving overall macroeconomic stabilization, or saving for future generations. These attempts have been mostly unsatisfactory.

Papua New Guinea's Mineral Resource Stabilization Fund of the 1970s was depleted by withdrawals and excessive public spending and was finally used up in 1999 to retire debt that had then reached 25 percent of GDP. Ghana's Mineral Fund is a source of controversy because its recipients, both mining communities and the Ministry of Finance, have mishandled its system of resource-rent sharing. Kazakhstan's National Oil Stabilization Fund, created in 2001 to reduce the negative impact of oil revenues on the domestic economy and provide for the welfare of future generations, has yet

to evolve rules for transfer of funds and establish spending priorities and has already been criticized for misuse of funds. The Petroleum Stabilization Fund established by Ecuador in 1990 turned into an additional source of revenue to finance regular budgetary expenditures. In Equatorial Guinea, the government has established a Future Generations Fund in its overall scheme for the use of anticipated petroleum revenues, but no significant amounts have been deposited.

In general, the same elements of disciplined economic management are needed to make a success of a resource fund as are needed to run an economy effectively. Thus, recourse to resource funds is unlikely to yield better results than pursuing equitable distribution and effective utilization of EI revenues through sound fiscal policies.

Sources: Country Case Studies; Davis et al. 2001; World Bank.

a history, the integration of resource funds with overall fiscal policy has proved problematic, and the stabilization of expenditure has remained elusive (see Box C10).

Revenue Generation

Project components designed to help resource-dependent countries improve the generation and accounting of fiscal revenues from resource extraction were included in 10 of the completed projects in the portfolio. These components focused on improving the capacity of governments to negotiate with investors and on upgrading accounting procedures to international standards.

Six of the completed Technical Assistance Loans helped to improve negotiating capacity and four others helped upgrade accounting procedures. Three projects, in Georgia (Oil Institution Building TA), Papua New Guinea (Petroleum Exploration TA), and Peru (Peru's Energy/Mining TA), helped build negotiating capacity through improved data collection and economic analysis for exploration and development. Capacity was developed in Russia for working with foreign suppliers and organizing bidding (Oil Sector Rehabilitation I and II projects) and in Equatorial Guinea (Petroleum TA project) for maintaining a dialogue on long-term development plans with oil companies.

Four completed projects supported the adoption of international accounting practices by state enterprises for improving transparency and compatibility with foreign investors: Azerbaijan's Petroleum TA with respect to the State Oil Company of Azerbaijan, the Mongolia Economic Transition Support project for the planning and restructuring of operations of the ERDENET copper mine, and Thailand's Gas Transmission I and II projects with respect to the Petroleum Authority of Thailand. The results are reported to have been satisfactory.

Efforts to improve capacity for negotiating with private investors and for adopting international accounting practices have yielded generally favorable results, mainly because the client governments and implementing agencies recognized the immediate benefits of attracting higher private investment and gaining more favorable contractual terms. The lesson is that where such conditions are stipulated, these project initiatives seem to be straightforward and effective.

Revenue Distribution

A distribution of EI revenues among federal, state, and local governments that is broadly acceptable and sustainable to key stakeholders is critical for converting the revenues into sustainable development and poverty reduction. In general terms, an acceptable distribution of revenues is one that is consistent with national developmental priorities, subject to (i) entitlements of legal, customary, and traditional owners of resource rights, and subnational units of the government, as recognized under national laws and (ii) compensation for negative environmental and social impacts. An additional negotiated premium to local communities and governments also may be appropriate, depending on national priorities. While the perception of equity will vary, the experience of several countries shows that it is important that none of the claimants gets an excessive share, poor governance does not constrain the actual transfer of funds, and there are clear regulatory provisions for using the funds in the intended manner (see Box C11).

Issues relating to distribution of revenues among owners of resource rights and different levels of government figured in six of the completed projects in the portfolio—with largely satisfactory outcomes—and two active projects relating to the Chad-Cameroon pipeline. The six completed projects—in Bolivia, Papua New Guinea, and Russia—contained provisions for distribution of revenues from resource extraction to meet entitlements, compensation, and other national priorities. Of the six projects, four had satisfactory outcomes in terms of achieving their distributional objectives.

Revenue Utilization

Developmentally efficient use of EI revenue can stimulate broad-based and sustainable economic development that goes beyond the EI sectors. Approaches to better use of EI revenues are discussed in CASs for 6 out of 26 EI-dependent

Box C11 — Distribution of Extractive Industries Revenues — Striking the Right Balance

Striking the right balance in distribution of EI revenues involves many complex issues and needs firm institutional arrangements and provisions for consultations among stakeholders to arrive at equitable and sustainable arrangements.

The government of Papua New Guinea (GOPNG) has handed over a greater share of the resource rent to the provincial governments and landowners since pioneering an innovative Development Forum in 1989 to represent their interests. In a recent project, GOPNG ceded 30 percent of its equity to the landowners, though the 1998 Oil and Gas Act had established a cap of 20 percent. Neither side has demonstrated effective use of these resources, and the distribution of revenues has not yet been settled to everyone's satisfaction.

In Equatorial Guinea, all oil revenues accrue to the central government, which exclusively decides their allocation, though local municipalities are deeply affected by the oil economy. In Chad, just under 5 percent of anticipated oil revenues are allocated to the local authorities in the oil-producing region and 70 percent to poverty sectors throughout the country (including the oil-producing region).

The experiences of Nigeria and Peru illustrate how revenue distribution can go awry for lack of proper implementation and proper regulatory mechanisms. In Nigeria, federal revenues, predominantly from oil, appear to be reasonably shared among the federal government (49 percent), state government (24 percent), and local government (20 percent). In practice, these shares are not realized because of prior appropriations, which are taken off the top, effectively reducing the share of state and local governments, making the issue one of actual implementation and quality of governance rather than a lack of appropriate constitutional provisions. In Peru, since 2001, the law requires a 50 percent of mining profits taxes to be plowed back into local communities. Yet few of these funds appear to reach the communities, primarily because the federal government retains them to pay ancient debts.

In Ghana, the constitution explicitly reserves all mineral rights for the state. Nevertheless, public sentiment has favored local communities receiving a direct share in royalties paid to the government of Ghana by mining companies. As a result, the government set up a Mineral Development Fund (MDF), which restored a traditional practice of payments to custodians of the mining land. The MDF receives 20 percent of all mining royalties, of which 9 percent goes to mining communities, which in turn is subdivided between local authorities. The other 11 percent goes to mining sector institutions and mineral-related investment projects. In practice, however, the discretion given to the Ministry of Finance in handling the MDF together with the lack of clear expenditure guidelines for the local authorities has resulted in little benefit to the local communities.

The distribution of oil rents in Ecuador is considered the most centralized and least transparent of the four Andean countries (ESMAP 2000). Over 1995–2000, an average of 90 percent of available oil rents was assigned to the central government and its institutions, 62 percent to the central budget, 7 percent to the armed forces, and 23 percent to the universities. Producing provinces and municipalities averaged 1.2 and 2.4 percent, much below the Andean countries' average of 18.9 percent and 9.5 percent. Although a large share of local government resources come from other central government transfers, they account for less than 1 percent of central government expenditures.

Sources: Country Case Studies; World Bank.

countries. The approaches include improving capacity for public finance management and developing a strategy for poverty-oriented use of revenues (Chad), resisting the unwise expenditure of oil revenues (Azerbaijan), managing resource rents effectively (Mongolia), and directing revenues toward sustainable use (Kazakhstan). Once again, there is little evidence in the CASs of lending or nonlending activities that follow directly from these discussions. Only three active projects relating to the Chad-Cameroon pipeline contain explicit provisions

---

| Box C12 | **Applying Extractive Industries Revenues to the Right Developmental Priorities** |

Issues related to use of EI revenues are intertwined with those of public expenditure policies. However, depending on the relative importance of EI revenues and the nature of developmental and macroeconomic priorities, sector-specific strategies need to be devised.

In Papua New Guinea, a large proportion of EI revenues went toward nonproductive uses in the 1990s, a period of poor economic growth for the country. This was due to inadequate institutional capacity as well as government preoccupation with macroeconomic imbalances, which distracted it from the scope and quality of public expenditure. Since 2000 the government of PNG has been consciously redirecting recurrent expenditure toward development projects.

In Equatorial Guinea, after a long period of poor economic growth, there have been visible signs of infrastructure improvements since 1995 that support the oil and the associated service industry and access roads in agricultural areas. The investment budget—which reflects a 1997 commitment to give priority to essential infrastructure and to alleviate poverty through investments in social services and agricultural diversification—is allocated among administration (20 percent), the productive sectors (13 percent), health (10 percent), education (15 percent), and infrastructure (32 percent). While the allocation appears appropriate for Equatorial Guinea's development needs, much needs to be done to develop the capacity of the sector ministries to implement such a large investment program efficiently.

In Bolivia and in Ghana, EI revenue enabled the government to increase spending on social programs and begin to alleviate poverty, but poverty remains entrenched in both countries. In Ecuador and PNG, poverty alleviation is an even more distant hope. In Kazakhstan, poverty assessments were undertaken only in the late 1990s, and their conclusions have been incorporated into World Bank strategy, but the Bank has little leverage after abundant oil revenue reduced the government's commitment to reform.

Chad's ongoing Petroleum Revenue Management project contains a detailed Revenue Management Plan that allocates prospective revenue from petroleum projects to poverty-related sectors such as education, health, rural development, and infrastructure (70 percent), civil sector operation expenditure (15 percent), a future generations account (10 percent), and a supplement to the producing region (5 percent). Capacity-building and institutional arrangements for transparent allocation and utilization are in process.

In Ecuador, a Bank review concluded that most of the country's oil capital was being used to finance government consumption, including widespread overstaffing in the public sector, growth in inefficient public enterprises and low levels of non-oil taxation, and high levels of subsidies for petroleum.

Source: Country Case Studies.

---

for allocating fiscal revenues from extractive industries (see Box C12).

Coordination across the World Bank Group

Aside from serving as an instrument for integrating activities within the Bank, the CAS is expected to strengthen coordination and cooperation between the Bank and IFC/MIGA. However, the review of CASs of EI-dependent countries found that, while the discussion of linkages with the Bank's EI activities has been very modest, the EI activities of IFC and MIGA are not always mentioned, even in joint CASs.[132] In response to a survey question about the coordination across the WBG on important issues affecting the EI sectors, 52 percent of Bank staff and 100 percent of MIGA, but only 48 percent of IFC staff, responded that it was adequate. In response to a question about factors that constrain the WBG's ability to help client countries enhance the contribution of the EI sectors to sustainable development, Bank and MIGA staff tended to point to the inadequate linkage between EI activities and sustainable development (50 percent and 56 percent, respectively, versus 42 percent of IFC staff), while IFC staff pointed to the inadequate level of support from the Bank's Country Departments and Country

Management Units (55 percent versus 52 percent of Bank staff and 29 percent of MIGA staff). These findings also point to a need for greater integration of EI sectoral and macro interventions in the Bank's assistance strategies, especially for IFC activities.

Conclusions

At the country level, the majority of CASs in EI-dependent countries recognized one or more issues related to the management of fiscal revenues from resource extraction, but in only a few instances was the discussion linked to specific interventions to address them. Also, the Bank's overall lending to EI-dependent countries experiencing negative growth has been substantially lower than average, with no indications of compensating non-lending interventions[133] and no evaluative evidence on the results of such interventions. A desk review of Bank interventions in five EI-dependent countries found that governance was the key to the successful management of EI revenues and fed into the quality of revenue distribution and the efficiency of its use in support of broad-based and sustainable development.

The CAS review and the staff survey findings point to a need for greater integration of EI sectoral and macro interventions in the assistance strategies. The evidence suggests that only half of WBG staff believed the actual level of coordination to be adequate , with inadequate linkages between EI activities and sustainable development and inadequate support from the Bank's country units emerging as the main areas for improvement. The joint CAS process, which has not been much used in EI-dependent countries, would appear to be an important instrument to achieve integration.

Taken together, these findings suggest that, while the Bank has been reasonably effective in the few cases when it addressed revenue generation and distribution issues at the project level, it has yet to formulate and implement a strategy to consistently transform resource rents into sustainable development, particularly in the most poorly performing EI-dependent countries where the need is greatest. If the Bank is to have a more effective role in such countries,

it will likely require government commitment as well as the full leverage of the Bank to achieve both sound fiscal management and a supportive governance framework. The best place to clarify the linkages between resource rents and sustainable development is the CAS, which can then be used to guide the design of specific projects and the monitoring and evaluation of results.

The strategic approach needs to ensure that project-specific interventions are effectively integrated with a macro-level effort to manage the revenues for sustainable development. Projects and analytical and advisory activities to strengthen policies and institutions to ensure that the management and use of EI revenues is efficient and transparent should play a major role. Projects to close uneconomical mines and mitigate pre-existing environmental and social conditions, including the integration of artisanal and small-scale mining within the formal sector, also will be important where such problems exist. Projects to establish a legal and regulatory framework that is appropriate, stable, and consistently enforced and that will facilitate the privatization of ongoing activities also should be expected to make a major contribution. Where the Bank can be confident that the incremental revenues will support sustainable development, it should continue to promote private investment for sector expansion.

6. Addressing the Challenge of Governance

High dependence on revenues from extractive industries has been associated with corrosive effects on economic and political life, including rent-seeking and government ineffectiveness, in many countries. Indeed, a review of the literature and feedback from NGOs suggest that good governance is central to creating an environment that fosters sustainable and equitable development and is an essential complement to sound revenue management and safeguard policies. Figure C11 shows the association between the quality of governance and EI dependence.[134]

Countries such as Botswana and Chile[135] have successfully leveraged their wealth into sustainable growth through investment-friendly policies, fiscal discipline, and long-term planning.

Figure C11	Worse Country Governance with Greater EI-Dependence

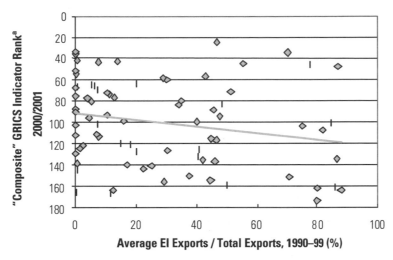

a "Composite" GRICS ranks are a simple average of individual GRICS rankings for 2000/2001 for Voice and Accountability, Political Stability, Government Effectiveness, Regulatory Quality, Rule of Law, and Control of Corruption.

Source: http://www.worldbank.org/sbi/governance/pdf/2001 kkzcharts.xls

While the highest quality of overall and sectoral governance may not be required for an EI project to be beneficial to a client country, some minimum conditions should exist to help ensure that the benefits of EI projects are not squandered and the citizens left with costs that can include environmental damage, health risks, and war.

Governance, defined as how power is exercised in the management of a country's economic and social resources for development, has been an explicit concern for the World Bank at least since 1990, when the Bank's General Counsel articulated the legal basis for its work in this area. This was followed by a Board Paper on "Governance and Development"[136] that outlined the Bank's general approach to improving governance. Before this time, the Bank had undertaken many initiatives that addressed institutional and policy aspects related to governance. They included projects to reform public sector policies and institutions and to create an enabling environment for private sector development. Since the early 1990s, much effort has been devoted to strengthening complementary process-oriented aspects of governance, including public participation, information disclosure, transparency promotion, and corruption reduction.

Project Components Relating to Governance and Transparency

The Portfolio Review found that about 41 percent of extractive industry projects had at least one component that bears directly or indirectly on improving governance and transparency. The relevant project components address sectoral governance issues such as (i) the institutional and policy framework and related capacity-building for clarification of property rights and improved accounting and auditing standards and practices and (ii) strengthening governance processes, including public consultation and participation, information disclosure and dissemination, transparency promotion, and corruption reduction.

Institutional and Policy Framework: Property rights issues relating mainly to clarification and administration of exploration rights and access to pipelines were addressed in nine completed and five active projects and had generally satisfactory outcomes. Cadastre and registry systems were formulated or upgraded (Argentina, Ecuador, Peru), and institutional capacity was improved for enforcement of laws and regulations, as well as for administering mine titles (Albania, Bolivia, Guinea, Peru, Russia, Zambia). Ongoing efforts among active projects included strengthening mining cadastral systems and related institutional capacity (Madagascar, Mozambique, Romania). In addition, components addressing the management of fiscal revenues were included in 10 projects (see Chapter 5).

Public Consultation and Participation: Consultative and participative decisionmaking processes involving all important stakeholders—local community, government, and industry—recently have emerged as important in a strategy to strengthen governance processes. In the portfolio of completed projects, public consultations of varying levels and in different forms, beyond the minimum requirements of the Bank's EA policy, were undertaken in only four projects. The Bolivia-Brazil Gas Pipeline project involved creating community-based organizations and committees and consulting the public on draft regulations and the project's environmental assessment. The Georgia Oil Institution Building project provided for training in stakeholder analysis and public consultation to maximize public participation in environmental decisionmaking. During the India Jharia Mine Fire Control project, effective public consultation processes included concerned state government, union leaders, tribal communities, and NGOs. The Russia Coal Implementation TA project supported stakeholders' participatory activities, especially local trade unions and the Association of Mining Cities.

Among the active projects, the Chad-Cameroon Pipeline project has involved public consultations in the preparation of the project's Environmental Assessment and Environmental Management Plan. Extensive and frequent public consultation also has taken place on the subject of likely project impacts and compensation measures. Compensation rates for all crops, trees, and other assets have been well researched and discussed with affected people in all categories of land tenure. The private sponsors will pay compensation at real market values, which are over and above government schedules.

Overall, while public consultation and participation has helped project implementation where it was carried out, it was quite rare across the portfolio of EI projects. This is an important gap in a sector where production and rehabilitation activities directly affect the livelihood and environmental and social well-being of large numbers of people and where benefits need to be shared in a cooperative and transparent manner to prevent rent-seeking behavior. The prominent examples of public consultation have occurred in countries with relatively higher levels of education and per capita incomes. In light of this finding, it is important to develop suitable mechanisms to ensure that affected people who are less literate and economically weak are given appropriate and fair means to register their feedback on issues that effect them. The provisions established for the Chad-Cameroon projects represent a particularly important pilot experience in this area.

Disclosure and Information Dissemination: Public disclosure and information dissemination, including conducting opinion surveys, figured in only six completed projects. Opinion surveys of project beneficiaries were conducted in six projects in Albania, Peru, Poland, and Ukraine. Public information and communications campaigns were mounted in six completed projects in Albania, Bolivia, Peru, Poland, and Zambia, with mixed results. Among active projects, the four projects associated with the Chad-Cameroon pipeline contain exemplary provisions for public disclosure and information dissemination.[137]

In Albania, as part of the Structural Adjustment Credit project (in which mining was only one component), the government conducted a survey of citizens' satisfaction with services, governance, and institutional reform strategy and received generally favorable feedback. A survey of beneficiaries and stakeholders was made under Poland's Coal SECAL I and II projects, while Poland's government also initiated an intensive dialogue with representatives of local government, labor unions, and NGOs. In the Ukraine Coal Pilot and Coal SECAL projects, an independent institute was involved in monitoring social rehabilitation efforts with affected parties and obtained generally positive feedback from project beneficiaries. A public opinion survey was conducted following the Privatization Adjustment project in Peru.

A public information campaign was mounted in Poland's Hard Coal SECAL I, and Albania began a program to survey citizen's satisfaction with key public services and publicized reviews of the impact of each element of its governance and institutional reform strategy (Albania Structural Adjustment Credit project). Following a controversy over its mapping work, the Ecuador Mining/Environment TA project began a dissemination effort to present scientific facts through various public forums. Bolivia's public information campaign on the benefits of the reform was not sufficient or effective enough to answer public criticism of the Regulatory Reform and Capitalization projects regarding benefits of newly capitalized firms. Zambia's efforts to produce an NGO policy paper proved insufficient to bridge the gap between the complex groups of NGOs and the government. Ukraine failed to respond adequately with appropriate information or disclosure to damaging reports in the media on the conduct of coal sector reform and may have invited political opposition to the reform process.

Promoting Transparency and Reducing Corruption:
Promoting transparency and reducing corruption did not figure as explicit objectives in any of the completed projects that were reviewed, with the exception of the Russia Coal SECAL I and II projects. However, some technical assistance components, such as those relating to accounting standards, bidding processes, and better management practices, had the effect of improving transparency, some of which may have lasting effects. There was one instance of misuse of project funds that was addressed eventually. Overall, 16 projects had components related to transparency or corruption, some of which were minor in scope.

An important objective of Russia's Coal SECAL I and II projects was the establishment of a transparent mechanism for the allocation and effective monitoring of subsidies. During these projects, the government of Russia took a series of radical and far-reaching steps that enhanced transparency and accountability through transfer of subsidy administration to government ministries and created mechanisms for direct payment of entitlements to individuals and job creation programs to local administrations.

The Bank's funding for Peru's Committee for Promotion of Private Investment helped it function with greater independence during the sale of state-owned enterprises (Peru's Privatization Adjustment project). Open and transparent bidding was used for the first time for petroleum imports, which helped to reduce costs of petroleum purchases (Petroleum Sector Reform project). Transparency was improved through upgrading accounting and auditing procedures during Azerbaijan's Petroleum TA and Thailand's Gas Transmission project, as well as under Madagascar's Petroleum Sector Reform project.

A notable achievement of the Peru Energy/Mining TA was that the government and public have accepted the concept of autonomous regulatory operators with stable and nondiscriminatory rules. The funds for the Miners' Separation Package scheme under Poland's Hard Coal SECAL were properly accounted for through audits, and accountability of mining companies was improved through more transparent company business plans and operating plans.

In the Ukraine Coal SECAL, the small business component saw some fraud in applications for micro-credit and employment subsidies, but follow-up measures to prevent recurrence were effective. Some administrative problems were encountered during audits of the employment restructuring funds and mine liquidation funds in Poland's Coal SECAL I and were satisfactorily resolved, and it was confirmed that the funds had been used properly.

There were some less successful experiences, as in Zambia's Second Economic and Social Adjustment project, where bilateral donors suspended program lending because of their concerns about governance issues. The Bank's sector policy initiatives in Russia helped underline the importance of institutional regulations surrounding transparent allocation of quotas and access to export pipeline facilities (Oil Sector Rehabilitation

I and II projects), though a draft law for this purpose fell short of expectations. Albania's Anti-Corruption Plan supported an array of measures to increase transparency, such as deregulation, more transparent privatization and licensing procedures, public administration reform, and judicial reform, which had an impact on all sectors, including hydrocarbon and mining.

In Bolivia's Regulatory Reform and Capitalization Assistance projects, detailed asset valuation helped set a benchmark to ensure that a fair bidding process and the privatization process were considered most transparent by investors. However, the government's scheme for sharing the proceeds of capitalization with specified sections of the population was marred by cases of fraud by claimants who falsified their ages to claim benefits. During the Guinea Mining Sector Investment project, the Ministry of Mines negotiated mining rights with potential private investors in a nontransparent way with respect to bauxite and alumina concessions, especially for the Dian Dian deposits. Though outside the scope of the project, these actions could well have affected the interest of potential investors in project activities. However, on another count, budgetary transparency was improved by the elimination of the Agency for the Management of Mines Infrastructure. Under the Mongolia Coal project, modern financial accounting, budgeting, and cost accounting have been introduced and adopted.

Overall, the scope of the project components relating to governance and transparency tended to be narrow, relating to specific steps in the sequence of project-related activities. In most cases, the link with better governance and transparency was incidental and did not follow from a stated objective of the project. None of the projects have any stated objectives dealing with larger governance or transparency issues, though these issues are recognized in many CASs. One reason for this could be the political sensitivity of this subject, making it difficult to convince client countries to adopt specific objectives in this regard. Another possibility is that these issues, being common to many sectors, may need to be dealt with at the macro level rather than through sectoral interventions.

Addressing Governance at the Country Level

Since major governance issues are most likely to be addressed through interventions that are not tied directly to EI projects, the Governance Study was undertaken to review the World Bank's assistance to six EI-dependent countries[138]—Chile, Ecuador, Ghana, Kazakhstan, Papua New Guinea, and Tanzania—in light of macro and sectoral governance problems. The study sought to understand the degree to which the Bank is factoring governance into its sectoral approach through governance-focused ESW, a governance-informed sectoral assistance strategy, and the design of projects. The study also makes an important distinction between macro and sectoral governance.

Macro Governance: Governance at the macro level covers all aspects of exercising authority through formal and informal institutions in managing a state's resources for sustainable development. Thus, the elements of macro governance include the creation of a favorable climate for economic growth, transparent budgetary and financial management, transparency in the political process, and a voice for all citizens, while providing them with effective social and environmental services. Many indicators have been developed for measuring the quality of macro governance in terms of its performance and process. Each indicator tends to cover one or two aspects of macro governance and the viewpoint of one or more important stakeholders—the government, civil society, or the business community. The World Bank Institute's Governance Research Indicators Country Snapshot (GRICS) estimates six dimensions—voice and accountability, political stability, government effectiveness, regulatory quality, rule of law, and control of corruption.[139]

Sectoral Governance: In contrast to macro governance, sectoral governance in the context of the EI sector is more closely concerned with a satisfactory legal, regulatory, and institutional framework to manage environmental and social risks; involving and protecting local communities against negative impacts of EI activities, including abuse of individual rights;[140] ensuring investor compliance with the law; and protecting investor contractual rights. This requires that appropriate environmental, financial, and compensation regulations exist and are enforced, with the effective participation of the local communities, while the rights of investors are respected. The structure and process of good sectoral governance can be ensured through government capacity-building and appropriate policy, legal, and institutional reforms, preferably in the overall context of good macro governance. In the absence of indicators specific to sectoral governance, they may need to be derived from those for macro governance, but extra efforts may be needed to tailor them to the specific situations and for data collection.

From Governance Awareness to Project Design

The Governance Study found that most of the Bank's EI projects are not the result of a governance-informed sector strategy. There is no indication that the decision to support increased investment or structural adjustment loans was preceded by an analysis that considered the likely governance benefits and risks of such investments. It is recognized that most of the EI projects under review predate the Bank's sharpened focus on governance in the later 1990s.[141] The Bank's apparent lack of integration of governance concerns into the lending program is reflected in recent OED CAEs covering the 1990s that found fault with the Bank for a belated, indirect, or muffled response to obvious governance issues in Ecuador, Ghana, Kazakhstan, and Papua New Guinea.

PNG presents a rare case where a link can be discerned between governance ESW, a governance-informed strategic approach to the EI sectors set out in the CAS, and the design of EI projects in the period under review. Both of PNG's Petroleum TA projects predated the Bank's increased focus on governance. But despite the success of these projects in building Papua New Guinea's petroleum sector, OED's CAE found that "progress in managing the growth of the oil and gas industry has not led to sustained economic benefits to the country because of macroeconomic mismanagement of oil revenues" and recommended that "the Bank should intensify its non-lending assistance, but restrain its lending services." Although both later operations, the 2000 Mining Sector Institutional TA Project and the 2000 Gas Development TA project, are primarily intended to increase private investment in their respective sectors, they also include components to address macro and sectoral governance issues.[142] The Governance Study, however, found no indication that the Bank considered the likely benefits of such increased investment in light of governance risks.

In Kazakhstan, while a public sector reform loan achieved the technocratic reforms it sought, it did not achieve its stated purpose of improving the effectiveness of resource mobilization and the efficiency of the use of resources because of the absence of system-wide checks and balances.[143] Papua New Guinea and Kazakhstan are not isolated cases.

The findings of the Governance Study are broadly similar to those of the Stakeholders' Survey, but WBG staff involved in EI projects and countries tend to be more sanguine. The survey of participants in the EIR's Stakeholder Workshops found that, while 83 percent of respondents expressed the need for the WBG to become involved in improving governance and transparency, only 41 percent felt that the level of effort and 26 percent that the level of success had been adequate. The survey of WBG staff found that 90 percent of respondents felt that improving governance and transparency in EI-dependent countries was important, and 64 percent said that these issues had been adequately addressed in projects. Here again, the survey findings confirm that there is room for significant improvement in strengthening the linkage between EI activities and governance issues.

Sequencing EI Lending with Regard to Improved Macro and Sectoral Governance

In pursuing lending interventions in EI without paying sufficient attention to governance, the World Bank risks a situation where a country is unable to capture the benefits or control the risks. Historically, the Bank's approach to the EI sectors has promoted private investment for sector expansion as a major objective on the basis that state enterprises in the sector had not been managed to maximize productivity and were subject to corruption and political interference. The rationale was that private sector development was desirable because it would be better managed and produce more fiscal revenue, but no explicit linkage was made to the efficient use of these revenues. This focus on expanding production through PSD predates the institutional changes in the late 1990s that allowed governance to be diagnosed, analyzed, and considered, and it may predate much of the debate on the development impact of EI sectors.

The Bank has no strategy for sequencing governance interventions in the EI sectors or coordinating them with work done in other sectors. Instead, the sequence of Bank actions has been shaped by the evolution of its understanding of the issues and its mandate. As a consequence, where the Bank sought to increase investment in the EI sectors, it pursued this objective either before supporting better risk management, or simultaneously. But as the experiences in Papua New Guinea and Kazakhstan illustrate, working to establish the prerequisites for good development outcomes from EI investments in parallel with, or after supporting expansion of the sector, poses a major challenge and is a high-risk strategy in countries with poor macro and sectoral governance.

Finally, countries are likely to be less receptive to improving governance in revenue and safeguards after the major investments have been made and incremental revenues are flowing. Yet no awareness of such logic is evident in the portfolio under review, nor is there any indication from ESW that the World Bank considered a sequencing of its interventions to mitigate the attendant risks. The decision to focus the policy dialogue with Equatorial Guinea, Kazakhstan, and Papua New Guinea on governance issues came after private investments in resource development had made the Bank unimportant as a source of finance. In hindsight, the experience in these countries points to the need for the Bank to develop a more selective and sequenced approach that takes macro and sectoral governance issues into account and gives priority to improving management of existing sectoral revenue flows and environmental and

social risk ahead of promoting new investments in expanding the EI sector. Alternatively, effective measures need to be taken to ensure that revenues from new production are used to promote development and reduce poverty.

Conclusions

While the Bank has long been aware of the importance of addressing the governance challenge for ensuring the transformation of resource rents into sustainable development, there is little evidence of sector-specific governance strategies in CASs of EI-dependent countries. The Bank's project-level interventions tend to be sporadic and narrow in scope, with few cases where a link can be discerned between these interventions and governance ESW or a governance-informed strategic approach to the EI sectors set out in the CAS. Where some links can be observed, as in Papua New Guinea and Kazakhstan, their experience suggests that governance issues take a long time to address, and working to establish good governance in parallel with, or after supporting increased investment in EI, is a high-risk strategy in countries with poor macro and sectoral governance.

The priority of supporting increased investment in the EI sectors needs to be based on an assessment of the quality of macro and sectoral governance. Where sectoral governance is poor, the Bank may focus its efforts on helping the borrower better capture the benefits and control the risks of EI projects in preparation for greater investment. Where macro governance is also weak, however, the Bank's decision to support sectoral reforms must be undertaken strategically with an understanding of their likely impact.

To assess the quality of macro and sectoral governance, the Bank needs to develop appropriate diagnostic instruments that take key indicators into account, supplemented by additional analysis. Key indicators of macro governance relate to the quality of public financial management and rule of law[144] as a measure of the government's ability to address problems through institutional reforms. At present, while there is substantial Bank ESW focused on the quality of public financial management, there is no diagnostic instrument to evaluate the rule of law or the quality of sectoral governance. Both of these gaps would need to be addressed for the Bank to be able to take macro and sectoral governance into account, at least in EI-dependent countries.

Given an assessment of the quality of macro and sectoral governance, a three-tiered approach would seem appropriate:

- For countries with sound macro and sectoral governance, the Bank should support the country as needed to attract investment to expand the sector or further improve management of resource revenue flows and environmental and social risks.

- For countries with sound macro governance and weak sectoral governance, the Bank should focus its support on strengthening sectoral governance, including management of environmental and social risks, and support significant sector expansion only in conjunction with adequate provisions to compensate for sectoral governance weaknesses.

- For countries with weak macro and sectoral governance, where the government lacks the ability to manage revenues well, increased investment designed to augment government revenues will have little benefit, and the Bank should focus its support on strengthening governance and managing of environmental and social risks.[145] The promotion of investments for significant sector expansion should be avoided, except where the Bank can adequately mitigate the risk that fiscal revenues from new investment may not be used for the country's development priorities. The Chad-Cameroon model represents an important test case for such a holistic approach.[146]

7. Recommendations

How effectively has the World Bank assisted its client countries in improving the contribution of the extractive industries to sustainable development? On the one hand, with its global mandate and experience, comprehensive country development focus, and overarching mission to fight poverty, the Bank is well positioned to help countries overcome the policy, institutional, and technical challenges to transforming resource riches into sustainable benefits, and its achievements are many. Overall, nearly 80 percent of the Bank's EI projects had at least moderately satisfactory outcomes, and the performance of this portfolio has been consistently and significantly above Bank-wide averages in terms of outcome, institutional development impact, and sustainability. The Bank's research made major contributions to broadening and deepening understanding of the disappointing performance of resource-abundant countries. It has helped set standards in the formulation and implementation of guidelines for the mitigation of environmental and social impacts. More recently, it has begun to address the challenge of governance with a variety of innovative tools.

On the other hand, the Bank can do much more to improve its performance in enhancing the EI sector's contribution to development and poverty reduction by (i) formulating and implementing integrated corporate- and country-level strategies for addressing the broader developmental issues that lie at the heart of many resource-rich countries' inability to achieve sustainable development; (ii) strengthening the implementation of the Bank's projects based on its policies for mitigating environmental and social impacts and for monitoring and reporting economic, environmental, and social results; and (iii) engaging stakeholders to develop stronger and widely accepted governance frameworks to assist the transformation of resource endowments into sustainable development.

Given the size and complexity of the World Bank Group and the diversity of issues that need to be addressed, the responsibility for following up on these recommendations is not expected to rest exclusively with the sector specialists in the Energy and Mining Sector Board and the Oil, Gas, Mining, and Chemicals Global Products Group.[147]

Recommendation 1: Formulate an Integrated Strategy

The Bank has not devoted enough attention to the developmental needs of the poorly performing resource-abundant countries, many of which experienced negative growth during the 1990s. To address this gap, the Bank Group needs to formulate and implement integrated strategies, at both the corporate and country levels, for transforming resource endowments into sustainable development. Such an integrated strategy will start with the presumption that successful EI projects—whether financed by the Bank or not—have to provide revenues to governments, mitigate negative environmental and social effects, and benefit local communities. It also will need to address governance squarely and help to ensure that EI revenues are used effectively to support development priorities. It also will require much better cooperation within the WBG and with other stakeholders.

(a) Formulate a sector strategy: The Bank, together with other members of the World Bank Group, needs to design and implement a sector strategy that closely integrates resource extraction with sustainable development through the effective management of EI revenues in support of developmental priorities and the reliable mitigation of adverse environmental and social impacts.[148] Where macro and sectoral governance are weak, the Bank's assistance should focus on strengthening macro and sectoral governance. In such cases, the Bank should carefully assess and report on the risks that EI fiscal revenues may not be used for development priorities.[149] The Bank should not support significant sector expansion unless it can adequately mitigate these risks.[150] Where macro governance is sound but sectoral governance is weak, the Bank should focus on improving sectoral governance.

(b) Address extractive industries in CASs: For all resource-rich countries, the Bank should explicitly address extractive industries in the CASs.[151] The CAS should discuss the sector's economy-wide linkages (such as the importance of government revenues, their management, and distribution) and reference the underlying governance assessment. This should guide future project design, facilitate monitoring and evaluation, and provide a framework for WBG-wide coordination and collaboration in the EI sector.

(c) Promote improved governance where governance is weak: The Bank should compensate for the lower level of lending that may be appropriate for resource-rich countries with weak macro and sectoral governance[152] by devoting greater management attention and an administrative budget for advisory and analytical activities aimed at improving the policy, institutional, and governance framework for EI. This would enable the Bank to establish and maintain continuity of engagement and facilitate a quick response to opportunities for assistance when they arise.[153]

(d) Support private sector development and environmental sustainability: In all countries, the Bank should be ready to support the closure of uneconomical mines, reform and privatization of state-owned enterprises, and mitigation of pre-existing environmental and social problems. Where appropriate, the Bank should help integrate ASM with the formal sector and internalize its environmental and social impacts, while at the same time creating alternative employment opportunities and supporting the consolidation of ASM activities for greater efficiencies and economies of scale.

Recommendation 2: Strengthen Project Implementation

The Bank needs to strengthen the implementation of its existing policy framework and ensure that it remains up-to-date with evolving needs. Given the potential impacts of resource extraction and the controversy surrounding the sector, rigorous implementation of safeguard policies is a minimum requirement for the Bank to operate in a world concerned with sustainable development. In addition, in light of growing concerns about the sustainability of EI-based development, the Bank needs to define, monitor, document, and report on the economic, social, and environmental impacts of its projects more systematically. Specifically, the sharing of benefits, identified by many stakeholders as a very important issue for resource extraction, needs to be explicitly monitored and evaluated.

(a) Improve upstream project screening: The Bank should provide clearer and more consistent guidance for the categorization of sectoral adjustment and technical assistance projects, the identification of applicable safeguards at the initial project screening, the appropriate

scope and nature of the EA instruments, and the reporting and evaluation of safeguards implementation. This needs to be followed up through the entire implementation framework, from good practice guidelines to appropriate monitoring and training.

(b) Provide for adequate specialist involvement at every stage: The Bank should strengthen the implementation of its safeguard policies by providing adequate resources for the participation of qualified environmental and social specialists in the preparation, appraisal, and supervision of all projects that are likely to have adverse impacts. This will ensure that such impacts are addressed adequately through the upstream design of appropriate mitigation strategies or project alternatives, as well as through the retrofit of timely remediation measures should unexpected impacts materialize during project implementation.

(c) Enhance reporting of results: The Bank should strengthen the implementation of its completion reporting requirements by (i) ensuring that project completion reports include the calculation of an ex-post economic rate of return or net present value or, where that is not feasible, a cost-effectiveness analysis to determine whether the project represented the least-cost solution to attain its objectives and (ii) preparing an activity completion summary for every significant nonlending activity.

(d) Evaluate the sharing of benefits: At appraisal and project completion, the Bank should systematically estimate the distribution of project benefits among different stakeholder groups—government at different levels, private companies, and local communities—evaluate its sensitivity to different scenarios and discuss its acceptability with key stakeholder groups.

Recommendation 3: Engage the Stakeholders

Often in collaboration with other organizations, the Bank has brought together diverse stakeholders in extractive industries to address issues at the local, national, regional, and global levels. The Bank's convening role has been actively sought and has been significant because of its access to all stakeholders, private and public development experience, and ongoing involve-ment with project investment and technical assistance in the sector. But the Bank has addressed some areas inadequately—notably governance and revenue management. The Bank's performance in these areas can be enhanced by improving consultation with stakeholders, including local communities, and by systematically and transparently reporting on key sustainability indicators. Such an approach also is likely to raise standards and practices of the sector as a whole.

(a) Update policy framework: In consultation with its stakeholders, the Bank should adjust its policy framework for extractive industries periodically to ensure that they remain up-to-date with evolving industry practice. It should resolve remaining inconsistencies within the WBG[154] and address identified gaps.[155] It also should recognize the expanding awareness of the human rights dimension of Bank policies and projects and explore possible avenues for addressing the issues, especially where it lags industry best practice.

(b) Promote disclosure of fiscal revenues from EI: The Bank should vigorously pursue country- and industrywide disclosure of government revenues from EI and related contractual arrangements (such as production-sharing agreements, concession, and privatization terms).[156] It should work toward and support disclosure of EI revenues and their use in resource-rich countries.

(c) Define and monitor sustainability indicators: Together with other stakeholders, the Bank should define indicators of economic, social, and environmental sustainability,[157] establish baseline data, provide for adequate monitoring over the life of the project, and report and evaluate on the results during supervision and in project completion reports. The Bank also should encourage more independent outside monitoring, ideally using local capacity (which may have to be developed).

(d) Increase local community participation: The Bank should support enhanced community consultation and participation throughout the life cycle of EI-projects. The Bank should assist countries to increase involvement by local communities in EI decisionmaking processes and ongoing consultation throughout the project life cycle, including closure.

Total Number of Projects: 76
Oil and Gas (Completed 24; Active 15); Mining (Completed 24; Active 13)

Oil and Gas: Completed Projects

Project title	Region	Country	Lending instrument	FY approval	FY completed	EA category	Project cost	WB loan
Petroleum Technical Assistance II	AFR	Equatorial Guinea	Technical Assistance	1993	1998	C	3	3
Calub Energy Development	AFR	Ethiopia	Specific Investment	1994	2001	A	14	14
Petroleum Sector Reform	AFR	Madagascar	Sector Investment and Maintenance Loan	1993	1999	B	6	5
Petroleum Sector Rehabilitation	AFR	Tanzania	Specific Investment	1991	2001	B	0	0
Petroleum Rehabilitation	AFR	Zambia	Specific Investment	1994	2000	B	19	4
Petroleum Exploration & Development Technical Assistance	EAP	Papua New Guinea	Technical Assistance	1994	2001	C	13	11
Petroleum Distribution & Sector Management	EAP	Republic of Korea	Specific Investment	1993	1999	A	653	112
Bongkot Gas Transmission	EAP	Thailand	Specific Investment	1993	1996	A	334	92
Second Gas Transmission	EAP	Thailand	Specific Investment	1995	1998	A	482	111
Clean Fuels and Environment Improvement	EAP	Thailand	Specific Investment	1995	2000	A	41	38
Petroleum Technical Assistance	ECA	Azerbaijan	Technical Assistance	1995	2001	C	10	20
Natural Gas System Reconstruction	ECA	Bosnia-Herzegovina	Emergency Rehab.	1997	2000	B	44	10
Oil Institution Building Technical Assistance	ECA	Georgia	Technical Assistance	1997	2001	C	1	1
Petroleum Technical Assistance	ECA	Kazakhstan	Specific Investment	1994	2000	C	14	13
GHG Reduction in Natural Gas (GEF)	ECA	Russian Federation	Global Environment Facility	1996	1999	C	1	1
Oil Rehabilitation Project	ECA	Russian Federation	Specific Investment	1993	2000	A	1035	414
Second Oil Rehabilitation Project	ECA	Russian Federation	Specific Investment	1994	2000	A	678	346
Third Structural Adjustment Loan	ECA	Russian Federation	Structural Adjustment	1999	2001	U	1500	1500
Oil Pipeline Engineering Project	ECA	Turkey	Technical Assistance	1997	1999	C	3	3
Hydrocarbon Sector Reform & Capitalization Technical Assistance	LAC	Bolivia	Technical Assistance	1996	1999	B	9	11
Gas Sector Development Project	LAC	Brazil	Specific Investment	1997	2001	A	1594	130
Energy Technical Assistance	LAC	Colombia	Technical Assistance	1995	2002	B	12	11
Energy and Mining Technical Assistance	LAC	Peru	Technical Assistance	1993	1999	B	16	11
Gas Infrastructure Development	SAS	Bangladesh	Specific Investment	1995	2000	A	135	68

Oil and Gas: Active Projects

Project title	Region	Country	Lending instrument	FY approval	EA category	Project cost	WB loan
Oil Spill Contingency	AFR	Africa	Global Environment Facility	1999	C	5	3
Petroleum Environment Capacity Enhancement Project	AFR	Cameroon	Technical Assistance	2000	C	11	6
Chad/Cameroon Pipeline	AFR	Cameroon	Specific Investment	2000	A	3500	90
Chad Petroleum Power Engineering	AFR	Chad	Specific Investment	1991	C	14	22
Petroleum Development & Pipeline Project	AFR	Chad	Specific Investment	2000	A	3724	93
Petroleum Sector Capacity-Building	AFR	Chad	Specific Investment	2000	C	26	24
Management of the Petroleum Economy Project	AFR	Chad	Specific Investment	1999	C	19	18
Gas Engineering	AFR	Mozambique	Specific Investment	1994	B	49	30
Songo Songo Gas Development and Power Generation Project	AFR	Tanzania	Specific Investment	2001	A	313	183
GEF Sichuan Gas Development & Conservation	EAP	China	Specific Investment	1994	A	945	265
Gas Development Technical Assistance	EAP	Papua New Guinea	Technical Assistance	2000	C	8	7
Energy Transit Institutional Building	ECA	Georgia	Technical Assistance	2001	C	12	10
Uzen Oil Field Rehabilitation	ECA	Kazakhstan	Specific Investment	1997	A	136	109
Petroleum Sector Rehabilitation	ECA	Romania	Specific Investment	1994	B	346	176
Emergency Oil Spill Mitigation	ECA	Russian Federation	Emergency Rehabilitation	1995	C	140	99

(continued)

Mining: Completed Projects

Project title	Region	Country	Lending instrument	FY approval	FY completed	EA category	Project cost	WB loan
Mining Sector Development & Environment	AFR	Ghana	Specific Investment	1995	2002	B	13	9
Mining Sector Investment Promotion	AFR	Guinea	Technical Assistance	1996	2001	C	16.8	23
Mining Sector Development	AFR	Tanzania	Technical Assistance	1995	2002	B	13	12
Second Economic and Social Adjustment Credit	AFR	Zambia	Structural Adjustment	1996	1998	U	90	90
Econ. Recovery and Inv. Promotion Credit	AFR	Zambia	Sectoral Adjustment	1996	1998	C	140	140
Public Sector Reform and Export Promotion Credit Project	AFR	Zambia	Structural Adjustment	1999	2001	U	170	170
Economic Transition Support	EAP	Mongolia	Rehabilitation Investment	1994	1997	U	26	23
Mongolia Coal Project	EAP	Mongolia	Specific Investment	1996	2002	B	61.9	0
Structural Adjustment Credit	ECA	Albania	Structural Adjustment	1999	2001	U	45	45
Hard Coal Sectoral Adjustment	ECA	Poland	Sectoral Adjustment	1999	2001	B	300	300
Hard Coal Sectoral Adjustment II	ECA	Poland	Sectoral Adjustment	2002	2002	B	100	100
Coal Sectoral Adjustment	ECA	Russian Federation	Sectoral Adjustment	1996	1997	B	500	500
Coal Sector Restructuring Implementation Assistance Project	ECA	Russian Federation	Technical Assistance	1996	2003	C	31	17
Coal Sectoral Adjustment II	ECA	Russian Federation	Sectoral Adjustment	1998	2002	B	800	800
Priv. Impl. Assistance & Social Safety Net	ECA	Turkey	Technical Assistance	1994	2000	C	129	30
Coal Pilot	ECA	Ukraine	Specific Investment	1996	2001	B	28	13
Coal Sectoral Adjustment	ECA	Ukraine	Sectoral Adjustment	1996	2000	B	300	300
Capitalization Program Adjustment Credit	LAC	Bolivia	Sectoral Adjustment	1996	1999	B	147	65
Reg. Reform and Cap. TA	LAC	Bolivia	Specific Investment	1994	1999	C	30	15
Env Conservation and Rehabilitation	LAC	Brazil	Specific Investment	1996	2000	B	87	36
Mining Dev and Env Control TA	LAC	Ecuador	Technical Assistance	1994	2001	A	24	11
Privatization Adjustment Loan	LAC	Peru	Sectoral Adjustment	1993	1998	C	280	280
Coal Sector Rehab	SAS	India	Specific Investment	1998	2001	A	1697	263
Jharia Mine Fire Control TA	SAS	India	Technical Assistance	1993	1999	B	11	8

Mining: Active Projects

Project title	Region	Country	Lending instrument	FY approval	EA category	Project cost	WB loan
Mining Capacity-Building	AFR	Burkina Faso	Specific Investment	1997	C	22	21
Mining Sector Reform Project	AFR	Madagascar	Learning and Innovation Loan	1998	C	22	21
Mining Sector Capacity	AFR	Mauritania	Technical Assistance	1999	C	16	15
Mineral Resources Project	AFR	Mozambique	Technical Assistance	2001	C	33	18
Economic Recovery and Investment Promotion TA	AFR	Zambia	Technical Assistance	1996	C	27	23
Mine Township Services Project	AFR	Zambia	Specific Investment	2000	B	38	38
Mining Sector Institutional Strengthening TA	EAP	Papua New Guinea	Technical Assistance	2000	B	12	10
Mine Closure	ECA	Romania	Specific Investment	2000	B	62	44
Privatization Social Support	ECA	Turkey	Specific Investment	2001	C	355	250
Mining Sector Development	LAC	Argentina	Technical Assistance	1996	B	40	30
Mining Technical Assistance	LAC	Argentina	Technical Assistance	1998	B	46	40
Energy & Mining TA Loan	MNA	Algeria	Technical Assistance	2001	C	22	18
Coal Environment & Social Mitigation	SAS	India	Specific Investment	1996	C	84	63

Attachment 2   Extractive Industries–Dependent Countrie

Country	Oil and Gas				
	Average oil and gas share of total exports[1] 1990–99 (%)	Population 2002[2] (millions)	Population below poverty line[3] (%)	Gross national income capita[2] (US$: 1999)	Average GDP/capita growth,[2] 1990–99 (%)
Yemen	89.0	17.5	19	390	1.46
Congo, Rep.	88.1	50.9	..	560	−3.27
Nigeria	86.8	126.9	34	250	0.2
Oman	86.4	10.8	..	n/a	0.95
Angola / Cabinda	83.5	1.6	..	410	−2.03
Iran	82.0	63.7	..	1,600	3.01
Turkmenistan	74.5	5.2	..	640	−7.11
Gabon	73.8	1.2	..	3,300	−0.07
Venezuela	56.9	24.2	31	3,730	0.16
Syria	48.9	16.2	..	930	3.19
Cameroon	33.5	14.9	40	600	−2.11
Ecuador	30.4	12.6	35	1,330	−0.27
Algeria	28.7	30.4	23	1,540	−0.49
Kazakhstan	23.1	14.9	35	1,290	−4.36
Papua New Guinea	20.0	4.8	..	770	2.26
Trinidad / Tobago	16.3	1.3	..	4,660	2.01
Russian Federation	16.2	145.6	31	1,750	−4.9
Azerbaijan	15.8	8.0	68	570	−2.18
Vietnam	15.8	78.5	51	370	5.51
Colombia	14.7	42.3	18	2,150	0.92

Note: ".." = not available.

Sources: World Bank and International Finance Corporation (2002)[1]; World Development Indicators, Central Database, World Bank[2]; World Development Indicators, World Development Report 2003.[3]

Country	**Mining**				
	Average mining share of total exports[1] 1990–99 (%)	Population 2002[2] (millions)	Population below poverty line[3] (%)	Gross national income capita[2] (US$: 1999)	Average GDP/capita growth,[2] 1990–99 (%)
Guinea	84.7	7.4	40	490	1.42
Congo (Dem. Rep.)	80.0	51.4	..	100	−6
Zambia	74.8	10.1	86	320	−2.3
Niger	70.6	10.8	63	190	−1.5
Botswana	70.0	1.6	..	3,040	2.53
Namibia	55.4	1.7	..	2,100	1.6
Jamaica	51.3	2.6	19	2,400	−0.13
Sierra Leone	50.0	5.0	68	130	−6.31
Suriname	48.3	0.4	..	1,350	2.71
Chile	46.6	15.2	21	4,600	4.86
Mauritania	46.0	2.7	57	390	0.55
Papua New Guinea	44.8	4.8	..	770	2.11
Peru	43.7	25.7	49	2,130	1.5
Mongolia	43.0	2.4	36	390	−1.64
Central Afr. Republic	42.1	3.6	..	290	−0.82
Ukraine	40.0	40.6	32	770	−8.63
Mali	40.0	10.8	..	240	0.69
Togo	37.7	4.7	32	310	−1.27
Bolivia	35.6	8.3	..	990	1.63
Guyana	35.0	0.9	..	760	4
Ghana	34.0	19.2	31	400	1.55
South Africa	30.0	42.8	..	3,160	−0.67
Jordan	28.9	4.9	12	1,630	0.4
Kazakhstan	23.2	14.9	35	1,290	−4.36
Kyrgyz Republic	21.2	4.9	51	300	−4.58
Morocco	20.0	28.7	19	1,190	0.73
Armenia	20.0	3.8	..	490	−2.6
Uzbekistan	18.4	24.7	..	640	−2.46
Cuba	17.8	11.2	..	500	5.6
Tanzania	15.8	33.7	42	260	0.36

Note: ".." = not available.

Sources: World Bank and International Finance Corporation (2002)[1]; World Development Indicators, Central Database, World Bank[2]; World Development Indicators, World Development Report 2003.[3]

Attachment 3   OED Evaluation Guidelines

OED's guidelines for evaluating the outcome, sustainability, and institutional development impact (IDI) of projects are summarized below:

Outcome

Definition: *The extent to which the project's major relevant objectives were achieved, or are expected to be achieved, efficiently.*

The outcome criterion is assessed on a six-point scale—highly satisfactory, satisfactory, moderately satisfactory, moderately unsatisfactory, unsatisfactory, and highly unsatisfactory. These differentiations reflect the large amount of information contained in the assessments of the three criteria supporting the outcome assessment (relevance, efficacy, and efficiency). The guiding principles provided below cover a high proportion of likely project evaluation scenarios.

Ratings

Highly Satisfactory: Project achieved or exceeded, or is expected to achieve or exceed, all its major relevant objectives efficiently without major shortcomings.

Satisfactory: Project achieved, or is expected to achieve, most of its major relevant objectives efficiently with only minor shortcomings.

Moderately Satisfactory: Project achieved, or is expected to achieve, most of its major relevant objectives efficiently but with either significant shortcomings or modest overall relevance.

Moderately Unsatisfactory: Project is expected to achieve its major relevant objectives with major shortcomings or is expected to achieve only some of its major relevant objectives, but it is expected to achieve positive efficiency.

Unsatisfactory: Project has failed to achieve, and is not expected to achieve, most of its major relevant objectives with only minor development benefits.

Highly Unsatisfactory: Project has failed to achieve, and is not expected to achieve, any of its major relevant objectives with no worthwhile development benefits.

Institutional Development Impact

Definition: *The extent to which a project improves the ability of a country or region to make more efficient, equitable, and sustainable use of its human, financial, and natural resources through (a) better definition, stability, transparency, enforceability, and predictability of institutional arrangements and/or (b) better alignment of the mission and capacity of an organization with its mandate, which derives from these institutional arrangements. IDI includes both intended and unintended effects of a project.*

Development can be defined as a process of institutional transformation through which scarce resources are used to enhance human welfare over the long term. This transformation involves changes in values, customs, laws and regulations, and formal and informal rules, as well as periodic realignments of organizational mandates, objectives, competencies, and resources. A development intervention has a positive institutional development impact if it effects such a transformation and thereby enhances the ability of a country or region to make more efficient, equitable, and sustainable use of the human, financial, and natural resources at its disposal. Accountability, good governance, the rule of law, and the participation of civil society and the private sector are prominent characteristics of an effective institutional environment.

Ratings

High: Project as a whole made, or is expected to make, a critical contribution to the country's/region's ability to use human, financial, and natural resources effectively, either through the achievement of the project's stated institutional development (ID) objectives or through unintended effects.

Substantial: Project as a whole made, or is expected to make, a significant contribution to the country's/region's ability to use human, financial, and natural resources effectively, either through the achievement of the project's stated ID objectives or through unintended effects.

Modest: Project as a whole increased, or is expected to increase, to a limited extent the country's/region's ability to use human, financial, and natural resources effectively, either through the achievement of the project's stated ID objectives or through unintended effects.

Negligible: Project as a whole made, or is expected to make, little or no contribution to the country's/region's ability to use human, financial, and natural resources effectively, either through the achievement of the project's stated ID objectives or through unintended effects.

Sustainability

Definition: *The resilience to risk of net benefits flows over time.*

Sustainability is evaluated by assessing the risks and uncertainties faced by a project and by ascertaining whether adequate arrangements are in place to help avoid known operational risks or mitigate their impact. The rating helps to identify projects that require close attention by the borrower, the Bank, and other partners in managing risks that may affect the flow of net benefits. Sustainability says nothing about the absolute level of the net benefits in relation to economic justification thresholds. It focuses on the features that contribute to the maintenance of operational achievements over the long term and the adaptability of operational designs and implementation arrangements to deal with shocks and changing circumstances.

Ratings

Highly Likely: Project net benefits flow meets most of the relevant factors determining overall resilience at the "high level," with all others rated at the "substantial" level.

Likely: Project net benefits flow meets all relevant factors determining overall resilience at the "substantial" level.

Unlikely: Project net benefits flow meets some but not all relevant factors determining overall resilience at the "substantial" level.

Highly Unlikely: Project net benefits flow meets few of the relevant factors determining overall resilience at the "substantial" level.

Not Evaluable: Insufficient information available to make a judgment.

Attachment 4   Background Papers

Thematic Studies

1. World Bank. 2002. *Evaluation of the World Bank Group's Activities in the Extractive Industries: Review of the Portfolio of World Bank Extractive Industries Projects.* OED Background Paper, World Bank.

2. Luis A. Ramirez. 2002. *Review of the World Bank's Assistance on Revenue Management Issues in Resource Abundant Countries.* OED Background Paper, World Bank.

3. Melissa A. Thomas. 2003. *Factoring in Governance: The World Bank and Extractive Industry Projects.* OED Background Paper, World Bank.

4. Roger J. Batstone. 2003. Review of Implementation of Safeguard Policies of World Bank Extractive Industries Projects. OED Background Paper, World Bank.

Country Case Studies

1. World Bank. 2003. *World Bank Group's Activities in the Extractive Industries: Ecuador Country Case Study.* OED Background Paper, World Bank.

2. World Bank. 2003. *World Bank Group's Activities in the Extractive Industries: Equatorial Guinea Country Case Study.* OED Background Paper, World Bank.

3. World Bank. 2003. *World Bank Group's Activities in the Extractive Industries: Ghana Country Case Study.* OED Background Paper, World Bank.

4. World Bank. 2003. *World Bank Group's Activities in the Extractive Industries: Papua New Guinea Country Case Study.* OED Background Paper, World Bank.

5. World Bank. 2003. *World Bank Group's Activities in the Extractive Industries: Kazakhstan Country Case Study.* OED Background Paper, World Bank.

Project Performance Assessment Reports

1. World Bank. 2003. *Project Performance Assessment Report: Brazil Gas Sector Development Project (L4265), Brazil Hydrocarbon Transport/Processing Project (L3376), and Brazil Natural Gas Distribution Project—Sao Paulo (L3043).* Draft Report. Operations Evaluation Department, World Bank.

2. World Bank. 2003. *Project Performance Assessment Report: Ecuador Mining Development and Environmental Control Technical Assistance Project (L3655).* Draft Report. Operations Evaluation Department, World Bank.

3. World Bank. 2003. *Project Performance Assessment Report: Equatorial Guinea Second Petroleum Technical Assistance Project (Credit 2408).* Report No. 24430. Operations Evaluation Department, World Bank.

4. World Bank. 2003. *Project Performance Assessment Report: Ghana Mining Sector Rehabilitation Project (C1921) and (L3927).* Draft Report. Operations Evaluation Department, World Bank.

5. World Bank. 2003. *Project Performance Assessment Report: Kazakhstan Petroleum Technical Assistance Project (Loan 3744).* Draft Report. Operations Evaluation Department, World Bank.

6. World Bank. 2003. *Project Performance Assessment Report: Papua New Guinea Petroleum Exploration Technical Assistance Project (Credit 1279) and Petroleum Exploration*

and Development Technical Assistance Project (Loan 3670). Report No. 24405. Operations Evaluation Department, World Bank.

6. World Bank. 2003. *Project Performance Assessment Report: Ukraine Coal Pilot Project and Coal Sector Adjustment Loan (Credit 4016 & 4118)*. Report No. 24928. Operations Evaluation Department, World Bank.

Attachment 5   References

Auty, R. 2000. "How Natural Resources Affect Economic Development." *Development Policy Review* 18(4):347–64.

Davis, Graham A., and John E. Tilton. 2001. *Should Developing Countries Renounce Mining? A Perspective on the Debate.* Colorado School of Mines.

Davis, Jeffrey, Rolando Ossowski, James Daniel, and Steven Barnett. 2001. *Stabilization and Savings Funds for Nonrenewable Resources: Experience and Fiscal Policy Implications.* International Monetary Fund, Washington D.C.

ESMAP (Energy Sector Management Assistance Program). 1997. *Kazakhstan Natural Gas Investment Strategy Study.* ESMAP Report No. 199.

Friends of the Earth. 2001. "Phasing out International Financial Institution Financing for Fossil Fuel and Mining Projects, Demanding Local Community Self-Determination." Position paper.

Gelb, A. 1984. *The Oil Syndrome: Adjustment to Windfall Gains in Oil Exporting Countries.* Development Research Department. The World Bank.

_____. 1988. *Oil Windfalls: Blessing or Curse?* World Bank research publication (0-19-520774-2). Oxford University Press.. The World Bank.

Isham, J., M. Woodcock, L. Pritchett, and G. Busby. 2002. *The Varieties of Rentier Experience: How Natural Resource Endowments Affect the Political Economy of Economic Growth.* Draft. The World Bank. <http://www.worldbank.org/research/growth/pdfiles/rentier.pdf> Accessed July 9, 2003.

MMSD (Mining Minerals and Sustainable Development). 2003. *Breaking New Ground: The Report of the MMSD Project.* Earthscan Publications.

Onorato, W., P. Fox, and J. Strongman. 1998. *World Bank Group Assistance for Minerals Sector: Development and Reform in Member Countries.* World Bank Technical Paper No. 405. The World Bank.

Ross, M. 2001. *Extractive Sectors and the Poor.* Oxfam of America.

Sachs, Jeffrey D., and Andrew M. Warner. 1995. *Natural Resource Abundance and Economic Growth.* NBER Working Paper No. 5398, 1–48.

van der Veen, Peter et al. 1996. *A Mining Strategy for Latin America and the Caribbean.* World Bank Technical Paper No. 345. The World Bank.

Weber-Fahr, M. et al. 2000. "Mining." Chapter 4.5 in *Poverty Reduction Strategy Sourcebook.* World Bank Group Mining. <www.worldbank.org/poverty/strategies/chapters/mining/mining.htm> Accessed July 9, 2003.

World Bank and International Finance Corporation. 2002. *Global Mining: Treasure or Trouble? Mining in Developing Countries.* Mining Department, The World Bank Group.

World Bank. 2002a. *World Development Indicators.* The World Bank.

_____. 2002b. *World Bank Group Work in Low-Income Countries under Stress: A Task Force Report.* The World Bank.

_____. 2001a. *Poverty Reduction Strategy Sourcebook: A Resource to Assist Countries in Developing Poverty Reduction Strategies.* The World Bank.

_____. 2001b. *Republic of Kazakhstan: Strategic Review of the Mining and Metallurgy Sector.* Europe and Central Asia Region. Unpublished. The World Bank.

_____. 2001c. *Fourth Quality-at-Entry Assessment.* Quality Assurance Group. The World Bank.

_____. 2000. *Fuel for Thought: An Environmental Strategy for the Energy Sector.* The World Bank.

_____. 1994a. *Kyrgyzstan: Mining Sector Review.* Agriculture, Mining, and Finance Division. Country Department III. Europe and Central Asia Department. The World Bank.

_____. 1994b. *Russian Federation: Restructuring the Coal Industry—Putting People First.* Vols I & II. Infrastructure, Energy, and Environment Division. The World Bank.

_____. 1992. *Strategy for African Mining.* Technical Paper No. 181. The World Bank.

_____. 1991. *Environmental Assessment Source Book.* Technical Papers 139, 140, and 154 (including update). Environment Department. The World Bank.

_____. 1984. "Guidelines for Petroleum Lending." Operations Manual Statement (OMS) 3.82. November 1984. The World Bank.

World Commission on Environment and Development. 1987. *Our Common Future.* Oxford University Press. New York.

Operations Evaluation Group:
Evaluation of IFC's Experience

- Following a peak in 1991 ($400 million), IFC approved investments of about $250 annually in EI.
- The share of EI has declined from over 20 percent in 1991 to around 5 percent in the last three years.
- Approvals were concentrated in oil and gas (54 percent), gold (14 percent), and copper (10 percent).
- Approvals were concentrated in Latin America (34 percent) and Sub-Saharan Africa (30 percent).

- Approvals were concentrated in countries with high country risk, much more so than IFC's overall approvals; these countries also predominantly feature poor governance.
- IFC's portfolio in EI (as of June 2002) was $628 million, or 6 percent of IFC's total portfolio.
- Just over 60 percent of the EI portfolio was in mining, and just under 40 percent was in oil and gas.
- Just over half was loans, just under half was equity.

Declining share since 1992

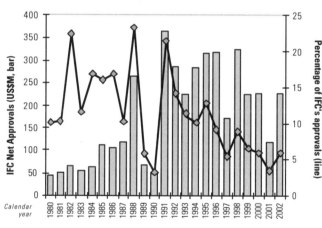

Concentrated in oil and gas, gold and copper

IFC approvals since inception ($4.3 billion)

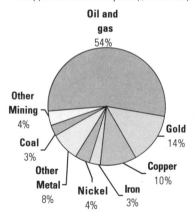

Concentrated in countries with poor investment climates

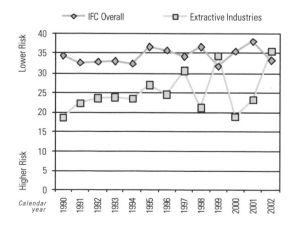

Concentrated in Latin America and Sub-Saharan Africa

IFC approvals since inception ($4.3 billion)

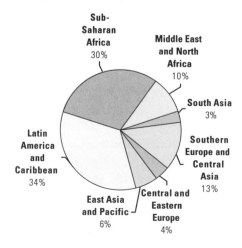

1. Introduction

Summary: Overall, IFC support for EI has been effective, but implementation can be improved, broader sustainability issues better addressed, and results better tracked and reported. Projects usually generated large revenues for governments and opportunities for people. IFC generally has added value, particularly in improving the environmental[158] and social aspects of projects, but given the sector's high-impact potential, it needs to prevent or mitigate negative impacts better and more systematically. IFC also needs to ensure that its environmental and social guidelines and procedures continue to set standards and adapt to rapidly improving industry standards, and that its projects adapt with them. In pursuit of its sustainability agenda, IFC needs to do more to address the risks that government revenues may not be used effectively for development and poverty reduction, that benefits may not be distributed transparently, and that local communities may not benefit tangibly from EI projects. To enhance the contribution of IFC's projects and the sector to sustainable development requires further improvements in project implementation, effective cooperation within the WBG, and full engagement of all stakeholders.

OEG's evaluation is based on the premise that IFC should support EI projects only if it can help improve the sector's contribution to sustainable private sector development. Promoting sustainable private sector development, and ultimately reducing poverty and improving people's lives, is IFC's mission. Some people feel that the exploitation of nonrenewable natural resources and sustainable development are an inherent contradiction. But most realize that, over the next decades and probably centuries, we will all need oil, gas, minerals, and metals, and that exploration, development, and use will continue with or without IFC and the WBG. The question is whether the WBG and IFC can improve the sector's development potential by enhancing positive and mitigating negative aspects. While IFC and the WBG finance only a small share of the sector's investment, their actual and potential influence is often much larger.

Sustainable development defined for this evaluation. Sustainable development "meets the needs of the present without compromising the ability of future generations to meet their own needs." An individual mine or oil field will eventually be exhausted, but EI projects can still contribute to sustainable development and thus provide a role model for other private investment if they are—

- economically sound, providing adequate revenues for host countries, which in turn are used for the benefit of current and future generations;
- financially sound, providing sufficient returns to reward investors for risk;
- environmentally sound, adequately mitigating negative environmental effects[159]—and, where possible, improving the environment; and
- socially sound, adequately mitigating negative social effects and providing tangible and sustainable benefits for local people.

The focus on sustainability in IFC's EI activities has increased over the past decade. IFC's sector strategy[160] has consistently emphasized the sector's contribution to government revenues and has focused on countries and projects where the value added by IFC is greatest. Initially, IFC mainly saw its role as funding projects without access to commercial finance and acting as a neutral party between government and investors. In the mid-1990s, the strategy was expanded to highlight environmental issues, later to social issues, and later still to governance and revenue management—how host countries distribute and manage the revenues from EI. In recent years, IFC's environmental and social specialists have devoted more time to the sector than to any other and have frequently improved EI projects beyond the requirements of IFC's policies and guidelines.

This increased focus on sustainability reflects the evolution in IFC and the industry. Over the past decade, environmental, social, and sustainability concerns have become more prominent in the sector. Industry has responded by developing and implementing better standards and techniques to reduce the environmental impacts of its operations.[161] Leading industry players now report on sustainability indicators—health, safety, environmental, and most recently social indicators—of their operations and are working on standardizing the reporting.[162] Industry also recognizes that it must do more to retain its "social license to operate," particularly to broaden the benefits of wealth creation and thereby contribute to poverty reduction.[163] Similarly, IFC's sustainability initiative, started in the past few years, has heightened the focus on sustainable development results within IFC and beyond. IFC's EI operations were often among the first to develop or implement new programs, such as SME linkages or IFC and AIDS. Under the sustainability initiative, IFC developed a position paper on revenue management in 2002, which recognized that large government revenues, as they typically occur in EI projects, require special attention—particularly where country governance is poor. Indeed, this is an area deserving special attention from IFC and the WBG.

2. From Economic Benefits to Sustainable Development

Development results in EI were the same as in other sectors. IFC synthesizes development results of four indicators—economic sustain-

ability, private sector development, business success, and environmental and social effects—into one "development outcome," which measures a project's overall impact on a country's development. Fifty-nine percent of the 22 evaluated EI projects achieved positive results, compared with 60 percent for all other IFC projects.[164] The development success rate for all 45 studied projects (65 percent) is slightly higher.[165] The "win-win" outcomes—positive development results and good investment results for IFC—are about the same when only evaluated projects are considered and slightly better for all studied projects (Figure D1). While there is room for improvement, it is important to note that this success rate has been achieved in very difficult country environments, where many development institutions are struggling to achieve positive results.[166]

About three-quarters of IFC's EI projects were economically attractive; results in mining were the same as in other sectors, those in oil and gas significantly better. Seventy-three percent of the evaluated EI projects had adequate economic returns—real economic rates of return over 10 percent—compared with 57 percent for other projects. The success rate for oil and gas (83 percent) was significantly[167] higher than that for mining (60 percent) and other sectors. Again, these results were achieved in difficult countries, but it is also important to note several limitations of the economic rate of return:

- It does not take into account the distribution of benefits—a dollar for the investor is treated the same as a dollar for government or a dollar spent on a social program for the poorest.
- It does not address how government revenues are used.
- Accounting for the depletion of natural resources in economic rate of return calculations is difficult. IFC uses a depletion premium to account for the non-renewable nature of the resource.[168]
- Compliance with IFC's environmental and social requirements was interpreted as an indication that negative externalities had been adequately mitigated; where appropriate, we imputed costs of cleanup as economic costs;

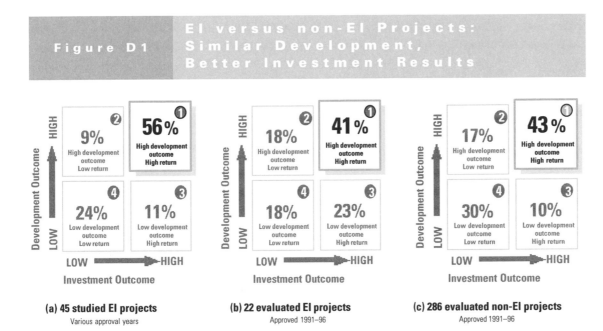

Figure D1 EI versus non-EI Projects: Similar Development, Better Investment Results

(a) 45 studied EI projects
Various approval years

(b) 22 evaluated EI projects
Approved 1991–96

(c) 286 evaluated non-EI projects
Approved 1991–96

however, it is difficult to quantify environmental and social externalities, and data are scarce.

Financial and economic project success were closely linked. All 12 projects that were financially successful also provided adequate economic returns.[169] In addition, 4 out of 10 projects that were not successful for investors still had adequate economic rates of return (greater than 10 percent). In three of them, the government retroactively changed earlier agreements, making otherwise viable projects financially unattractive.

Most projects generated large revenues for governments, sometimes even when private investors did not do well. These revenues come in many different forms[170] but usually as income taxes and royalties.[171] Governments sometimes get revenues even when investors do not do well. For example, IFC has funded projects that failed or ran into financial difficulties. Often, but not always, these companies continue to pay all taxes, including royalties, duties, and transit fees, while investors lose money. In other cases, governments faced with the potential loss of jobs and community livelihood agreed to forgo some taxes until a project turned around. In Eastern Europe, some IFC clients faced increasing tax demands that led to financial losses from otherwise viable projects. A Latin American oil company failed, but its assets were bought and rehabilitated, and the new company contributed more than $30 million in royalties in 2000. A mining company lost more than $30 million in four years, but was expected to pay about US$5.5 million in taxes.

All stakeholder groups recognize that the distribution of benefits and costs is the crucial issue in EI. We surveyed stakeholders from many backgrounds—government, industry, NGOs, and the WBG.[172] Among a wide range of questions covering economic, environmental, social, and governance aspects (Attachment 6A), equitable distribution of benefits was perceived to be the most important overall; it was also among the top two issues in every stakeholder group.

But IFC—and the WBG—has not adequately addressed distribution. In several projects, people outside and even inside the WBG questioned ex-post whether benefits of EI projects were distributed fairly.[173] For example, where governments had taken a large equity share, but commodity prices—and fiscal revenues—dropped below expectations, they were later disappointed, or where they had granted income tax exemptions for the first years—often the most profitable for a gold project. We surveyed 33 IFC staff—all EI sector investment staff and all regional economists or strategists. Only half of the respondents indicated that distribution was adequately addressed in IFC's EI projects—or in CASs. Responses by World Bank staff were similar (Attachment 6C). Recognizing the importance of distribution in EI, IFC usually identifies the share of net benefits that accrues to government. But IFC typically has not compared the benefits with other EI projects or stated whether it perceives the distribution of benefits to be reasonable—and has been criticized for this in the case of the Chad-Cameroon pipeline.[174] IFC also has not systematically tracked actual government revenues during supervision.[175] Recognizing the uncertainty about commodity prices, resource quality, and many other factors, IFC typically addresses downside risks for investors in a sensitivity analysis, but IFC did not address how such risk factors affect the distribution of benefits.

Transparency and improved analysis of the distribution may help prevent later conflicts. Because of variations in country and project characteristics (e.g., resource quality, taxation regimes, legal entitlements, country risk), some people question the reliability and relevance of distributional comparisons. But given the importance of rent distribution—and the history of conflicts over it[176]—more comparative analysis is warranted. Attempts have been made to compare distributions across countries, both in the WBG and elsewhere.[177] World Bank staff we interviewed stated that they could and should be cited to provide a frame of reference when presenting IFC projects for approval. More transparency on how the distribution was arrived at, comparing it with other projects, and testing its robustness under different scenarios would help reduce potential conflicts and disputes.[178]

"Insufficient" benefits for local communities are an important development issue—and a commercial risk—that has not always received enough attention. IFC typically has not calculated shares accruing to different levels of government or accruing directly to local communities. It is difficult to define "sufficient" benefits. At the least, they should compensate local communities for negative impacts and maintain or improve their living standards. Where local people oppose projects, businesses risk costly interruption and property damage. In EI, environmental problems often trigger the opposition. However, such opposition often can be traced to deeper social issues; for example, a long-standing perception of insufficient benefits. In such situations, companies sometimes spend a lot to build trust or defend themselves—money that could be better spent on community development. Where IFC client companies proactively engage the community and provide benefits for local people—for example, increased employment or sales, better infrastructure, schools, and housing—they reduce risk for their operations. But private companies cannot be expected to take over government responsibilities—for financial reasons, and because such a solution is not sustainable.

Benefits from government revenues do not always reach local communities. In many countries where IFC operates, government revenues are not being used effectively for the benefit of local communities. In some countries, communities received only a very small share of fiscal revenues—which led to problems. For example, in one case, the "legal" distribution to the provincial authorities was only a small share of royalties; even that was not consistently distributed, and communities accused local leaders of embezzlement. In another case, the "legal" distribution to the region was quite high but usually not forthcoming. Even where money was distributed to the provincial governments, people affected by EI did not necessarily benefit, because of mismanagement, lack of transparency and possible corruption, allocation of the money to other parts of the province, or its being used for recurrent administrative expenditures instead of invested to provide sustainable benefits.

Volatility of revenues is also a problem but may be easier to fix. The discussion during taxation conferences[179] tends to focus on managing the volatility of revenues from EI, caused by changing commodity prices and the exhaustibility of the resource. Several "technical" solutions—for example, funds for stabilization or for future generations—are well understood, but the record of such solutions is poor, owing in part to the secular decline in commodity prices and in part to poor governance.

3. Private Sector Development and Benefits to Investors

EI investments were often among the first attractive investment opportunities for private investors and IFC. In at least a dozen countries,[180] IFC's first investment was in EI. IFC's EI investment also was often the first private investment in the sector, providing important demonstration effects. Investments in other sectors—by IFC and others—often followed. In recent years, IFC has focused increasingly on enhancing SME linkages in connection with its EI investments (Box D1) and on supporting EI-related projects with trust funds.

Financial returns—for IFC and other investors—were better than for other sectors ... OEG evaluates both business success—whether projects were attractive for all investors[181]—and IFC's own investment results. Business success was better in EI (55 percent positive) than in other sectors (44 percent). While this result is not significantly different, it was achieved in very difficult country circumstances. Controlling for country risk, the business success of EI projects was significantly better than for other projects, indicating that EI projects can be among the few attractive investment opportunities in difficult countries. IFC's investment results on a portfolio basis also are substantially better than in other sectors, enhancing IFC's overall profitability and helping to support IFC's activities in other sectors.

... but financial risks also were higher. For investors, the sector is riskier than others. For example, while EI projects featured more extremely positive financial results (financial rates of return > 20 percent), they also featured more financial losses (Figure D2). IFC's equity investments in EI are as likely to succeed as those in other sectors—about one-third of the time—but successful investments are more likely to result in large returns. IFC's strong portfolio results are carried by a handful of very big winners. In all of the projects, IFC invested early in the project's development, taking considerable risk. Overall, such winners tended to be concentrated in Latin America, in countries with at least reasonable governance, and in oil, gold, and copper—the largest exposures by subsector.[182]

The main drivers of project business success were quality of management and the resource, commodity prices, and the country's governance and investment climate. Among the studied projects, the following tended to be the main business success drivers:

- Quality of management: Strong management and a financially committed sponsor are crucial to deal appropriately with production challenges and market downturns—but were sometimes missing.

- Quality of the resource: Only resources that are globally cost-competitive are likely to result in attractive financial returns. IFC and the sponsors sometimes have overestimated the quality of the resource or—put differently—underestimated the difficulties and costs to extract and process it.

- Commodity prices: The 1990s were a decade of falling prices for many commodities. For example, from 1990 to 1998, oil prices dropped in real terms by over 40 percent, gold by over 20 percent, and copper by almost 40 percent. This has had negative effects on the projects IFC supported and shows the importance of investing in the lowest-cost producers. Several commodity prices have since recovered, so the current outlook is probably brighter than at the evaluation stage.

- The host country environment: Taxation regimes are an important determinant of returns to investors, as are other features of the enabling environment. In several cases, viable projects had poor returns to investors because of government actions, such as retroactively increased taxation or transit fees. Better regulatory qual-

Box D1	Value-Added SME Linkages

IFC's environmental and SME departments increasingly work with project sponsors, aid agencies, and NGOs to develop programs promoting sustainable economic development in areas affected by EI projects. Examples of programs to set up or strengthen micro-finance organizations, training programs, and technical advice for local businesses include the following:

Mozal Aluminum Smelter, Mozambique

- IFC worked with Mozal to develop local business capacity to compete for product and service contracts—transport, catering, cleaning, and security. For these, Mozal broke its contracts down into smaller components (to attract local competition) and now spends about US$35 million annually with private local companies. As part of Mozal's Community Development Trust, which tries to maximize positive impacts for the local community, farm extension services have been provided to 1,200 farmers.
- An ongoing linkage supply program developed by the IFC-managed Africa Project Development Facility helps small businesses win and deliver Mozal phase II construction contracts.

Chad-Cameroon Petroleum Development and Pipeline Project

- The WBG worked closely with the sponsors to put in place features to ensure economic benefits for local businesses—to date more than $340 million has been spent, more than $139 million in Chad alone. Ongoing training enables SMEs to win pipeline-related contracts. IFC launched The Support and Training Entrepreneurial Program in Chad to train university graduates to consult, train, and develop small and

micro-enterprises. Already 14 field officers are working with more than 150 enterprises.
- IFC is working with the U.S. organization Africare to implement a project to provide food to petroleum workers in the short term and to the general population in the long term. Eight enterprises have been created and more than 120 people have received training and financing.

Yanacocha Gold Mine, Peru

- IFC is working with Yanacocha to implement a Rural and an Urban Development program. Many program components have been implemented with NGOs, rural communities, and the city of Cajamarca. Yanacocha and external donors have provided more than $15 million and $7.3 million respectively, for this program.
- Local SMEs supplying goods and services participate in quality management training focused on international business practices and environmental and safety standards to improve productivity and win Yanacocha contracts. A training program equips tradesmen to participate in the construction of a housing complex that will be developed over the next five years. Also, SME suppliers of components, such as window frames, are being assisted.
- Another program has been established to build local farmers' capacity to supply the mine's canteen and hotels. Similarly, local artisans in ceramics and textiles have been identified for training in design, production, and marketing and are supported at local and international trade fairs.

Note: Data provided by the WBG's SME department and summarized by OEG.

ity was significantly correlated with better financial results, as was political stability, which also was significantly correlated with better development results and environmental effects.

4. Environmental and Social Issues— From "Do No Harm" to Sustainability

IFC has continually expanded the scope of its environmental and social assessment. In

1988–89, IFC began its own reviews and appointed its first environmental advisor.[183] Initially, IFC followed the World Bank's safeguard policies, guidelines, and procedures, but gradually IFC developed its own, better adapted for the private sector. From 1993, IFC developed sector-specific guidelines for areas not covered by the World Bank's existing guidelines and adopted specific procedures for environmental review in 1992–93. In 1998, after exten-

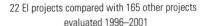

Figure D2   **Extractive Industries: Riskier than Others**

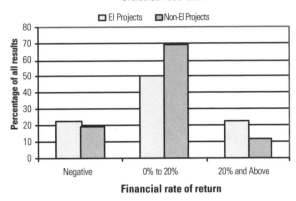

22 EI projects compared with 165 other projects evaluated 1996–2001

sive consultation, IFC revised its review procedures and adapted several safeguard policies for the private sector. It also developed a policy statement on harmful child and forced labor (the World Bank lacks such a policy).[184] Also in 1998, the World Bank updated its Pollution Prevention and Abatement Handbook[185] (PPAH), providing industry-specific guidelines that apply to WBG projects. IFC continues to modify its operating procedures and to develop additional industry-specific guidelines.[186]

Lessons from experience lead to changes in policies, guidelines, procedures, and practices. Based on past evaluation findings, OEG has made numerous recommendations with respect to environmental and social safeguard policies, guidelines, and procedures, many of which have been implemented. IFC's Environmental and Social Development Department also feeds lessons from practical experience and research into upgrading procedures within the department. For example, IFC introduced a guideline on hazardous materials handling, in part motivated by the Yanacocha mercury spill and the Kumtor cyanide spill. IFC produced a guideline for offshore oil and gas projects before investing in Early Oil, Azerbaijan. Thus, the body of policies, documents, and procedures that codifies IFC's environmental and social operating procedures and practices

is adapting constantly. The recently completed safeguard policy review by the CAO is likely to result in changes also.

IFC increased staffing in support of the increased focus on environmental and social issues. Starting with one staff member, IFC hired additional environmental, and later social, experts between 1990 and 2002 and currently employs almost 40 specialists. Their role is to appraise and supervise projects to ensure that projects financed by IFC meet the applicable environmental and social safeguard policies and guidelines and improve projects "beyond compliance." In recent years, IFC's environmental and social experts have spent more time on EI than on any other sector, highlighting the sector's high-impact potential in this area.

IFC categorizes projects on the basis of their potential environmental and social impact. When a project is first presented to IFC, the environmental and social specialists categorize it according to its potential negative impact. The categorization determines how IFC appraises and supervises a project and which actions will be sought from the clients. A Category 'A'[187] project—considered likely to have significant adverse environmental and social impacts, unless prevented or mitigated—requires peer review and triggers a detailed and disclosable assessment document (environmental impact assessment), a public consultation process, and frequent supervision throughout the life of the project. A Category 'B' project—with lesser potential impact than Category 'A'—has a narrower environmental assessment, requires only submission of an environmental summary, and, in practice, receives less direct supervision. Some NGOs have criticized IFC for "under-categorizing" projects and have argued that all EI projects should be Category 'A.' Management—and the CAO—maintains that projects should be categorized to reflect their impact potential. OEG usually found projects to be appropriately categorized, but given unclear guidance and lacking documentary explanation it is sometimes difficult to understand the rationale for categorizations.[188] Even so, IFC sometimes goes beyond the requirements for Category 'B' projects; for example, subjecting them to independent audits.

EI projects have high potential for negative environmental and social impact. About 40 percent of IFC's EI investments are Category 'A' (most others are 'B'), compared with 3 percent of IFC's non-EI investments. More than 40 percent of IFC's total Category 'A' investments are thus in EI. This indicates the high environmental sensitivity of the sector and IFC's commitment to thorough environmental review and monitoring of the sector. In support of this commitment, IFC's environmental and social specialists spent one-third of their time on the EI portfolio in fiscal year 2002.

Resource-rich countries are more likely to have problems achieving important development goals. The WBG has assessed the likelihood that countries will achieve important Millennium Development Goals.[189] OEG then analyzed whether EI-dependent countries were more or less likely to achieve the Millennium Development Goals than other developing countries. Only the goal of reduced child malnutrition was much more likely to be achieved in EI-dependent countries (likely or possible in 67 percent of countries) than in others (51 percent). EI-dependent countries were less likely to

achieve almost all other goals, most notably increasing access to clean water (58 percent versus 72 percent) and reducing child mortality (46 percent versus 65 percent), maternal mortality (45 percent versus 59 percent), and HIV/AIDS (50 percent versus 63 percent). IFC recently has started an initiative against HIV/AIDS, with 6 of 14 engagements with client companies working in the EI sector (Box D2).

IFC's Results in Mitigating Negative and Enhancing Positive Impacts

Mixed environmental and social results for EI projects. Using only the random sample of detailed evaluations,[190] the results for mining (4 of 10 projects, or 40 percent rated positive) are significantly worse and those for oil and gas (11 of 12, or 92 percent positive[191]) are significantly better than those for other projects (65 percent). Using the broader, but less in-depth analysis of the entire portfolio,[192] the positive results for oil and gas (94 percent positive) are confirmed, and mining projects (62 percent positive) are not different from the IFC average (65 percent). For mining, the better performance of the broader portfolio of studied projects, compared with the evaluated sample, indicates that performance has improved.[193] To validate results from the evaluations and desk reviews, OEG staff visited 13 EI projects (Box D3). Each field visit included an environmental specialist with EI experience or a mining engineer. For the most part, the field visits confirmed the information in IFC's files.

IFC's oil and gas projects performed well, but there are issues beyond compliance. The oil and gas sector is dominated by multinationals that in recent years have stated their commitments to improve performance and enhance sustainability and are also disclosing results achieved. OEG's analysis also found that the performance of projects sponsored by major multinationals was much better than that of projects sponsored by smaller companies. IFC could transfer knowledge and disclosure standards from these companies to less progressive companies to improve overall sector performance.[194] While oil and gas projects have an

Box D2 — Extractive Industries and HIV/AIDS

The majority of the private sector, including most of IFC's clients, still is not meaningfully involved in counteracting HIV/AIDS, a disease that affects communities, workers, and managers. Businesses will feel the impact of HIV/AIDS most clearly through their workforce, with direct consequences for profitability. Some sectors are more risky than others regarding HIV transmission. Extractive industries tend to be particularly at risk, because they usually pay salaries that are significantly higher than those of the general population and their operations also rely on a workforce separated from their families for long periods of time. Such conditions have contributed systematically to high-risk behavior, in extractive industries and in related activities, such as infrastructure construction and transportation. The rural settings of EI operations, which—unlike more urbanized areas—often lack government health, education, and prevention programs, further increase the risk. Thus, the communities in which extractive industries operate have a heightened AIDS risk. The figure below also illustrates that resource-rich countries are less likely to achieve the Millennium Development Goal of halting or reversing AIDS by 2015.

HIV/AIDS: Worse in resource-rich countries
Likelihood of achieving the Millennium Development Goal of halting or reversing AIDS by 2015

32 resource-rich countries
(Excludes 17 countries without data)

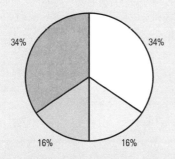

52 resource-poor countries
(Excludes 54 countries without data)

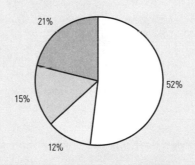

□ Likely   □ Possible   □ Unlikely   ■ Very Unlikely

The program IFC Against AIDS guides its clients in designing and implementing education, prevention, and care programs in support of employees and the communities in which they work and live. Under this initiative, IFC has to date worked with 10 clients (4 in EI) on HIV/AIDS programs and is starting to engage with 4 more (2 in EI). With the help of trust funds, IFC also is working on putting together an HIV/AIDS toolkit that would help mining companies become effective partners in the prevention and treatment of HIV/AIDS, both for the mining workforce and the communities dependent on the mines. The assignment is to identify, evaluate, and disseminate selected examples of public-private partnership approaches to HIV/AIDS prevention and treatment in the mining sector that have proved to be workable and cost-effective. Among the clients with which IFC has worked is Mozal, an aluminum producer in Mozambique, which has a strong HIV/AIDS program that includes educating and raising awareness, voluntary testing and counseling, and supplementing medication available at local hospitals. For more information on the program, see Mozal's Health, Safety, Environment and Community Report (www.mozal.com).

Note: For more information on IFC's initiative, see www.ifc.org/test/sustainability/docs/IFC_against_AIDS.pdf.

Box D3	Observations from OEG's Site Visits and Country Studies

OEG staff visited 13 projects in 6 countries.[a] Evaluators analyzed the overall country and sector context, reviewed firsthand the impact of IFC's projects (and, to a lesser extent, other projects), and asked representatives from government, civil society, industry, and the WBG about their perceptions. The main observations were as follows:

- EI projects, their relations with communities, and their impacts are extremely complex.
- For the most part, the field visits confirmed information in IFC's files, but they also found surprises—good and bad—demonstrating that, even with diligent supervision from Washington and occasional field visits, IFC will always be struggling to remain fully informed.
- IFC projects usually brought direct jobs and other opportunities; most projects improved access to infrastructure and services for many people, often in remote areas.
- Some client companies were especially proactive in trying to increase opportunities for local people by providing training for potential employees and suppliers—sometimes with IFC's help.
- Opportunities attracted people from outside the project area; their influx sometimes caused environmental and social problems for the existing community. In particular, where the capacity of local governments was weak, companies found it difficult to cope.
- Not everyone benefited, and negative environmental and social impacts were not always adequately mitigated.
- IFC-supported projects appeared to operate to higher standards than others; nevertheless, NGOs focused their criticism on projects supported by IFC, other international financial institutions, and multinational companies, perhaps because they felt they had more leverage there than at the national level.
- NGO criticism alerted IFC to problems on several occasions, but some criticism was unwarranted, and views expressed by different NGOs—for exam-

ple, local versus international—sometimes differed substantially.
- The very strong contribution by IFC's environmental and social development specialists in several projects was acknowledged by clients and communities with whom they interacted.
- But these interactions often came late, responding to problems rather than preventing them proactively—which would have been more effective and cheaper; more systematic tracking of key risk factors could have prevented some problems.
- Companies that consulted early and continuously with the local community had more effective support programs that did not necessarily cost a lot but established trust and support.
- Once the trust of the local community is lost—for example, following an accident—companies find it very costly to regain it.
- Affected communities usually saw few benefits from the taxes and royalties companies paid to governments—either little money flowed back or it was not effectively used.
- Companies were expected to make up for the lack of government services, and many of them did a lot: providing roads, water, or power, or supporting education and health services for the community. But companies are wary of taking on too much: not only can it be costly and create further expectations, it also creates an unsustainable dependency on a limited-life EI project.
- Several clients asked OEG about best practices with respect to social, environmental, health, and safety issues. There is much potential to share best practices among IFC's client companies; for example, one mining company gave sewing machines to village women who, once they had developed skills making uniforms for the mine, began to export clothing.

a. Argentina, Brazil, Ghana, Kazakhstan, Kyrgyz Republic, Peru. In one country (Kyrgyz Republic), the focus was mainly on the environmental and social performance of the project.

almost spotless compliance record, OEG observed one instance of noncompliance with respect to wastewater discharges, which was later corrected. In another case, an oil pipeline (replacing truck traffic) in an area later designated as a national park raised complex environmental and social issues. When IFC exited two years after disbursement, the project was not in full compliance with IFC's requirements, but the sponsor was working toward it. Other projects raise issues beyond IFC's requirements:

- First, several projects feature routine gas flaring. When the projects were approved, this was not covered by a specific guideline. Even today, the WBG guidelines for onshore oil and gas projects are not very specific on this issue, particularly compared with more recent IFC offshore guidelines.[195] In any event, it was difficult to establish the extent of the problem, because IFC management does not systematically track gas flaring—or GHG emissions—for all portfolio projects. IFC will calculate GHG emissions for future projects (see Box D4 on climate change), but it is unclear whether they will be tracked during supervision. Also, the WBG is leading a global gas flaring reduction initiative, which includes—as a first step—tracking gas flaring, followed by a number of possible steps to reduce the problem.[196]
- Second, transportation of oil could have been addressed more thoroughly in some cases. For example, NGOs raised concerns about spills from pipelines used by, but not part of, IFC projects. In another project, OEG discovered that environmental staff were unaware that a project had started to transport oil using trucks and rail rather than the originally anticipated pipeline, and environmental management of this transport mode appeared insufficient. The environmental impact of the transportation infrastructure for IFC's oil and gas projects has not always been a focus in the past, but IFC has begun to pay more attention to this issue. However, it can be a difficult issue to address, as it is often "beyond the fence line" of control by the project sponsors.

Mining projects, particularly gold, had some environmental problems. The broad range of environmental and social issues facing mining projects requires a strong focus by the sponsoring company just to achieve compliance with IFC's guidelines. Gold mining projects—the largest share of IFC's mining projects—had a higher incidence of reported problems. Gold production usually involves toxic materials (e.g., cyanide, mercury, arsenic), and weaknesses in their han-

---

Box D4	**IFC's Position on Climate Change (excerpts)**

IFC recognizes the long-term risk from climate change. While the Kyoto Protocol puts the main responsibility for reducing GHG emissions on developed countries, IFC believes it can have a role in reducing the GHG intensity of economic activity in developing countries. IFC requires that environmental assessments for each project consider global environmental aspects, including climate change. GHG emissions are quantified and disclosed for projects with potentially significant emissions. IFC actively promotes market-based solutions. In particular, IFC

- Seeks to reduce methane and carbon dioxide emissions in hydrocarbon extraction projects;
- Will invest in cleaner coal projects that demonstrate best practice in addressing environmental and social issues;
- Will support low-cost energy solutions for developing countries (in parallel with WB policy reform);
- Pursues projects generating GHG emission reduction credits and establishes relationships with potential buyers;
- Uses concessional funding (Global Environment Facility) to promote renewable energy and energy efficiency where appropriate;
- Devotes substantial resources to find, develop, and fund projects for renewable energy;
- Will support funds to purchase GHG emissions credits when the market is ready; and
- Pursues projects that reduce losses in power transmission and distribution.

Source: http://www.ifc.org/test/sustainability/docs/Climate_Change_IFC.pdf

dling were the most frequent problem. In response, IFC has developed a hazardous materials management guide but has not yet urged all its existing client companies to follow it. IFC also participated in the steering committee developing the Cyanide Management Code.[197]

For a positive rating, projects need to be, over their lifetime, in material compliance with IFC's at-approval requirements, which are a proxy for what IFC considered acceptable environmental performance. Projects are thus not measured against current requirements, unless at-approval requirements were clearly out of line with sound environmental practice in place at the time.[198] Thus, some projects rated satisfactory would not comply with current standards. Given the rapid evolution of industry standards, IFC may consider

- Continuously updating guidelines and policies as industry standards evolve,
- Routinely advising clients when IFC updates guidelines,
- Identifying and documenting any shortfalls against the latest guidelines during supervision and urging clients to comply voluntarily, and
- Contractually requiring clients on future projects to achieve compliance with updated guidelines; however, this may be difficult to negotiate, as clients are unlikely to subscribe to a "moving target."

IFC Helping to Generate Sustainable Benefits

Community Development—the shift from "do no harm" to "doing good." IFC's previous focus on mitigating negative impacts to ensure compliance with safeguard policies is moving increasingly toward a focus on enhancing positive socioeconomic impacts in its EI projects as part of a broader sustainability initiative. For example, in 2000, IFC issued guidance on community development.[199] The WBG's Small and Medium Enterprise (SME) Department has worked with several communities to assist in the development of small businesses in connection with high-profile projects, with a particular focus on EI.[200] IFC policy encourages community development plans but has not made them mandatory for EI projects.[201]

IFC often goes beyond the guidelines and policies. OEG has observed that in many cases, IFC establishes internal procedures for appraisal and supervision of projects that go beyond the minimum standards of the published guidelines. For example, even where they were not required, IFC has

- Helped clients implement community development plans, sometimes using trust funds (see Box D5 and Attachment 5);
- Helped clients with HIV/AIDS initiatives (see Box D2);
- Requested cumulative EIAs; and

Box D5

Donor-Supported Trust Funds Contribute to IFC's Sustainability Initiative

Since 1994, through IFC's Trust Fund Unit, donors have spent $3.5 million to support technical assistance for 22 EI-related projects—mostly in the past three years (Attachment 5). Increasingly, technical assistance supports sustainable development, including a conference in China to improve the investment climate for sustainable mining and a global initiative to disseminate examples of successful approaches to HIV/AIDS prevention. So far, the projects appear to have been broadly successful. However, because Project Completion Reports have often not been prepared, OEG was unable to assign project ratings. Technical assistance demand by the EI sector—focusing on social and environmental development—is likely to grow. Through better tracking, IFC would be in a better position to understand and communicate the impacts of its technical assistance program to its donors and the public.

- Encouraged some clients to adopt the new hazardous materials management guidelines.

The WBG has developed policies, guidelines, practices, and procedures that are setting standards and helping to improve the sector's contribution to sustainable development. Many observers—international organizations, government, industry, and NGOs—concur that the World Bank Group's requirements and guidelines set a high standard.[202] A 2001 United Nations Environment Program (UNEP) study observed that the participation of multilateral financial institutions significantly raises a project's environmental and social standards. Other multilateral (e.g., European Bank for Reconstruction and Development, Inter-American Development Bank) and bilateral institutions reference and some use IFC and World Bank guidelines. Several government officials have commented that WBG guidelines are an important benchmark when setting local standards. Industry also sees value: 95 percent of clients in EI saw IFC's requirements as primarily helpful to their long-term interest, compared with only two-thirds of all clients.[203] Some clients and even other companies list in their annual reports that they comply with IFC guidelines,[204] and several industry representatives commented that IFC's and the WBG's guidance materials—particularly on social issues—are very helpful. For example, IFC has published good practice manuals on public consultation, resettlement, HIV/AIDS, child labor, and community development.[205] By publishing guidance[206] on topics such as mine closure and community development and by hosting workshops and participating in or leading sector initiatives, the WBG is highly visible, taking a leadership role in improving environmental and social impacts. In 2003, some of the largest private project finance banks have committed to adopting IFC safeguard policies and guidelines, thus broadening their reach.[207] Nevertheless, many other financial institutions and export credit agencies still lack such standards (Box D6).

Nevertheless, some guidelines are inconsistent, incomplete, or missing. Given the WBG's high visibility, it is particularly important that its guidelines be updated regularly and conform to at least good practice standards in the industry and among financial institutions. IFC did not update its safeguard policies for several years, and some are now inconsistent with World Bank guidelines.[208] For example, staff told OEG that IFC projects now must comply with a draft, nonpublic version of the 1999 policy on safety

---

Box D6	Lack of Similar Standards in Other Financial Institutions

Many businesses recognize that "addressing sustainable development is critical to their long-term survival, and to delivery of enhanced shareholder value."[a] But there is also much concern that similar standards do not apply to everyone. NGOs use WBG guidelines to point out weaknesses in other financial institutions' requirements and are concerned about a "race to the bottom."[b] UNEP noted in 2001 that, despite some progress since 1999, most export credit agencies were lacking adequate environmental and social requirements—all the more worrisome because their investment volume in the sector is much larger than that of the multilateral institutions. Some IFC investment staff expressed concerns about losing business to financial institutions with lower standards when IFC cannot convince potential clients that IFC's guidelines are in their own long-term interest. OEG found that NGOs are often vocal critics of projects supported by international financial institutions and multinational corporations but do not necessarily raise similar concerns about local or state-owned companies with worse performance.

a. *Mining & Minerals Sustainability Survey 2001:* A PriceWaterhouse Coopers survey of 32 world-class mining and minerals organizations.
b. Numerous examples include ECA-Watch (www.eca-watch.org/problems/impacts.html) demanding to "stipulate World Bank and OECD DAC [Development Assistance Committee] standards as the minimum acceptable" for export credit agencies.

of dams, not with the 1996 version on IFC's Web site, nor with the 2001 World Bank policy. Similarly, IFC does not use the "new" World Bank 2001 involuntary resettlement policy but the "old" 1990 policy, combined with a resettlement handbook, which is appreciated by practitioners but not mandatory. While OEG was told that what applies is clear to IFC's specialists, to any outsider it must appear extremely confusing. There are also numerous examples of inconsistent or incomplete IFC guidelines. For example, requirements for closure plan funding differ for different types of mines (coal, open pit mining, base metal mining). IFC promised specific guidelines for cyanide leaching in gold mining in 1998, but they have yet to be published. Ongoing consultations are seen as critical for enhanced community development but are not required. Social issues are recognized as crucial for mine closure but are not addressed in the requirements. IFC's 2001 guidelines for offshore oilfields place much more emphasis on reducing gas flaring and other sources of greenhouse gas emissions than the applicable 1998 WBG guidelines for onshore oilfields. IFC's requirements for identifying and controlling impacts of downstream transportation of oil and gas projects are generally adequate but may need to be more specific on road and rail transport of oil, oil products, and gas. Some areas, such as human rights, are not covered by IFC's guidelines but are being addressed by the industry or other bilateral or multilateral institutions.[209]

Leading EI companies have signed on to "Voluntary Principles on Security and Human Rights," but IFC has no such requirements. Human rights organizations have repeatedly noted violations of the rights of individuals in connection with EI projects, particularly in the oil sector.[210] EI projects involve large investments, often in countries where security, including the threat of war or terrorist attack, is a concern. IFC has approved projects in several such countries, where sponsors were working with the army or private security forces to protect their property. Because IFC usually leaves security issues up to client companies, there is potential for problems to develop. A few IFC clients have been accused of human rights violations, and IFC has been criticized for supporting projects that could lead to such violations. Following an initiative led by several countries, many industry leaders and NGOs have signed on to "Voluntary Principles on Security and Human Rights."[211] However, IFC currently has no policy or guidance on country-internal conflicts[212] or potential human rights abuses and does not usually specify how its client companies should protect staff and assets. Given the potential risks for people in the host country and for IFC's own reputation, this appears to be a significant gap and an area where WBG standards and guidelines do not reflect corporate best practice.

Policies, guidelines, and best practice must produce results in the field. Operational policies and guidelines provide direction to IFC staff and clients. But the ultimate test of their usefulness is whether they improve results in the field. Safeguards are useful, but identification of potential problems by investment officers is equally important so that these issues are not overlooked. Therefore, additional training of investment staff to recognize social and environmental issues in EI projects throughout the project cycle would be useful. Investment officers need not have the expertise to replace environmental and social development specialists, but they should have sufficient skills to recognize problems and the benefits of getting specialists involved in internal and external project preparation as early as possible. Particularly, investment staff intervention to bring specialists into early contact with sponsors and to encourage sponsors to retain skilled and experienced social specialists in relevant situations is of prime importance. Strong management support and recognition of investment officers who proactively engage with sponsors to address social and environmental issues are essential for improved sustainability of IFC projects.

Problems can arise when IFC's environmental and development specialists are not involved early enough. Several projects had problems that could have been prevented or more easily mitigated had there been early interaction between IFC's social specialists and the project sponsor. For example, in one Latin American project, IFC became involved in the early 1990s, but the first social development specialist input from IFC came many years later, because IFC did not hire social specialists until the mid-1990s. IFC's specialist recommended that the sponsor employ more social specialists to adequately address community issues, including conflict resolution. But this recommendation was taken seriously only after the social and environmental impacts of a subsequent spill became apparent. The sponsor now has a very proactive social department of 15 people who consult with both rural and urban stakeholders about the project.

Supervision for EI projects is better than for the overall IFC portfolio, but gaps remain.

IFC's supervision for EI projects was significantly better overall than for other sectors, with 82 percent (versus 59 percent) rated satisfactory. In part, this reflects the necessity of closer supervision of environmental and social aspects, as many EI projects face complex environmental and social issues. Nevertheless, there are important gaps:

- IFC had insufficient information to assess the environmental performance of several EI portfolio projects, often where IFC had only an equity investment or in older projects preceding the introduction of IFC's 1998 procedures.[213]

- IFC was caught unaware because of weak monitoring, or less than full disclosure by companies, of problems relating to handling of hazardous materials, mine closure plans, acid rock drainage, tailings impoundments, IFC's resettlement policy, gas flaring, and transportation of oil.

- While project-level supervision overall was strong, IFC's management and information systems do not provide adequate centralized data on environmental and social issues for the portfolio. For example, management is only now starting to develop overview reporting templates specifying which safeguard policies and guidelines apply to specific projects and whether projects comply with them, which mining projects have appropriate mine

closure plans and funding in place, and which oil and gas projects involve routine flaring. IFC's new management information system will address some, but not all, of these issues.

Many of IFC's EI projects are in countries with inadequate environmental and social governance; this strongly challenges IFC in terms of resource allocation, reputation risk, and responsibility. Many host countries lack adequate environmental laws, regulations, and enforcement. Previous OEG studies[214] have found significantly worse performance in such countries. EI projects are particularly concentrated there, and IFC's potential added value is thus also greatest. But substantial resources are required for IFC to ensure compliance. It is unclear whether IFC will ever—or should—be in a position to replace host country enforcement. In addition, even if IFC can ensure compliance while it is an investor, it typically cannot influence performance after exiting its investment.[215] Also, some issues (e.g., new settlement in areas of resource development) are difficult for IFC and its clients to deal with in the absence of government support. Yet IFC does not consistently assess the institutional capacity of national government agencies. In some cases there was a preceding or concurrent World Bank involvement to upgrade government capacity, but this is not the norm.[216] This raises the question whether IFC ought to seek World Bank assistance more routinely to upgrade government's environmental review capacity where it is found lacking. A complementary action that would reduce the burden on IFC would be to require that clients subscribe to international standards of independent monitoring.[217] In all new Category 'A' projects (and for some Category 'B' projects), IFC requires independent audits or at least independent verification of the Annual Monitoring Reports (AMRs). Such requirements could reduce the supervision load and reputation risk for IFC, but this has to be balanced against the higher cost for the client—who also benefits from improved performance.

Baseline data are important but were not always established or tracked sufficiently.

EIAs prepared for Category 'A' projects are

required to include a comprehensive baseline survey of environmental and social conditions. Yet for several past projects either this had not been completed or it did not provide enough information.[218] A detailed inventory of the environmental and social conditions before breaking ground for exploration is crucial to track development results, and it is also in the self-interest of the company. Local communities—understandably—highlight areas where they want improvements and do not necessarily give credit for past improvements achieved. It is common for the EI industry to be charged with polluting air and water, degrading land, destroying structures, and, in general, worsening livelihoods. While many claims are real, some cannot be substantiated.[219] Extensive baseline data, later tracked in ongoing monitoring programs, would help distinguish real from false claims and make it possible to appropriately compensate for negative impacts. They also would help the company—and IFC—to demonstrate positive developments.[220] On the other hand, monitoring and baseline surveys are costly. It is therefore important to establish the most important environmental and socioeconomic indicators in the EIA and identify how they should be tracked later. IFC has started to track development results more systematically in its supervision, and well-designed EIAs and AMRs could help in this respect.

Challenges in Meeting IFC's Environmental and Social Development Objectives

Funding mine closure—difficult to implement. Mine closure is a major environmental and social issue. Abandoned mines represent an environmental hazard to the country and potentially significant cumulative cleanup costs associated with long-term environmental and social damage. Since 1982, the WBG has therefore required concrete and detailed plans for reclamation and funding, with the goal of returning land to conditions supporting prior land use (or better uses). Since 1998, IFC's guidelines have required that money be reserved over the life of the mine to cover closure cost.[221] However, IFC's experience has shown in several

cases that this approach can be problematic—when commodity prices declined, the ore body was less valuable and the mine life thus shorter than anticipated. While IFC eventually secured funding for mine closure in several such cases, this clearly represented a risk, and mine closure issues have not been resolved for all portfolio projects.[222] Another difficulty for implementing sustainable solutions for mine closure is that IFC generally exits from its investments when its role is completed—often well before the mine closes—and therefore loses any influence over the mine operator. The WBG has developed good practice guidance, covering different options for securing funding that may offer solutions,[223] but this guidance is not mandatory. There is clearly an urgent need to identify solutions (e.g., financial instruments) to ensure that mines will be closed properly, even if a company becomes insolvent.

Social issues related to mine closure—not covered and even more complex. The social issues surrounding mine closure are not covered in IFC's guidelines. They revolve around communities being able to deal with loss of jobs, economic activity, revenues, and services associated with mine closure. To address them requires the cooperation of multiple stakeholders, including local communities, mining companies, and different levels of government. The WBG has developed guidance on this issue, including the respective roles of different stakeholders and "checklists" on handling social and environmental mine closure issues. Like all guidance notes, they are not mandatory for IFC projects.[224]

Longer mine life—more potential for sustainable development? IFC has funded mines with estimated lives exceeding 30 years where the mining company becomes a part of the community and can justify expenditures for improved infrastructure to support its operations. This allows more time to contribute to sustainable development and prepare for mine closure but may increase the community's dependence. IFC also funds mines with relatively short lives. The compressed life can exaggerate some of the social and environmental issues associated with mining, including mine closure and reclamation risk. One African company told OEG that it wished it had invested in local community development earlier. It did not, in part because it had expected to close down within a decade, but it will now continue to operate following the acquisition of an adjacent mine.

Tailings dams—the Achilles' heel of mining projects but few problems in IFC's portfolio. In 1996, Comsur, an IFC client, experienced a tailings dam break. In the same year, IFC also discovered through an evaluation that the client of one of its older investments was discharging tailings straight into a river—without a tailings dam.[225] Following this, a 1999 draft Policy on Safety of Dams (OP4.37) was prepared that includes tailings dams. The environmental assessment must now provide information on the tailings dam. IFC's mining engineers and environmental staff are expected to review tailings dam safety at appraisal and during supervision. While there were no problems until recently, IFC just discovered a problem with a leaky tailings impoundment.[226] Tailings dams often remain following closure, posing a potential threat to the community. It is thus important to assess the public risks from potential tailings dam failure, starting from the EIA.

Private ownership can improve environmental performance, but this often means addressing the environmental legacy of past practices—a challenge. Several IFC investments have been in newly privatized but existing operations. The past practices of the former government managers had left a legacy of environmental problems (oil pits, leaking pipelines, contaminated waterways, leaking tailings dams), often passed on to the new owners charged with the cleanup. Environmental performance invariably improved under the new ownership, reversing most of the negative impacts, but in some cases bringing the operation into compliance proved difficult and prolonged.

Going beyond the fence line. Current industry practice places an imaginary fence line around the project, with activities outside the fence line

not considered part of the project's impact. While there has to be a cut-off, defining the fence line is difficult. For example, a country's ability or lack thereof to clean up a spill can have effects well beyond what may be considered the confines of the project, particularly with respect to transport—by rail, road, pipelines, and sea. Transport often is contracted to or is the full responsibility of third parties. Two IFC projects experienced high-profile hazardous materials spills, Minera Yanacocha, Peru, and Kumtor Gold, Kyrgyz Republic. Both featured road transport mishaps outside what had been defined as the fence line. On the basis of these experiences, IFC has extended its appraisal and supervision reach to cover some of the operations of suppliers and shippers, applying environmental guidelines to these activities. Nevertheless, the debate will remain over the point of transfer of responsibility.

Challenges when IFC enters late in the process. IFC can have a major influence if involved in the project from inception. In several cases, however, IFC was not approached until after the sponsors had advanced the project, not always in accordance with IFC's guidelines, particularly in relation to public consultation. In such cases, IFC faces a choice between turning down a project and losing the opportunity to add value, or imposing what may be costly conditions on the client for proceeding. Current guidance on what to do in such circumstances is unclear.

Ensuring sound environmental and social performance equity investments. IFC has several equity-only investments, with little legal leverage to influence the project and no legal right to obtain Annual Monitoring Reports. IFC could use "moral suasion" but has not always done so. In some cases, the appropriate environmental and social terms and conditions were in the loan documents, but they expired upon repayment of the loan. If the company is delinquent in its environmental or social responsibilities, IFC will bear some reputation risk, whether it remains an investor or exits. Even today, IFC does not always include contractual environmental and social requirements for equity. OEG pointed out this problem in its first Annual Review in 1997. IFC management responded that it would look into this issue, but that there were complex commercial and other considerations. But IFC's 1998 environmental and social review procedures do not distinguish between investment instruments and do not address this issue. It is difficult to negotiate appropriate requirements for equity investments (e.g., shareholders' agreement, put option in case of environmental default), but lack thereof makes it difficult, if not impossible, for IFC to comply with its own procedures. Also, there are no guidelines establishing how active IFC should be as a shareholder; for example, whether IFC should routinely ask for information about a client's environmental practices and raise this issue at shareholder meetings.[227]

New approvals—similar difficulties. Since 2001, IFC has approved funding for five projects to help the EI sector with services, loans, or seed capital. These projects could create jobs, establish new ventures, and improve services. As yet, there have been few disbursements under these projects, but when they or similar projects are disbursed, they could present unique challenges for monitoring and enforcing compliance under IFC's safeguards policies and guidelines, because of IFC's indirect relation to the underlying projects and lack of contractual leverage. Similar issues apply to EI projects approved through financial markets operations, which were not covered in this evaluation.

ASM can give rise to major environmental and social problems and sometimes pose a reputation risk for IFC's clients. ASM features prominently in a number of countries where IFC has EI investments. Authorities sometimes consider ASM a stopgap measure for poverty prevention and leave it untouched, even if they oppose its practices. ASM is often illegal and involves very unhealthy and unsafe working conditions, including child labor. ASM can cause major environmental damage, degrade land beyond rehabilitation, and pollute waterways with heavy sediment, heavy metals, hazardous materials (mercury), and acid rock drainage. Sometimes

ASM precedes large mines, and government regulation often requires eviction of miners; at other times, ASM is attracted by large-scale mining activity. In either case, large mining companies face a dilemma—evicting ASM operators is difficult and results in poor community relations, while letting them operate results in reputation risk—being blamed for the poor environmental and safety record of ASM.[228] In one case, an IFC client wanted to help artisanal miners with better equipment and guidance but realized that even improved conditions would still constitute too great a reputation risk. Dealing with ASM often has proved beyond the capability of industry. But governments also are struggling with it. Observers suggest a twofold solution: one, create alternative employment opportunities; two, help "upgrade" this subsector: provide assistance to transform artisanal miners into safer, small-scale miners who are regulated and abide by improved environmental standards. Experience beyond IFC's portfolio suggests that private companies can engage constructively with ASM operators (Box D7), as does other WBG work.[229]

5. Disclosure and Consultation

IFC's disclosure requirements have increased. IFC adopted its first disclosure policy in July 1994 and revised it in 1996 and 1998.[230] Under the policy, IFC balances accountability as a public institution—favoring disclosure—with the need to protect commercially sensitive information. EI projects are particularly sensitive, and IFC frequently signs confidentiality agreements. Disclosure in IFC has increased substantially since the early 1990s, when almost none was required. Recognizing the fundamental importance of accountability and transparency in the development process, IFC requires disclosure of the following:

- **Summary of Project Information**—a brief factual summary of the evolving project.
- **Environment-Related Documents**—Category 'A' projects: environmental impact assessment, released at least 60 days before the Board date; Category 'B' projects: summary of the key findings of the environmental review, released at least 30 days before.

Disclosure is only required before approval; public information is thus often outdated, but this aspect has improved recently. In several projects reviewed by OEG, project scope or design had substantially changed, but the publicly available information had not been updated.[231] Publicly available project documents usually addressed planned measures to address environmental effects, not whether these measures have been effectively implemented. Such issues usually would be covered in an AMR supplied by the client to IFC, but AMRs are not publicly available.[232] While disclosure has to be balanced against commercial confidentiality, lack of disclosure diminishes trust.[233] For some recent IFC projects, updated environmental and social information has been disclosed.[234]

IFC protects its clients by keeping project information confidential—but is that in their best interest? Leading industry players see value in disclosure. IFC, at EIR workshops and other consultations, has been criticized—sometimes based on misconceptions about specific EI projects. More information could diminish such misconceptions, but IFC does not disclose, even in aggregate form, noncompliance by its clients.[235] There are no guidelines on whether, or under what circumstances, IFC should notify local authorities or the public of known compliance shortfalls. Many IFC clients have started to voluntarily disclose detailed social, environmental, and financial reports, recognizing that openness and transparency increases trust and is in their long-term interest. Others, such as one client who asked OEG's advice about best practice in sustainability reporting, are considering it,. Leading industry players publish independently verified, detailed sustainability reports, including, for example, sites with independent audits and mine closure plans; injury rates; land, water, and energy use; spill incidents, gas flaring, carbon dioxide, and greenhouse gas emissions; and environmental and noncompliance incidents. IFC has begun to insist on disclosure of ongoing environmental and social information in a few high-profile projects, but this is not the norm.

In several cases, IFC clients have gone beyond the disclosure requirements.[236] One client is now the only company in the country that audits and discloses environmental performance reports. In a few recent cases, IFC has agreed with the client on independent monitoring and disclosure of the AMR. In several cases, IFC has gone beyond the minimum requirements; one example being the Chad-Cameroon Pipeline project, with a 19-volume environmental management plan and ongoing independent review. Some other IFC clients also disclose substantial amounts of information about their environmental and social activities.[237] Such information often can be found on IFC's or the clients' Web sites.

Build community trust through open, honest, respectful, and ongoing consultation. But IFC's requirements fall short of its own good practice guidance on public consultation and disclosure plans.[238] The guidance defines consultation as "a wider continuous process of participation of all stakeholders in the decisions throughout the formulation and execution of a project." IFC's preapproval disclosure and consultation requirements may not be enough to achieve trust in the community. In particular, ongoing consultations are not required (unless a project involves resettlement or indigenous peoples),[239] nor is disclosure.

Good communication can improve the effectiveness of assistance programs and reduce anxiety if problems occur. Unilateral company decisions on what is best for the community are likely to be misguided and expensive and cause discontent. For example, when a mining company used tanks to temporarily restore water supply to villagers without consulting them, they accused it of treating them "like refugees." But another mining company consulted extensively with the community and, for a few hundred dollars, developed a project that recycles engine oil for coastal fishermen, reduces coastal pollution, and has strong community support. Companies that communicate poorly can face the high costs of project interruptions and community relations turned sour.[240] From field visits, desk reviews, and the literature, it is clear that IFC clients that consult, disclose, and communicate well are better off than those that do it poorly.

Public consultation can be complex, confusing, and difficult for both the company and the stakeholders. Some multinationals have geared up for this important part of doing business, but others are struggling and even with the best of intentions are finding themselves running into difficulties. Some have requested assistance from IFC.[241] To consult with the companies on an equal footing, the communities and other stakeholders may need assistance and training to understand the business and technology. Independent experts can help, but who pays for them? If the sponsor provides the funding, the expert may be perceived as compromised, but alternative funding sources are scarce. IFC has worked with a number of clients and communities to facilitate the consultative process, sometimes using trust funds (Attachment 5), sometimes with the help of the CAO—and OEG has witnessed positive effects in several projects.

6. Governance and Challenges of Managing Revenues from Extractive Industries

Extractive industries—large revenues for countries with poor governance. The economic sustainability section of this report indicated that most of IFC's EI investments created large revenues for host countries, particularly in oil and gas, sometimes even when investors did not achieve satisfactory returns.[242] There is abundant evidence that such large revenues, which, tend to be volatile and finite, create particular challenges for resource-rich countries. While IFC usually analyzed the financial, social, and environmental aspects of a project thoroughly, it has, in the past, not approached revenue management and distribution with the same rigor. Because IFC's EI projects are highly concentrated in risky countries that tend to suffer from weak governance, the issue becomes particularly important. Since fiscal year 1993, half of IFC's EI approvals were in countries in the worst governance quartile, compared with only one-quarter of all non-EI approvals.[243] To recommend not investing in countries with poor governance sounds tempting, but the WBG's mission is to reduce poverty and improve people's lives—and hundreds of millions of people live in resource-rich countries with poor governance. While the WBG alone may not be able to improve governance, by using its unique position as global player with the convening power to engage both public and private stakeholders, it can effect change.

Challenges of investing in countries with the poorest governance. Countries with poor governance often lack transparency, adequate laws, financial capacity, and regulations to allow regulators and judiciary systems to cope adequately with large EI projects. If corruption is an issue, customs agents, transport companies, regulators, and government officials could exert significant pressure on projects, causing delays and additional costs. From a development perspective, corruption is bad for growth and tends to reduce economic growth and private sector investment.[244] Resource-rich developing countries that are often cited among the best examples for the positive contribution of the EI sector—such as Botswana and Chile—are all considered to have relatively little corruption.[245]

Results—for development, IFC's bottom line and the environment were closely correlated with governance quality. OEG analyzed the results of the 45 studied projects using different governance indicators.[246] Development results were significantly better in countries with good government effectiveness, political stability, and regulatory quality (Figure D3). It is also worth noting that investing in countries with poor governance is not necessarily financially attractive for IFC. In fact, none of IFC's 10 most successful EI investments were in a country with the highest corruption.[247] IFC's equity returns were worst in countries with the poorest control of corruption and the best in countries with the highest control (Figure D4).[248] Environmental results were significantly better with better political stability.

Bribes are common in EI, particularly in oil and gas. According to Transparency International,[249] the oil and gas sector is perceived as third most likely to involve bribes, following only public works contracts and arms deals. Mining ranks seventh. The Organisation for Economic Co-operation and Development (OECD) Convention on Combating Bribery of Foreign Public Officials in International Business Transactions[250] entered into force in February 1999. Thirty-five countries have ratified the convention, and most have already enacted legislation to make it a crime for businesses to bribe foreign public officials. Quite a few countries already had laws outlawing corruption abroad.[251]

Figure D3 — Better Development Results with Better Governance (45 studied EI projects)

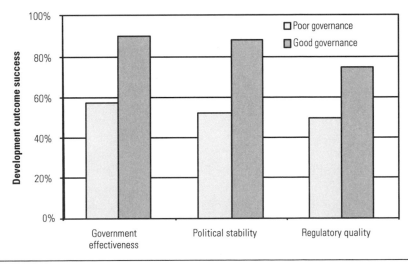

Source: WBI Grics-II

133

Figure D4 — Better Country Governance — Better IFC Equity Returns for EI and for Other Sectors

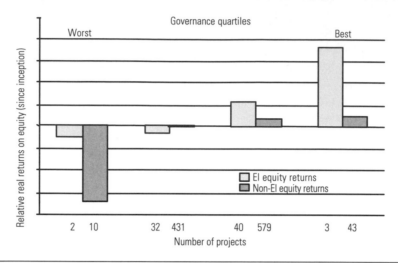

Note: 175 countries were sorted based on the average of their respective GRICS indicators (Voice and Accountability, Political Stability, Government Effectiveness, Regulatory Quality, Rule of Law, and Control of Corruption) and divided into quartiles.

Source: World Bank Institute. Governance Research Indicators Country Snapshot (GRICS) Dataset, 2001.

Nevertheless, paying bribes still appears to be common.

IFC takes precautions against corruption, but it is clearly a risk. IFC projects provide a demonstration effect for others, and it is therefore imperative that the projects are implemented transparently and honestly. IFC usually explicitly requires sponsors to abide by host country laws and regulations, which often outlaw corruption. During appraisal, IFC typically checks the background and reputation of its sponsors and how licenses were awarded. To that end, IFC has, on several occasions, hired private investigators. IFC also typically requires that its clients' financial statements be audited, which may reduce but not eliminate the scope for irregularities. OEG reviewed project files and had informal discussions with IFC staff, project sponsors, and third parties knowledgeable about the sector. OEG found no evidence that IFC clients were paying bribes but did not conduct an audit. However, particularly because IFC projects are taking place in countries with high perceived levels of cor-

ruption, there is clearly a risk. OEG's field visits and other research showed substantial differences with respect to the transparency and handling of EI sector revenues among different countries with IFC EI investments.

Corruption is linked to revenue management but is difficult to prove. International Monetary Fund (IMF) research has found that corruption distorts allocation of resources by governments. It is associated with higher public spending but poorer quality infrastructure. In countries with poor governance, it is therefore particularly important to address how governments manage fiscal revenues from EI. OEG visited several countries where little of the government revenues was flowing back to benefit communities next to EI projects. In some countries, there was a strong suspicion that government officials at different levels were corrupt. Without transparency about the resource flows, such allegations are difficult to prove or disprove. About 70 percent of government officials surveyed (Attachment 6B) saw a need for the IFC to help improve governance and transparency (the corresponding figure for the World Bank is 83 percent). One mining minister advocated disclosure of moneys provided to local authorities to better ensure local communities benefit from it.

IFC's recent efforts with respect to revenue management. The Chad-Cameroon pipeline is the first IFC project to proactively tackle revenue management.[252] This effort followed IFC's recognition that projects that devolve little or no benefit to local communities present both development and commercial risks. A recent IFC position paper on revenue distribution and management[253] (Box D8) states that, in high-impact projects in countries with poor governance and weak institutions, IFC will systematically assess the risks that governments would misuse payments or that intended benefits may not reach local communities. IFC would also, together with the Bank, IMF, and sponsors, consider mitigating measures. At this point, the position paper applies only to "high-impact" projects (substantial in relation to the nation's income), and none of the mitigating measures are mandatory.

Key issues in revenue management. A joint working group consisting of industry, civil society, and WBG staff considered the following

policies critical with respect to revenue management and utilization:[254] (i) the establishment of transparency and accountability with respect to revenues earned and their disposition, (ii) consultation with principal stakeholders in developing plans for the use of resource revenues, (iii) credible oversight and audit of the implementation of these plans, and (iv) serious attention to building local institutional capacity.

Disclosure of government revenues—a step toward better management? To date, neither the IMF nor the World Bank necessarily require that resource-rich countries disclose the revenues generated by EI, even though they sometimes recommend it. IFC's EI clients are also not required to disclose the revenues they generate for governments. However, several public campaigns have started to advocate disclosure of EI revenues.[255] But disclosure of government revenues can raise difficult issues. Governments in some countries even make it illegal, through confidentiality covenants in production-sharing agreements, for example. Industry is concerned that unilateral disclosure could create a competitive disadvantage. However, almost all industry representatives whom OEG interviewed in the course of this study would support industry-wide disclosure of government revenues. Most of them, however, emphasized that these were

Box D8 — IFC's Position Regarding Revenue Distribution and Management—Highlights

Revenue distribution and management in extractive industry projects are important development issues and have emerged as major risk factors for both the operation and the reputation of investors. Large revenues generated by these projects and accruing to government may be misused. Benefits from these revenues may not reach local communities. While revenue distribution and management are not issues in every IFC project, they can become problematic in high-impact projects; that is, *where revenues are substantial in relation to the nation's fiscal income.*

To deal with the problem, IFC proposes a number of steps that it may undertake for high-impact projects that will generate substantial revenues for host governments:
- Engage with the World Bank or IMF to coordinate issues beyond IFC's mandate.
- Consider other mitigation measures, such as sponsor's community development programs, when coordination may not achieve the necessary level of management.
- Seek funds or partners to assist a sponsor with capacity-building.

their personal, not necessarily corporate, views. Some companies operating in the EI sector have started disclosing government revenues even against host government concerns.

7. Issues Beyond the Control of IFC and Its Clients Require Effective Cooperation and Action Inside and Outside the World Bank Group

Issues beyond IFC's control require better cooperation among financiers and development partners. IFC has been more effective in EI projects than in other sectors in addressing most issues within its own control. More needs to be done to ensure that the sector and the projects IFC supports contribute to sustainable development. IFC can address some issues with its clients; for example, helping them to improve their environmental performance, community development activities, and consultation and disclosure—to serve as role models for sustainable development. IFC has done much[256] and can probably do even more to convince its clients that better environmental and social performance, while potentially entailing short-term costs, will ultimately be in their long-term interest. But to have even greater impact, IFC also needs to work on further improving its own environmental and social policies and guidelines and their implementation and—together with its member countries—help improve those of other international financial institutions. Little would be gained if IFC alone adds requirements and its potential clients seek financing elsewhere. But many of the issues discussed in this evaluation are beyond even the control of IFC's client companies. To resolve them will require close cooperation within the World Bank Group and with other stakeholders and partners—the IMF, IFC's member governments, and other international financial institutions. The recent adoption of IFC's policies and guidelines on environmental and social issues by several internationally active banks is an important step in that direction.

Merging World Bank and IFC units has improved sectoral cooperation, but cooperation with country departments and attention to revenue distribution and utilization, governance, and

transparency are still inadequate. To validate the findings of this evaluation, we surveyed all of IFC's sectoral investment staff and regional economists.[257] Almost 90 percent responded that merging IFC's and the World Bank's sector departments into one Global Product Group had improved coordination of sectoral issues. At the same time, less than half said that overall cooperation within the WBG was adequate; in their view, lack of support by the World Bank's country departments was the biggest internal constraint.[258] One likely explanation for the insufficient coordination is that the country directors lack the incentive to address EI issues: in the countries where IFC operates, the WBG's EI lending volume tends to be small, EI projects are considered environmentally risky,[259] and governments may not be receptive to WBG activity in this area. Of 24 IFC staff who responded, 63 percent considered host country governments' lack of support to be the biggest constraint to enhancing the contribution of the EI sector to sustainable development. Only about half of the IFC respondents said that revenue distribution and utilization, governance, and transparency were adequately addressed in EI operations. This response confirmed an analysis of CASs showing that weak country governance and revenue management in resource-rich countries often were not adequately addressed in CASs and subsequent WBG interventions; IFC's EI activities often were not even mentioned in CASs (see Annex C). This points to a need to address EI issues in country strategies more thoroughly, ideally in a Comprehensive Development Framework mode, also engaging other stakeholders beyond the WBG.

Perceptions of environmental and social performance differ. Well over 90 percent of IFC staff responded that environmental and social issues were adequately addressed in IFC's EI projects. This perception is better than our evaluation results suggest, but staff may have considered IFC's performance on current projects, whereas we evaluated past results. Certainly the perception of IFC staff is different from that of outside observers. Among the participants at the EIR workshops, only 44 percent (of 52) responded that IFC successfully addressed environmental impacts; 33 percent (of 48) responded positively for social impacts. Views among NGOs were the worst—15 percent and 7 percent positive, respectively. Responses from government and industry were around 50 percent positive, slightly better for environmental issues. This points to a need for improved performance compared with past results and also for much greater disclosure and engagement of stakeholders to address the poor perceptions where they are not warranted.

Even a concerted WBG effort is probably not enough. About two-thirds of IFC staff responded that the biggest factor keeping EI from contributing to sustainable development is the lack of support from the host country government. One respondent explained, "[The] main problem is governments in client countries don't want the Bank or IFC messing with their only independent source of revenues. Even when the Bank does intervene, it often does not have the leverage to engineer change." Some respondents commented that the IMF also needs to be involved and that continued engagement in the sector was important to maintain the country dialogue. An OED study also found that governance was key to successful management of fiscal revenues from EI but that government commitment or political will to address it was lacking in four out of five country cases (Annex C, Chapter 5).

The results confirm that closer cooperation is needed—within the WBG and beyond. The survey results confirm the evaluation findings—that important issues, such as revenue distribution, utilization, governance, and transparency, need to be better addressed. This will require closer cooperation within the WBG. But the WBG will also need to use its convening power and the help from its member governments, the IMF, industry, financiers, and civil society to break the resource curse and ensure that extractive industries contribute to sustainable development. Greater transparency about the resources generated for governments is likely to increase pressure on governments to account for the flow and effective use of those resources. Our evaluation results suggest that better country governance is not only likely to improve the development results of IFC's operations but also IFC's financial results.

IFC needs to better tackle transparency, government revenue distribution, and, more generally, sustainable development. Other stakeholders echoed the perceptions of IFC staff. NGOs, industry, and governments expressed a need for IFC to address these issues (Attachment 6B). But no group responded that there was enough IFC effort or success. NGOs were most critical (less than 10 percent said IFC successfully addressed these areas), but the perceptions of industry (about 20 percent) and government (about 40 percent) also indicate substantial room for improvement.

8. Conclusions and Recommendations

Overall, IFC has effectively supported EI operations, but it needs to further improve their implementation, better address broader sustainability issues, and, with its clients, better track and report on results achieved. Projects usually generated large revenues for governments and opportunities for people. IFC has generally added value, particularly in improving the environmental and social aspects of projects, but given the sector's high impact potential, IFC needs to help client companies prevent or mitigate negative impacts more effectively and systematically. IFC also needs to ensure that its environmental and social guidelines and procedures continue to set standards and adapt to rapidly improving industry standards and that its projects adapt with them. In pursuit of its sustainability agenda, IFC needs to do more to address the risks that government revenues may not be effectively used for development, that benefits may not be distributed transparently, and that local communities may not tangibly benefit from EI projects. To enhance the contribution of IFC's projects and the sector to sustainable development requires further improvements in project implementation, effective cooperation within the World Bank Group, and the full engagement of all stakeholders.

This evaluation found gaps in three areas: strategic gaps, resulting from inadequately addressing issues such as country governance and revenue management through effective action, both within the WBG and with other partners, and clearer project selection criteria; implementation gaps, which, if addressed, could enhance the performance of IFC's EI projects and, through the demonstration effects of IFC's projects and requirements, that of EI more generally; and gaps in engaging stakeholders, which, if addressed, would allow IFC and its clients to improve performance and better demonstrate contribution to sustainable development.

Recommendation 1: Formulate an integrated strategy

Address extractive industries in CASs. IFC should work closely with other parts of the WBG to ensure that CASs for resource-rich countries[260] explicitly discuss the EI sector's contribution to sustainable development (e.g., the importance of fiscal revenues and their management, distribution, and use for development priorities) and obstacles for enhancing its contribution. The CAS should provide an agreed framework for WBG-wide cooperation, with a particular focus on close interaction between IFC and the World Bank's country departments. IFC and the World Bank should routinely work together to enhance the development impacts of EI projects; for example, in the form of public-private partnerships with respect to community development programs.[261] IFC and the WBG should build on existing initiatives, such as Business Partners for Development and the Comprehensive Development Framework, to enlist the help of other stakeholders, such as the IMF, other bilateral and multilateral institutions, industry, and civil society.

Where country governance is weak, increase transparency and address the weaknesses. Together with the World Bank and other stakeholders, IFC should analyze all aspects of country governance quality and the risks that poor governance may detract from sustainable development. In particular, IFC should encourage enhanced transparency and disclosure concerning contractual agreements between investors and governments, the amount of fiscal revenues generated, and their distribution.[262] IFC—together with the World Bank and other stakeholders—should encourage such transparency sectorwide in the country. When financing projects whose major expected development contribution is the generation of revenues to governments, IFC should carefully review and discuss the governance risk that these revenues will not be used productively. Where such governance risk is high and the project's revenues are significant,[263] IFC should work with the government (in partnership with the World Bank and IMF) to put in place mechanisms to reduce this risk, including possibly ring-fencing of project revenue management. For all proposed EI investments, IFC should address these issues in Board Reports.

Support environmental and social sustainability. IFC should focus on projects that can serve as models for environmental and social performance, transparency, and disclosure. Where laws and regulations—or their enforcement—are weak, IFC should insist on special measures to ensure a project's sound environmental and social performance. Such measures could include building local monitoring capacity and disclosing independently audited and publicly disclosed monitoring reports. They could also include an explicit assessment of the risk of conflicts and measures to deal with them.

Recommendation 2: Focus on implementation

Improve project appraisal[264] and supervision.[265] IFC should continue to require high-quality environmental impact assessments that establish baseline data for relevant environmental and socioeconomic impact indicators. These indicators—compared with the baseline—should be consistently tracked[266] and aggregated for IFC's management. Appropriate requirements allowing IFC to adequately mitigate risks and monitor all its projects should be included for all investments, particularly equity.[267]

Where IFC finds poor environmental and social systems or performance, it should address them proactively and vigorously.[268] IFC's investment officers and nominees to company boards should be co-responsible with technical specialists for the environmental and social performance of their projects. Where possible, IFC should also develop and use local monitoring capacity.

Adequately involve specialists throughout. IFC needs to ensure that its environmental and social specialists are consulted as early as possible and throughout the project life and that investment officers fully share relevant information. To that end, investment officers need to be better trained to identify risks and opportunities. Making the investment officer and department explicitly accountable for environmental performance would likely provide a strong incentive for calling in the experts as early as possible, not after a problem has materialized.

Enhance reporting of results. IFC should develop a reporting template that specifies for each portfolio project which safeguard policies and guidelines apply, whether the company is in compliance with them, and how it performs with respect to key sustainability indicators for the industry. Where relevant, IFC should also include "beyond the fenceline" issues, such as transportation and project-related security issues.

Evaluate distribution of benefits. IFC should develop[269] global comparators for the distribution of benefits from EI—among investors, governments at different levels, and local communities. For its projects, IFC should analyze the distribution and compare it with other EI projects. At appraisal, IFC should include the distribution effects in its sensitivity and risk analysis (e.g., distribution of benefits at different levels of output and prices), track actual distribution during the project life, and aggregate the data at the country and sector level.

Recommendation 3: Engage the stakeholders

Update policies and guidelines. In consultation with stakeholders, IFC should continuously update its environmental and social safeguard policies, guidelines, and processes in line with evolving good practice in the industry.[270] The WBG should use its convening power and the help of its member governments to promote their use by governments, industry, and other financiers. IFC should develop, update, or clarify policies and guidelines on indigenous peoples (or "vulnerable people"), safety of dams, natural habitats (or biodiversity), security and human rights, HIV/AIDS prevention, mining (closure—funding and social issues, acid rock drainage, precious metal mining), and oil and gas (gas flaring, downstream transportation of oil).

Promote disclosure of fiscal revenues from EI. IFC should encourage—and consider requiring—its clients to publish such information. Where client confidentiality undertakings initially restrict disclosure, IFC could report results on an aggregate country, regional, or sectoral level and participate in initiatives advocating such disclosure. IFC needs to balance client confidentiality with its own accountability as a public institution and the public's desire to know more. On balance, increased communication and transparency are likely to help IFC and its clients and reduce misconceptions, distrust, and criticism.

Develop, monitor, and report on sustainability indicators. In consultation with other stakeholders, IFC should develop and track key sustainability indicators and consider disclosing them to demonstrate the economic, social, and environmental impacts of its EI projects.[271] Reporting on credible sustainable development indicators will help overcome the current inability to systematically demonstrate results achieved.

Increase local community participation. This evaluation found strong evidence that improved community consultation is in the best long-term interest of our clients. IFC should make community development programs with ongoing consultations the norm for EI projects. Such programs should start with a participatory assessment of the community's situation[272] and long-term development needs. They should include ongoing consultations, focus on sustainable solutions to meet these needs, and prepare communities for the time after the extractive operations cease. Good communication is also likely to improve results, as will listening to people and being exposed to public scrutiny and challenge.

Improve communications with clients. IFC should routinely share best practice among clients and encourage them to apply it. IFC should communicate its information needs better to its clients; for example, by tailoring reporting to their own requirements. Clients very much appreciated assistance they had received from IFC staff but were eager for more. IFC should build on its various initiatives to add value and further facilitate exchange of ideas among its clients, by organizing conferences and further developing toolkits on how to best address environmental and social issues, for example.[273]

Attachment 1   Evaluation Approach

For this study, OEG analyzed a random sample of IFC projects approved between 1991 and 1996 and evaluated at early operating maturity between 1996 and 2001. The performance of these 22 evaluated EI projects was compared with others evaluated in the same time period, using IFC's established evaluation framework (see www.ifc.org/oeg/xpsrs/xpsrs.html) under three performance dimensions: development outcome, IFC's investment outcome, and IFC's effectiveness (Attachment 4B). To validate the findings, OEG also conducted a desk review of all EI projects approved since fiscal year 1993 and older projects still in IFC's portfolio. The results of these 45 studied EI projects are summarized in Attachments 4C and 4D. OEG also reviewed IFC's strategy in the sector, technical assistance trust fund activities (Attachment 5), internal documents, and relevant literature.

OEG presented an analysis of IFC's investments in the sector in its approach paper for this study. More information can also be found in the WBG's background paper to the EIR. Both are available online. A brief summary of the analysis is in Attachment 3, and highlights are in Attachment 1.

Evaluators visited more than a dozen project sites in six countries to assess development results and to talk to representatives from industry, government, and civil society (see Box D3). We surveyed participants at the EIR workshops about their perceptions: initially, about the most important sectoral issues, to help guide the evaluation (Attachment 6A); then, at the regional workshops, about the need for, and effort and success of, IFC and the WBG in the sector (Attachment 6B). OEG also asked IFC staff to what extent the WBG was appropriately addressing key issues in the sector (Attachment 6C) and whether coordination in the WBG was adequate. OEG also sought feedback from numerous stakeholders knowledgeable about the sector, inside and outside the WBG.

Attachment 2   IFC's Investment in Extractive Industries

Approvals. In the 1960s and 1970s, few developing countries considered private sector development of their EI resources. IFC funded its first EI project, a Chilean copper mine, in 1958 and only five EI projects in the subsequent 12 years, three of them in the Chilean copper sector. As countries loosened control of their natural resources and permitted private sector investment, IFC became more active in the sector. Growth was initially slow. Prior to FY1980, IFC had approved only 17 projects for US$137 million. Growth then accelerated through 1991, when IFC's net approvals reached almost US$400 million. Approvals have, since 1991, fluctuated at around US$250 million annually, with a similar amount funded through the IFC B-loan syndication program. Compared with IFC's total approvals, the importance of EI projects declined substantially from around 15 percent in the 1980s to about 6 percent today. Since 1990, IFC has approved more than 140 extractive industries projects, predominantly in Latin American and Sub-Saharan African countries (about 30 percent each).

Products and funding instruments. IFC's EI approvals—about US$3.1 billion from 1990 to the end of 2002—were particularly concentrated in oil and gas production and development (61 percent).[274] Gold (16 percent) and copper (6 percent) were also important. IFC has provided loans, equity, quasi-equity, and syndicated investments (mostly loans) to EI projects. IFC approved relatively fewer equity investments in EI (12 percent) than in other projects (16 percent) since 1990. In IFC's outstanding portfolio, however, EI had a larger share of equity (34 percent)

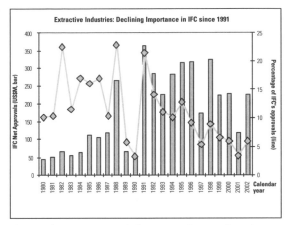

than other projects (26 percent). IFC has been successful in attracting participant funding to EI—participants approved funding for about as much as IFC approved for its own account.

Frontier countries. IFC's overall strategy does not emphasize EI as a sector. However, it does emphasize investments in "frontier countries," defined as countries with poor country credit ratings.[275] Investments in EI depend on the loca-

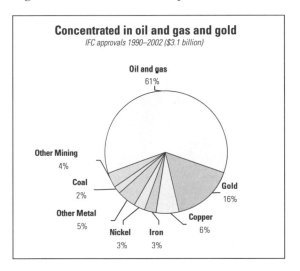

Extractive Industries - Outstanding Portfolio June 30, 2002		US$ millions	%
Mining	Loan	214	56%
	Equity/Quasi-Equity	170	44%
sub-total		384	4%
Change from previous year		-6%	
Oil and Gas	Loan	143	59%
	Equity/Quasi-Equity	101	41%
sub-total		245	2%
Change from previous year		5%	
All EI	Loan	357	57%
	Equity/Quasi-Equity	271	43%
sub-total		628	6%
Change from previous year		-2%	
Non-EI	Loan	6,511	65%
	Equity/Quasi-Equity	3,581	35%
sub-total		10,092	94%
Change from previous year		-1%	
Grand Total		10,720	100%

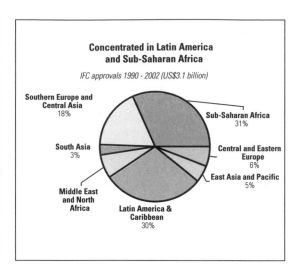

Concentrated in Latin America and Sub-Saharan Africa

IFC approvals 1990 - 2002 (US$3.1 billion)

Southern Europe and Central Asia 18%
Sub-Saharan Africa 31%
South Asia 3%
Central and Eastern Europe 6%
East Asia and Pacific 5%
Middle East and North Africa
Latin America & Caribbean 30%

tion of the natural resources. IFC's investments also depend on where IFC has a role to play. IFC's role and contribution in EI projects was significantly better (95 percent satisfactory or better) than in other projects (79 percent). On average, IFC's approvals in EI have been in countries 10 points riskier (on a scale of 0 to 100) than IFC's average approvals. Thus, operating in EI allows IFC to invest in risky countries, where it is often difficult to find other opportunities. For example, in at least a dozen countries, IFC's first approval was in EI,[276] and during the past decade, Sub-Saharan Africa received the largest share of IFC's EI approvals. In Sub-Saharan Africa, where foreign direct investment is scarce, IFC's extractive industries approvals have accounted for more than 40 percent of IFC's total approvals since 1956. IFC's outstanding EI portfolio on June 30, 2002, was concentrated in Latin America and Sub-Saharan Africa.

More analysis of IFC's approvals can be found in the WBG background paper for the EIR (www.eireview.org) and in OEG's approach paper (www.ifc.org/oeg). Further details on IFC's EI portfolio performance are included in the main report and in Attachment 4.

Attachment 3A   Summary Results—All EI Projects

This attachment combines all EI projects that OEG reviewed: evaluated projects (Attachment 4B) using IFC's established evaluation framework (www.ifc.org/oeg/xpsrs) and studied projects (Attachments 4C and 4D) using desk reviews and the simplified binary evaluation framework (Attachment 4H). Ratings in some cases refer to multiple investments in the same company.

Note that the comparator—IFC average and non-oil, gas, and mining projects—refers to projects approved 1991–1996 and evaluated 1996–2001, whereas studied extractive industries projects include both older and newer projects.

			Development outcome				IFC's investment outcome			IFC's effectiveness			
			Project	Economic sustainability	Environmental effects	PSD		Equity	Loan		Screening, appraisal, structuring	Supervision and administration	Role and contribution
Studied projects **(Various approval years)**													
Oil and Gas	Number rated	23	23	23	17	23	23	16	19	23	23	23	23
	Success Rate	70%	61%	78%	94%	65%	65%	50%	58%	78%	57%	83%	87%
Mining	Number rated	22	22	22	21	22	22	13	22	22	22	22	22
	Success Rate	59%	59%	59%	62%	77%	68%	46%	73%	73%	64%	86%	91%
All EI	Number rated	45	45	45	38	45	45	29	41	45	45	45	45
	Success Rate	64%	60%	69%	76%	71%	67%	48%	66%	76%	60%	84%	89%
Evaluated projects **(Approved 1991–96, Evaluated 1996–2001)**													
Oil and Gas (12)		67%	50%	83%	100%	58%	58%	25%	80%	92%	50%	92%	100%
Mining (10)		50%	60%	60%	40%	90%	70%	60%	78%	70%	70%	70%	90%
All EI (22)		59%	55%	73%	71%	73%	64%	44%	79%	82%	59%	82%	95%
IFC average **(Approved 1991–96, Evaluated 1996–2001)**													
1996–2001 evaluations (308)	Success Rate	60%	44%	58%	65%	72%	54%	28%	73%	62%	55%	60%	80%
...of which: non-EI (286)	Success Rate	60%	44%	57%	65%	72%	53%	28%	73%	60%	54%	59%	79%

Attachment 3B Performance Ratings for Evaluated EI Projects

The 22 EI projects were part of a random representative sample of 308 IFC projects approved 1991–1996 and evaluated 1996–2001. An evaluated project's development outcome was rated as one of the following: highly successful, successful, mostly successful, mostly unsuccessful, unsuccessful, or highly unsuccessful; indicators were rated excellent, satisfactory, partly satisfactory, or unsatisfactory. For a simplified presentation, the top half of the rating scale appears in the table as 'S' (satisfactory or better, also referred to as "positive" in the main text); the bottom half as 'LS' (less than satisfactory).

In 2002, OEG updated the evaluation framework to better align it with other IFC initiatives

	Type	DEVELOPMENT OUTCOME	Project business success	Growth of economy	Living standards	Environmental, social, health, & safety effects	Private sector development	IFC's INVESTMENT OUTCOME	Equity	Loan	IFC's EFFECTIVENESS	Screening, appraisal, & structuring	Supervision & administration	Role & contribution
1	Min	S	S	S	S	S	S	S	S	S	S	S	S	S
2	Min	S	S	S	S	S	S	S	S	S	S	S	S	S
3	Min	S	S	S	S	S	S	S	N/A	S	S	S	S	S
4	Min	S	S	S	S	LS	S	S	N/A	S	LS	S	LS	S
5	Min	S	S	S	S	LS	S	LS	N/A	LS	S	LS	S	S
6	Min	LS	LS	LS	S	S	S	S	N/A	S	S	S	S	S
7	Min	LS	LS	LS	S	LS	S	S	S	S	S	S	S	S
8	Min	LS	S	S	S	LS	S	S	N/A	S	LS	LS	LS	LS
9	Min	LS	LS	LS	S	LS	S	LS	LS	N/A	S	LS	LS	S
10	Min	LS	LS	LS	S	LS	LS	LS	LS	LS	LS	LS	S	S
11	OG	S	S	S	S	S	S	S	N/A	S	S	S	S	S
12	OG	S	S	S	S	S	S	S	S	S	S	S	S	S
13	OG	S	S	S	S	S	S	S	N/A	S	S	S	S	S
14	OG	S	S	S	S	S	S	S	N/A	S	S	S	S	S
15	OG	S	S	S	S	S	LS	S	N/A	S	S	S	S	S
16	OG	S	S	S	S	NOP	S	LS	N/A	LS	S	S	S	S
17	OG	S	LS	S	S	S	S	LS	N/A	LS	S	LS	S	S
18	OG	S	LS	S	LS	S	S	LS	LS	S	S	LS	S	S
19	OG	LS	LS	S	S	S	LS	S	N/A	S	LS	LS	S	S
20	OG	LS	LS	LS	S	S	LS	S	N/A	S	LS	LS	LS	S
21	OG	LS	LS	LS	LS	S	LS	LS	LS	N/A	S	LS	S	S
22	OG	LS	LS	S	S	S	LS	LS	LS	N/A	S	LS	S	S

(e.g., corporate and departmental scorecards, sustainability initiative). The major change was to reduce the development outcome indicators from six to four:

- "Economic growth" and "Living standards" were merged into one indicator—"economic sustainability"
- "Enabling environment" was merged into "Private sector development"

OEG's current evaluation framework is available at: http://www.ifc.org/oeg/xpsrs/NonfinMarkets/nonfinmktsinsts.html.

Type: **Min** = Mining; **OG** = Oil and gas
Outcomes/indicators: **S** = Satisfactory or better; **LS** = Less than satisfactory **NOP** = No opinion possible; **N/A** = Not applicable, as this operation featured none

Attachment 3C — Performance Ratings for Studied Oil and Gas Projects

Outcomes/indicators: **S** = Satisfactory or better; **LS** = Less than satisfactory; **NOP** = No opinion possible; **N/A** = Not applicable, as this operation featured none

	DEVELOPMENT OUTCOME	Project business success	Growth of economy	Environmental, social, health, & safety effects	Private sector development	IFC's INVESTMENT OUTCOME	Equity	Loan	IFC's EFFECTIVENESS	Screening, appraisal, & structuring	Supervision & administration	Role & contribution
1	S	S	S	S	LS	S	S	S	S	S	S	S
2	S	S	S	S	S	S	S	S	S	S	S	S
3	S	S	S	S	S	S	N/A	S	S	S	S	S
4	S	S	S	S	S	S	S	LS	S	LS	S	S
5	S	S	S	LS	S	S	S	LS	S	LS	S	S
6	S	S	S	S	S	S	N/A	S	S	S	S	S
7	S	S	S	S	S	S	S	S	S	S	S	S
8	S	S	S	S	S	S	S	LS	S	S	S	S
9	S	S	S	S	S	S	N/A	S	S	S	S	S
10	S	S	S	S	S	S	N/A	S	S	S	S	S
11	S	S	S	NOP	S	S	S	LS	S	S	S	S
12	S	S	S	S	S	S	S	LS	S	S	S	S
13	S	LS	S	S	S	S	N/A	S	S	LS	S	S
14	S	S	S	NOP	S	LS	LS	LS	S	S	LS	S
15	S	S	S	NOP	LS	LS	LS	N/A	LS	LS	S	LS
16	S	LS	S	S	S	LS	LS	LS	LS	LS	S	S
17	LS	LS	S	S	LS	S	N/A	S	S	LS	S	S
18	LS	LS	LS	S	LS	S	N/A	S	LS	LS	LS	S
19	LS	LS	LS	NOP	LS	LS	LS	N/A	S	S	S	S
20	LS	LS	LS	S	LS	LS	LS	N/A	S	S	S	LS
21	LS	LS	S	S	LS	LS	LS	LS	S	LS	S	S
22	LS	LS	LS	NOP	LS	LS	LS	N/A	LS	LS	LS	LS
23	LS	LS	LS	NOP	S	LS	LS	S	LS	LS	LS	S

| **Attachment 3D** | **Performance Ratings for Studied Mining Projects** |

Outcomes/indicators: **S** = Satisfactory or better; **LS** = Less than satisfactory; **NOP** = No opinion possible; **N/A** = Not applicable, as this operation featured none

	DEVELOPMENT OUTCOME	Project business success	Growth of economy	Environmental, social, health, & safety effects	Private sector development	IFC's INVESTMENT OUTCOME	Equity	Loan	IFC's EFFECTIVENESS	Screening, appraisal, & structuring	Supervision & administration	Role & contribution
1	S	S	S	S	S	S	S	S	S	S	S	S
2	S	S	S	S	S	S	S	S	S	S	S	S
3	S	S	S	LS	S	S	N/A	S	S	S	S	S
4	S	S	S	S	S	S	S	S	S	S	S	S
5	S	S	S	S	S	S	N/A	S	S	S	S	S
6	S	S	S	LS	S	S	S	S	S	LS	S	S
7	S	S	S	S	S	S	NOP	S	S	S	S	S
8	S	S	S	S	S	S	N/A	S	S	S	S	S
9	S	S	S	S	S	S	N/A	S	S	S	LS	S
10	S	S	S	S	S	S	N/A	S	S	S	S	S
11	S	S	S	S	S	S	N/A	S	S	S	S	S
12	S	S	S	LS	S	S	S	S	S	S	LS	S
13	S	S	S	LS	S	LS	N/A	LS	S	LS	S	S
14	LS	LS	LS	S	LS	S	S	S	S	S	S	S
15	LS	LS	LS	NOP	LS	S	LS	S	LS	LS	S	LS
16	LS	LS	LS	LS	LS	S	N/A	S	LS	LS	S	LS
17	LS	LS	LS	S	S	LS	LS	LS	S	S	S	S
18	LS	LS	LS	S	S	LS	LS	LS	S	S	S	S
19	LS	LS	LS	LS	S	LS	LS	LS	LS	LS	LS	S
20	LS	LS	LS	S	LS	LS	LS	LS	LS	LS	S	S
21	LS	LS	LS	LS	S	LS	LS	LS	LS	LS	S	S
22	LS	LS	LS	LS	LS	LS	LS	LS	LS	LS	S	S

Attachment 3E   Approved Projects Reviewed by OEG—Mining

Evaluated (in bold italics) and studied projects
Approved amounts may differ from disbursed amounts (US$ millions)

Country	Project Name	ID	Approval Date	Status	Project Size	IFC Gross	IFC Net	Loan	Equity	Quasi-equity	Other	Participants	Project Type	Environ. Category	Detail Sector
Bolivia	Comsur														
	COMSUR (II)	*3956*	*Sep-93*	*Active*	*55.5*	*12.3*	*12.3*	*11.0*	*0.0*	*1.3*	*0.0*	*0.0*	*Investment*	*B*	*Zinc*
	COMSUR III	4799	Aug-95	Active	22.0	13.3	8.3	7.5	0.0	0.8	0.0	5.0	Investment	A	Gold
	COMSUR V	9670	Dec-99	Active	22.7	10.0	10.0	10.0	0.0	0.0	0.0	0.0	Investment	B	Zinc
Brazil	Codemin														
	CODEMIN SA III	420	May-78	Active	98.4	62.9	8.9	5.0	3.9	0.0	0.0	54.0	Investment	N	Nickel
	CODEMIN III	658	Feb-83	Active	4.0	0.4	0.4	0.0	0.4	0.0	0.0	0.0	Rights Issue	N	Nickel
Brazil	MBR														
	MBR (II)	2649	Jun-92	Active	266.1	60.0	35.0	25.0	0.0	10.0	0.0	25.0	Investment	A	Iron
	MBR LTDP	9343	Jun-99	Active	342.0	140.0	25.0	20.0	0.0	5.0	0.0	115.0	Investment	A	Iron
Brazil	Para Pigmentos														
	PARA PIGMENTOS	*4494*	*Jun-94*	*Active*	*183.0*	*74.0*	*34.0*	*25.0*	*0.0*	*9.0*	*0.0*	*40.0*	*Investment*	*A*	*Misc. Ores*
Brazil	Samarco														
	Samarco	5036	Jan-97	Active	44.8	39.0	23.0	23.0	0.0	0.0	0.0	16.0	Investment	A	Iron
Chile	Escondida														
	ESCONDIDA COPPER	1081	Jul-88	Active	1,143.2	85.0	85.0	70.0	15.0	0.0	0.0	0.0	Investment	N	Copper
	Escondida RI	9209	Nov-98	Active	25.0	25.0	25.0	0.0	0.0	25.0	0.0	0.0	Rights Issue	C	Copper
Chile	Refimet														
	REFIMET SMELTER	*4802*	*Feb-95*	*Closed*	*91.2*	*79.0*	*20.0*	*10.0*	*0.0*	*10.0*	*0.0*	*59.0*	*Investment*	*B*	*Copper*
	Refimet (Rev)	*7346*	*Nov-95*	*Closed*	*6.0*	*5.0*	*5.0*	*5.0*	*0.0*	*0.0*	*0.0*	*0.0*	*Investment*	*C*	*Copper*
Gabon	COMILOG II														
	COMILOG II	*2772*	*Jun-91*	*Closed*	*35.4*	*9.0*	*9.0*	*9.0*	*0.0*	*0.0*	*0.0*	*0.0*	*Investment*	*U*	*Other Metals*
Ghana	Bogosu														
	BOGOSU GOLD	973	Jul-87	Active	6.0	0.6	0.6	0.0	0.0	0.6	0.0	0.0	Investment	N	Gold
	BOGOSU (V)-RESTR	4102	Jun-93	Active	0.0	0.0	0.0	0.0	0.0	0.0	0.0	0.0	Rescheduling	B	Gold
Ghana	GAGL														
	IDUAPRIEM GOLD	1231	Feb-90	Active	13.5	3.0	3.0	0.0	3.0	0.0	0.0	0.0	Investment	N	Gold
	IDUAPRIEM II	2386	Jun-91	Active	55.4	48.0	18.0	8.4	0.0	8.5	1.1	30.0	Investment	B	Gold
	GAGL III	4896	Jul-95	Active	11.5	10.1	10.1	0.0	0.0	2.6	7.5	0.0	Investment	B	Gold
	GAGL IV	7261	Mar-96	Active	13.5	4.5	4.5	4.5	0.0	0.0	0.0	0.0	Investment	B	Gold
	GAGL IV-Restr	10327	Jun-00	Active	13.5	0.5	0.5	0.0	0.0	0.5	0.0	0.0	Restructuring	C	Gold
Kyrgyz Republic	Kumtor														
	KUMTOR GOLD	*3966*	*Mar-95*	*Active*	*335.0*	*40.0*	*40.0*	*30.0*	*0.0*	*10.0*	*0.0*	*0.0*	*Investment*	*A*	*Gold*
Mali	SOMISY														
	SOMISY	*2429*	*Dec-91*	*Active*	*122.6*	*23.2*	*23.2*	*0.0*	*1.5*	*21.7*	*0.0*	*0.0*	*Investment*	*B*	*Gold*
	Somisy Capex	7975	Jun-97	Active	63.8	35.0	10.0	10.0	0.0	0.0	0.0	25.0	Investment	B	Gold
	Randgold RI	9342	Nov-98	Active	34.8	2.3	2.3	0.0	2.3	0.0	0.0	0.0	Rights Issue	C	Gold
Mali	Sadiola Gold														
	SADIOLA GOLD	*4360*	*Dec-94*	*Active*	*246.2*	*64.8*	*39.8*	*35.0*	*4.8*	*0.0*	*0.0*	*25.0*	*Investment*	*A*	*Gold*
Mozambique	Mozal														
	MOZAL	7764	Jun-97	Active	1,365.0	120.0	120.0	55.0	0.0	65.0	0.0	0.0	Investment	A	Aluminum
	Mozal II	10323	Apr-01	Active	1,024.0	25.0	25.0	25.0	0.0	0.0	0.0	0.0	Investment	A	Aluminum
Peru	Buenaventura														
	BUENAVENTURA 1	446	Dec-78	Active	10.0	3.5	3.5	2.0	1.5	0.0	0.0	0.0	Investment	N	Silver
	BUENAVENTURA III	1232	Mar-90	Active	6.0	0.6	0.6	0.0	0.6	0.0	0.0	0.0	Rights Issue	U	Silver
	BUENAVENTURA IV	4070	May-93	Active	105.8	0.7	0.7	0.0	0.7	0.0	0.0	0.0	Rights Issue	B	Silver
Peru	Minera Regina														
	MINERA LA REGINA	737	Jun-84	Active	21.4	5.2	5.2	5.0	0.2	0.0	0.0	0.0	Investment	N	Other Metals
	Regina Restr II	8888	Dec-97	Active	0.0	0.0	0.0	0.0	0.0	0.0	0.0	0.0	Restructuring	A	Other Metals
Peru	Yanacocha														
	YANACOCHA	2983	May-93	Active	45.0	24.7	12.7	12.0	0.3	0.3	0.0	12.0	Investment	A	Gold
	MAQUI MAQUI	*4449*	*May-94*	*Active*	*53.8*	*15.9*	*10.9*	*10.0*	*0.0*	*0.0*	*0.9*	*5.0*	*Investment*	*A*	*Gold*
	Yanacocha III	9502	Jun-99	Active	121.0	110.0	30.0	30.0	0.0	0.0	0.0	80.0	Investment	A	Gold
Tajikistan	Zeravshan														
	Zeravshan Gold	*7192*	*Oct-96*	*Active*	*127.0*	*7.5*	*7.5*	*0.0*	*1.2*	*6.3*	*0.0*	*0.0*	*Investment*	*B*	*Gold*
	Nelson Gold	7911	Oct-96	Active	0.0	2.1	2.1	0.0	0.0	0.0	2.1	0.0	Investment	B	Gold
	Zeravshan-Jilau	8579	Feb-98	Active	14.7	3.0	3.0	3.0	0.0	0.0	0.0	0.0	Investment	B	Gold
	Zeravshan-NGC	8823	Feb-98	Active	9.0	3.0	3.0	0.0	3.0	0.0	0.0	0.0	Investment	B	Gold
Turkey	Cayeli Bakir														
	CAYELI BAKIR	*2448*	*Jun-92*	*Active*	*144.5*	*75.0*	*30.0*	*30.0*	*0.0*	*0.0*	*0.0*	*45.0*	*Investment*	*B*	*Copper*
Uganda	Kasese														
	Kasese Cobalt	4895	Jun-96	Active	110.0	24.6	19.6	16.0	3.6	0.0	0.0	5.0	Investment	A	Other Metals
Venezuela	Minera Loma														
	Loma de Niquel	7343	Apr-97	Active	430.0	124.5	74.5	65.0	2.4	7.1	0.0	50.0	Investment	A	Nickel
	Minera Loma RI	10398	Jun-00	Active	98.4	0.3	0.3	0.0	0.0	0.3	0.0	0.0	Rights Issue	C	Nickel
Zambia	KCM														
	KCM	8570	Feb-00	Active	334.8	30.0	30.0	0.0	7.2	22.8	0.0	0.0	Investment	A	Copper
Zimbabwe	Wankie														
	WANKIE COLLIERY 2	3485	Oct-92	Closed	28.0	10.0	10.0	10.0	0.0	0.0	0.0	0.0	Investment	B	Coal Mining

Unrated projects, reviewed for issues and lessons
Approved amounts may differ from disbursed amounts (US$ millions)

Country	Project Name	ID	Approval Date	Status	Project Size	IFC Gross	IFC Net	Loan	Equity	Quasi-equity	Other	Participants	Project Type	Environ. Category	Detail Sector
Africa Region	**MACS**														
	MACS	9345	Apr-01	Active	100	74.0	34.0	30.0	4.0	-	-	40.0	Investment	B	Mining Services
Burkina Faso	**AEF FasoMine**														
	AEF FasoMine	9024	Sep-98	Active	5	1.5	1.5	1.0	0.5	-	-	-	Investment	B	Iron
China	**Daning Coal**														
	Daning Coal	10015	May-01	Active	75	30.0	15.0	13.0	2.0	-	-	15.0	Investment	A	Coal Mining
India	**Sarshatali Coal**														
	Sarshatali Coal	7984	Feb-99	Active	149	35.0	35.0	30.0	5.0	-	-	-	Investment	A	Coal Mining
Indonesia	**Dianlia**														
	Dianlia	9987	Feb-01	Active	10	5.0	5.0	4.0	-	1.0	-	-	Investment	B	Coal Mining
Mexico	**Mexcobre**														
	MEXCOBRE SX/EW	4313	May-94	Closed	75	60.0	25.0	25.0	-	-	-	35.0	Investment	B	Copper
	Pan American														
	Pan American	9800	Jul-99	Active	13	12.5	12.5	-	12.5	-	-	-	Investment	A	Silver
	La Colorada	10326	Feb-01	Active	51	28.6	10.3	4.0	-	6.0	0.3	18.3	Investment	A	Silver
	PanAme - La Colora	10856	Feb-01	Active	1	1.2	1.2	-	1.2	-	-	-	Investment	A	Silver
Peru	**Quellaveco**														
	QUELLAVECO	3823	Apr-93	Active	31	6.2	6.2	-	-	6.2	-	-	Investment	A	Copper
	QUELLAVECO - RI	7447	Mar-96	Active	27	5.3	5.3	-	-	5.3	-	-	Rights Issue	C	Copper
	Minera Q RI	10170	Jan-00	Active	3	0.6	0.6	-	0.6	-	-	-	Rights Issue	A	Copper
Russian Federation	**Julietta**														
	Julietta	10020	Sep-00	Active	77	10.0	10.0	8.5	-	1.5	-	-	Investment	A	Gold
	Bema Gold														
	Bema Gold	10655	Sep-00	Active	1	1.0	1.0	-	1.0	-	-	-	Investment	A	Gold
Sierra Leone	**Sierra Rutile**														
	SIERRA RUTILE 1	2609	Apr-92	Closed	71	20.0	20.0	20.0	-	-	-	-	Investment	A	Nickel
	SIEROMCO	3999	Jun-93	Closed	27	10.0	10.0	10.0	-	-	-	-	Investment	B	Other
	Sierra Restr	9148	May-98	Closed	0	0.0	0.0	-	-	-	-	-	Restructuring	N	Misc. Ores
Tunisia	**Miniere Bougrine**														
	MINIERE BGRN - RI	4677	May-94	Closed	8	0.9	0.9	-	-	0.9	-	-	Rights Issue	U	Zinc
Uzbekistan	**Amantytau Gold**														
	AMANTAYTAU GOLD	4323	Mar-94	Closed	6	1.2	1.2	-	-	1.2	-	-	Investment	C	Gold

Attachment 3F	Approved Projects Reviewed by OEG— Oil and Gas

Evaluated (in bold italics) and studied projects

Approved amounts may differ from disbursed amounts (US$ millions)

Country	Project Name	ID	Approval Date	Status	Project Size	IFC Gross	IFC Net	Loan	Equity	Quasi-equity	Other	Participants	Project Type	Environ. Category	Detail Sector
Albania	**Patos Marinza**														
	Patos Marinza	7429	Mar-98	Active	275.2	108.5	58.5	30.0	28.5	0.0	0.0	50.0	Investment	A	O & G Production
	Patos Marinza In	10885	Jun-01	Active	197.5	10.0	10.0	10.0	0.0	0.0	0.0	0.0	Investment	A	O & G Production
Argentina	**Bridas/PAE**														
	BRIDAS 2	3078	Jun-92	Active	238.0	130.0	50.0	35.0	0.0	15.0	0.0	80.0	Investment	B	O & G Production
	BRIDAS III	*5093*	*Jun-95*	*Active*	*221.3*	*70.0*	*30.0*	*20.0*	*10.0*	*0.0*	*0.0*	*40.0*	*Investment*	*B*	*O & G Production*
	Cadipsa														
	(SOP) CADIPSA	*2979*	*Oct-92*	*Closed*	*83.0*	*40.0*	*20.0*	*10.0*	*5.0*	*5.0*	*0.0*	*20.0*	*Restructuring*	*B*	*O & G Production*
	Capsa Diadema														
	Diadema Field	*7418*	*Jun-96*	*Active*	*70.0*	*60.0*	*20.0*	*15.0*	*0.0*	*5.0*	*0.0*	*40.0*	*Investment*	*B*	*O & G Production*
	Cia.Combustible														
	CIA. COMBUSTIBLE	4067	Dec-93	Closed	251.6	80.0	40.0	25.0	15.0	0.0	0.0	40.0	Restructuring	B	O & G Production
	Huantraico / Neuquen														
	Huantraico	2764	Oct-91	Active	60.0	17.0	17.0	0.0	17.0	0.0	0.0	0.0	Restructuring	A	O & G Production
	HUANTRAICO (II)	3262	Jun-92	Active	180.4	60.0	25.0	15.0	10.0	0.0	0.0	35.0	Investment	U	O & G Production
	Neuquen	7182	Mar-96	Active	186.0	26.4	26.4	0.0	26.4	0.0	0.0	0.0	Investment	B	O & G Production
	Neuquen Basin RI	9537	Jan-99	Active	5.0	5.0	5.0	0.0	5.0	0.0	0.0	0.0	Rights Issue	C	O & G Production
Azerbaijan	**Early Oil**														
	Early Oil:Amoco	7271	Jul-98	Active	650.0	65.7	32.8	32.8	0.0	0.0	0.0	32.8	Investment	A	O & G Production
	Early Oil: Exxon	9440	Jul-98	Active	305.4	30.9	15.4	15.4	0.0	0.0	0.0	15.4	Investment	A	O & G Production
	Early Oil:LUKOil	9441	Jul-98	Active	382.7	38.6	19.3	19.3	0.0	0.0	0.0	19.3	Investment	A	O & G Production
	Early Oil:TPAO	9442	Jul-98	Active	259.8	26.1	13.0	13.0	0.0	0.0	0.0	13.0	Investment	A	O & G Production
	Early Oil:Unocal	9443	Jul-98	Active	384.7	38.8	19.4	19.4	0.0	0.0	0.0	19.4	Investment	A	O & G Production
Cameroon	**Pecten**														
	PECTEN (II)	*3815*	*Feb-94*	*Active*	*135.0*	*105.0*	*40.0*	*40.0*	*0.0*	*0.0*	*0.0*	*65.0*	*Investment*	*B*	*O & G Production*
	Pecten Itindi	7621	Feb-97	Active	115.0	95.0	20.0	20.0	0.0	0.0	0.0	75.0	Investment	B	O & G Production
	Pecten - Mokoko	8498	Mar-98	Active	265.0	265.0	75.0	75.0	0.0	0.0	0.0	190.0	Investment	B	O & G Production
Congo	**Engen**														
	ENGEN/ENGEN CONG	*4981*	*May-95*	*Closed*	*99.8*	*91.4*	*46.4*	*15.0*	*2.9*	*28.5*	*0.0*	*45.0*	*Investment*	*B*	*O & G Production*
Cote d'Ivoire	**CI-11**														
	BLOCK CI-11	*3448*	*Mar-93*	*Active*	*45.5*	*11.4*	*11.4*	*0.0*	*11.4*	*0.0*	*0.0*	*0.0*	*Investment*	*A*	*O & G Production*
	BLOCK CI-11 OIL	*4603*	*Nov-94*	*Active*	*66.0*	*27.3*	*27.3*	*0.0*	*27.3*	*0.0*	*0.0*	*0.0*	*Investment*	*A*	*O & G Production*
	BLOCK CI-11-UMIC	4975	May-95	Closed	45.0	35.0	15.0	15.0	0.0	0.0	0.0	20.0	Investment	A	O & G Production
	Block CI-II-GNR	7018	May-95	Closed	25.0	17.5	7.5	7.5	0.0	0.0	0.0	10.0	Investment	A	O & G Production
	CI-II-Pluspetrol	7019	May-95	Closed	25.0	17.5	7.5	7.5	0.0	0.0	0.0	10.0	Investment	A	O & G Production
	BlockCI-11/12 RI	8233	Mar-97	Active	5.0	5.0	5.0	0.0	5.0	0.0	0.0	0.0	Rights Issue	C	O & G Production
	Block CI-11 RI 2	9171	May-98	Active	5.0	5.0	5.0	0.0	5.0	0.0	0.0	0.0	Rights Issue	FI	O & G Production
Ecuador	**Tripetrol**														
	TRIPETROL EXPLOR	*3251*	*Jul-92*	*Closed*	*32.0*	*10.0*	*10.0*	*6.0*	*0.0*	*4.0*	*0.0*	*0.0*	*Investment*	*B*	*O & G Production*
Egypt	**Apache Qarun Concession**														
	MELEIHA OIL EXPL	873	Jun-86	Active	180.0	79.5	49.5	30.0	19.5	0.0	0.0	30.0	Investment	N	O & G Production
	MELEIHA II	995	Sep-87	Active	36.0	9.2	9.2	0.0	9.2	0.0	0.0	0.0	Investment	N	O & G Production
	MELEIHA & AGHAR	2975	Jun-92	Active	36.4	13.0	13.0	0.0	13.0	0.0	0.0	0.0	Investment	B	O & G Production
	Meleiha														
	Phoenix Resource	5127	Oct-95	Closed	10.0	10.0	10.0	0.0	10.0	0.0	0.0	0.0	Investment	A	O & G Production
	Apache Qarun	*7211*	*Oct-95*	*Closed*	*51.6*	*27.5*	*12.5*	*12.5*	*0.0*	*0.0*	*0.0*	*15.0*	*Investment*	*A*	*O & G Production*
	PRC Qarun	7422	Oct-95	Closed	93.3	55.0	25.0	25.0	0.0	0.0	0.0	30.0	Investment	A	O & G Production
Guatemala	**Basic**														
	BASIC	3888	Jun-94	Closed	33.0	20.0	14.0	10.0	4.0	0.0	0.0	6.0	Investment	A	O & G Production
	BASIC II	7407	Jul-96	Closed	73.0	25.8	13.8	12.0	1.8	0.0	0.0	12.0	Investment	A	O & G Production
India	**Triveni**														
	TRIVENI	2202	Dec-90	Closed	20.6	0.6	0.6	0.0	0.6	0.0	0.0	0.0	Investment	U	Oilfield Services
Kazakhstan	**Akshabulak/Kazgermunai**														
	Akshabulak	7416	Mar-96	Active	266.9	65.7	65.7	0.0	0.1	65.6	0.0	0.0	Investment	A	O & G Production
Pakistan	**MariGas**														
	MARI GAS II	*2837*	*Dec-91*	*Closed*	*47.9*	*19.5*	*19.5*	*19.5*	*0.0*	*0.0*	*0.0*	*0.0*	*Investment*	*B*	*O & G Production*
	PPL														
	PPL	655	Nov-82	Active	176.6	163.4	17.0	15.5	1.6	0.0	0.0	146.4	Investment	N	O & G Production
	PPL-SUI LIME	*3911*	*Jun-94*	*Active*	*72.5*	*52.1*	*31.1*	*31.1*	*0.0*	*0.0*	*0.0*	*21.0*	*Investment*	*B*	*O & G Production*
	PPL-SUI LIME INC	4907	Oct-94	Active	2.0	2.0	0.0	0.0	0.0	0.0	0.0	2.0	Investment	C	O & G Production
Poland	**Amoco Poland**														
	COALBED METHANE	3471	Mar-94	Closed	86.5	8.7	8.7	0.0	0.0	8.7	0.0	0.0	Investment	B	O & G Production
Russian Federation	**Aminex (Russia/Tunisia)**		Oct-96												
	Aminex: Tunisia	7610	Oct-96	Closed	7.2	3.1	3.1	0.0	3.1	0.0	0.0	0.0	Investment	B	O & G Production
	Aminex: Kirtayel	7624	Oct-96	Active	85.2	20.1	20.1	17.0	3.1	0.0	0.0	0.0	Investment	B	O & G Production
	Aminex RI	9623	Mar-99	Active	1.1	0.1	0.1	0.0	0.1	0.0	0.0	0.0	Rights Issue	C	O & G Production
	Bitech														
	Bitech-Silur	8902	Mar-99	Closed	65.0	25.0	25.0	17.5	7.5	0.0	0.0	0.0	Investment	B	O & G Production
	Polar														
	POLAR LIGHTS	*4040*	*Jun-93*	*Closed*	*340.0*	*60.0*	*60.0*	*60.0*	*0.0*	*0.0*	*0.0*	*0.0*	*Investment*	*A*	*O & G Production*
	Vasyugan														
	VASYUGAN	*3532*	*Jun-93*	*Closed*	*37.1*	*11.5*	*11.5*	*10.0*	*0.0*	*1.5*	*0.0*	*0.0*	*Investment*	*B*	*O & G Production*

Unrated projects, reviewed for issues and lessons
Approved amounts may differ from disbursed amounts (US$ millions)

Country	Project Name	ID	Approval Date	Status	Project Size	IFC Gross	IFC Net	Loan	Equity	Quasi-equity	Other	Participants	Project Type	Environ. Category	Detail Sector
Africa Region	**SAPTFF**														
	SAPT FF	10145	Jun-00	Active	200	80	80.0	-	-	-	80.0	-	Investment	FI-2	Trade Finance
Bangladesh	**Jalalabad II**														
	Jalalabad II	9354	Mar-00	Active	163	70	40.0	30.0	-	10.0	-	30.0	Investment	A	O&G Production
Cameroon	**ChadOil -COTCO**														
	ChadOil-COTCO	11124	Jun-00	Active	-	-	-	-	-	-	-	-	Investment	A	O&G Production
Chad	**ChadOil**														
	ChadOil	4338	Jun-00	Active	3,274	400	10	100.0	-	-	-	30	Investment	A	O&G Production
	ChadOil -TOTCO	11125	Jun-00	Active	-	-	-	-	-	-	-	-	Investment	A	O&G Production
Colombia	**Harken**														
	Harken	9484	Jun-99	Closed	158	55	30.0	20.0	-	10.0	-	25.0	Investment	B	O&G Production
Kazakhstan	**Sazankurak**														
	Sazankurak	10056	Jun-00	Active	45	20	20.0	15.0	-	5.0	-	-	Investment	B	O&G Production
Kazakhstan	**FIOC**														
	FIOC	10411	Jun-00	Active	-	0	0.0	-	0.0	-	-	-	Investment	B	O&G Production
Nigeria	**Delta Contractor**														
	Delta Contractor	10683	Jun-01	Active	30	15	15.0	15.0	-	-	-	-	Investment	FI-2	Finance Companies
Pakistan	**Lasmo Pakistan**														
	Lasmo Pakistan	10408	Jun-01	Active	120	40	40.0	40.0	-	-	-	-	Investment	B	O&G Production

Attachment 3G	Reasons for Not Rating Projects or Companies		

	Country	Project name	Reason
Mining	Africa Region	MACS	No disbursement yet.
	Burkina Faso	AEF FasoMine	No disbursement yet.
	China	Daning Coal	No disbursement yet.
	India	Sarshatali Coal	No disbursement yet.
	Indonesia	Dianlia	No disbursement yet.
	Mexico	Mexcobre	Exited, loan prepaid in 1996.
	Mexico	La Colorada	Too early to evaluate. The Russian project did not proceed; Mexican project in early start-up.
	Peru	Quellaveco	No commercial activity.
	Russian Federation	Julietta Gold / OMGC	Too early to evaluate; commenced operations in late 2000.
	Russian Federation	Bema Gold	Too early to evaluate; disbursed in late 2001.
	Sierra Leone	Sierra Rutile	Original project ceased operations due to civil war. Expansion not yet disbursed.
	Tunisia	Miniere Bougrine	Project closed; no information available.
	Uzbekistan	Amantaytau	Exited original project;—a feasibility study—was closed. Follow-on project was dropped.
Oil and Gas	Africa Region	SAPTFF	No disbursement yet.
	Bangladesh	Jalalabad	No disbursement yet.
	Chad/Cameroon	ChadOil	Too early to evaluate; no first oil yet
	Colombia	Harken	Exited; no current information available.
	Kazakhstan	FIOC Sazankurak	Too early to evaluate; disbursed in late 2001.
	Nigeria	Niger Delta	No disbursement yet.
	Pakistan	Lasmo	No disbursement yet.

The companies and projects above were reviewed by OEG. They were considered inappropriate for rating purposes (i.e., too early, cancelled, insufficient information, etc.). They did provide valuable issues and lessons that have been used in this report.

I. Development Outcome Rating

The development outcome rating is a bottom-line, synthesis assessment of the operation's results, based on the following four development indicators:

- **Project Business Success** considers the narrow objectives supported by IFC's financing. The best measure of a project's business success is its FRR. Lacking the data to calculate an FRR, we based this rating on assessments of the inputs to an FRR—capital expenditures, cost overruns, capacity utilization, sales volumes, pricing, revenues, margins, profits, taxes, subsidies, and so forth.

  — Rates satisfactory when the inputs to an FRR suggest a satisfactory FRR.

- **Economic Sustainability** considers the project's net economic benefits to all members of society, which is best measured by an ERR. Lacking the data to calculate an ERR, we based this rating on assessments of the inputs to an ERR—the social benefits and costs, including taxes paid, benefits to suppliers, effects on competitors, consumer surplus, effects on input and output markets, and how competitive prices and quantities are determined in relevant markets. It also should capture non-quantified benefits. In particular, whether the project had a direct impact—positive or negative—on the poor or on living standards in the local community.

  — Rates satisfactory when the net economic benefits are positive and near expectations and, in marginal cases, where a project also has a demonstrably positive effect on society in the host country.

- **Project's Environmental Effects** are based on the project's compliance with WBG environmental requirements.

  — Rates satisfactory if the project is—and was over its lifetime—in material compliance with either IFC's current or at-approval requirements.

- **Private Sector Development** considers, as relevant, the upstream and downstream linkages to private firms, new technology, management skills and training, degree of local entrepreneurship and competition, demonstration effects, enhanced private ownership, capital markets development, and business practices as positive corporate role models. It also includes regulatory improvements, such as changes in government policy and legal, tax, and accounting frameworks and possibly project-related technical assistance or project activities that have changed the enabling environment to create conditions conducive to the flow of private capital, domestic and foreign, into productive investment.

  — Rates satisfactory when the project provides distinctly positive net contributions.

II. IFC Investment Outcome

  — Rates satisfactory when no loss reserves exist, loans are not in arrears, equity investments achieve a 5 percent real return, any loan rescheduling still provides the full margin originally expected, and any loan prepayment provides greater than 65 percent of the originally expected loan income.

III. IFC's Effectiveness

- **Screening, Appraisal, and Structuring**
  — Rates satisfactory if it met IFC's procedures and good practice standards.

- **Supervision and Administration**
  — Rates satisfactory if IFC was sufficiently informed to react in a timely manner to any material change in the project's and company's performance.

- **Role and Contribution**
  — Rates satisfactory if IFC's role and contribution were in line with its operating principles.

- **IFC's Effectiveness (Synthesis) Rating**
  — Rates satisfactory if IFC's performance was up to a high professional standard.

Attachment 4   **IFC's Technical Assistance Trust Fund Activities in EI Projects**

Trust Funds: IFC Donor-Supported TA Programs, through IFC's Trust Fund Unit, has approved TA of US$3.5 million for 22 EI projects since 1994. The majority (84 percent) of the funding was approved in the last three years and has increasingly supported sustainable development initiatives. Examples include funding for a conference to improve the investment climate for sustainable mining (China), support to bring a coal company into environmental and social compliance (Russia), dissemination of examples of successful approaches to HIV/AIDS prevention (global), and a range of programs for a gold and copper mining investment (Laos). In 2002, oil- and gas-related projects were approved to support an investment forum in Mongolia and privatization assistance in Mozambique. EI project approvals reached 12 percent of total approvals in 2002 but have accounted for only 3 percent of total approvals since 1994. It is likely, as EI projects include more social and environmental development, that demand for the Technical Assistance Trust Fund to support EI projects will grow. Because Project Completion Reports were generally not completed on the above projects, OEG did a desk review and some one-on-one consultations to better understand project results. Overall, the projects have been broadly successful, but based on the information received, OEG was unable to assign project ratings.

Year	Amount US$	%	Projects	Average %	US$	Country region
1994	100,000	3	1	5	100,000	Brazil
1995	225,000	7	1	5	225,000	Kazakhstan
1996	115,000	3	2	9	57,500	Albania, Tajikistan
1997	43,460	1	1	5	43,460	Mongolia (2)
1998	—	0	0	0	—	
1999	60,000	2	1	5	60,000	Africa Region
2000	318,000	9	3	14	106,000	Tajikistan, Albania, Kyrgyz Republic
2001	800,000	23	5	23	160,000	China (2), Kazakhstan, World Region/Global, Zambia, Lao People's Democratic Republic
2002	1,795,400	52	8	36	224,425	Mongolia, Mozambique (2), Lao People's Democratic Republic (2), World Region/Global, China (2) Russia
	3,456,860	100	22	100	157,130	

More than 50 stakeholders participated in the EIR Planning Workshop in Brussels (28–30 October, 2001): government entities (9), the private sector (15), nongovernmental organizations (21), and the World Bank Group (8). Over the course of the workshop, OED/OEG asked participants to rank the evaluative questions suggested in the approach paper by importance.

About half of the participants responded. The questions, and the final rankings based on the votes cast, are shown below:

1. ***Distribution of costs and benefits*** was ranked first overall and first or second by each group.
2. ***Environmental and social effects,*** including effects on local communities, indigenous peoples, biodiversity, and potential human rights abuses, were ranked second overall and among the top six questions by each group of respondents.
3. ***Appropriate mitigation mechanisms for environmental and social effects*** throughout the project cycle was ranked third, with some differences of opinion by the respondents.
4. ***The WBG's role in improving development impacts and minimizing risks*** was ranked fourth overall, with roughly equal importance across all groups.
5. ***Compliance with the WBG's safeguard policies*** was ranked fifth, with wider variation among the respondents.

EVALUATIVE QUESTIONS

		Rank (percentage of votes)
1. Project Context and Economic Effects		
1.1	What was the share of EI of export earnings, GDP, and government revenues in the respective country of WBG operation?	22
1.2	To what extent has there been an association between EI's share of GDP and the country's economic growth and income distribution?	12 (3%)
1.3	To what extent were the project's objectives consistent with the country's current development priorities?	6 (6%)
1.4	What were the net benefits generated by a specific WBG investment operation?	11 (3%)
1.5	How are benefits and costs distributed among central government, local government, local communities, and private shareholders? Is the distribution perceived to be fair by different stakeholder groups? Are there conflict resolution mechanisms in place, and, if so, have they worked? Are there lessons to be learned about the consequences of different types of distributions?	1 (13%)
1.6	Did the operation have impacts on private sector development in the host country beyond the operation itself (e.g., demonstration effects, linkages, infrastructure development, etc.)?	17
1.7	Are royalties effectively channeled for developmental purposes? Are independent arrangements for auditing, monitoring, and evaluation in place?	9 (5%)
2. Environmental and Social Effects		
2.1	What have been the environmental and social effects — positive and negative — of WBG activities in the sector? In particular, what were the effects on biodiversity, local communities (including indigenous peoples)? Have there been human rights abuses associated with WBG projects?	2 (11%)
2.2	Have WBG operations complied with relevant safeguard policies and adequate labor safety standards? How adequate are the measures taken to mitigate the most important negative environmental and social aspects, such as involuntary resettlement? How do WBG safeguard policies compare with local requirements?	5 (7%)

(continued)

2.3	Have expected environmental and social effects at each stage of the project cycle (construction, operation, closure and restoration) been adequately assessed and addressed at appraisal (e.g., through environmental assessments, public consultations, and project design and implementation arrangements)?	17
2.4	Have actual effects been adequately monitored during supervision?	20
2.5	Have appropriate mechanisms been put in place to handle environmental and social effects throughout the life cycle of oil, gas and mining operations (e.g., for compensation to adversely affected communities and for mine or field closure even beyond WBG involvement)?	3 (9%)
2.6	Was the operation affected by — or did it even contribute to — civil war?	26

3. Governance and Transparency

3.1	Did the operation contribute to capacity-building at the government (central or local), corporate, or voluntary agency level?	7 (6%)
3.2	Did corruption increase or decrease over the life of the project? Is this change attributable to the project?	17
3.3	Did the operation improve the framework for property rights in EI (e.g., is it clear who owns the resource and is it possible to transfer the rights)?	21
3.4	Were exploration and development rights awarded in a fair and transparent manner?	15
3.5	Disclosure: Were the benefits from development of the resource, and their distribution, disclosed? Was the use of the generated benefits transparently disclosed? What are the issues related to public disclosure?	8 (5%)

4. Role of the World Bank Group

4.1	Was WBG financing necessary for a particular project or activity to proceed?	12 (3%)
4.2	Did the WBG help improve the development impacts and minimize the risk associated with oil, gas, and mining activities? How and to what extent did the WBG affect the impacts from the point of view of government (central and local), civil society, and the companies? In particular, has the WBG helped improve positive environmental and social aspects and reduced potential negative aspects in the operations it supported? Has the WBG helped the country address macroeconomic consequences resulting from the volatility of commodities markets?	4 (7%)
4.3a	Did the WBG help improve the efficiency of the oil, gas, and mining sector and the investment climate in the sector, ...	15
4.3b	... and has this resulted in subsequent private investment without WBG support?	24
4.4	Did the WBG contribute to improved governance and increased transparency in the sector?	10 (4%)
4.5	Did the WBG assess whether the economic benefits from EI, which are retained in the host economy, are adequate compared with the value of the resources and, if so, how?	12 (3%)
4.6	Did the WBG address and influence the distribution of benefits and costs? Can one establish what impact this had on poverty reduction?	24
4.7	Has there been a trade-off between IFC profitability and development outcomes achieved in these sectors?	23

CONTACTS:

Andres Liebenthal, Operations Evaluation Department
World Bank
Phone/Fax: 1 (202) 458-2507 / 1 (202) 522-3123
e-mail: aliebenthal@worldbank.org

Roland Michelitsch, Operations Evaluation Group
International Finance Corporation
Phone/Fax: 1 (202) 458-0768 / 1 (202) 974-4302
e-mail: rmichelitsch@ifc.org

Attachment 5B	Perceptions of Survey Participants at the EIR Regional Workshops

The survey was conducted at the various EIR Regional Workshops. To date, the Latin America and the Caribbean, Eastern Europe and Central Asia, and Africa Workshops have been held in Rio de Janeiro, Brazil (April 15–19, 2002); Budapest, Hungary (June 18–22, 2002); and Maputo, Mozambique (January 13–17, 2003), respectively. Feedback from the Asia Workshop (March 2003) was not received in time to be included in this report. The purpose of the regional workshops is to engage the various regional stakeholders in the EIR. OED/OEG asked the participants to provide their impressions on the need, effort, and success of World Bank and IFC involvement in the EI in the region. The response rate for the survey was about 26 percent, as indicated in the table below.

TABLE 1. STAKEHOLDER SURVEY: RESPONDENT PROFILE

Respondent category	Venue				% of all respondents
	Rio	Budapest	Maputo	Total	
Local NGO	3	5	3	11	14
Global NGO	1	6	1	8	11
Industry	3	8	5	16	21
Government	11	1	19	31	41
World Bank Group	2	U	1	3	4
Other	1	4	2	7	9
No. of respondents	21	24	31	76	100
No. of workshop participants	85	80	127	292	
% of respondents to participants	25	30	24	26	

Responses pertaining to IFC	Perception Survey Results - All Workshops by Participant Type											
QUESTIONS	All NGO		Industry		Government		WBG		Other		Total	
Responses primarily based on:												
(1) General knowledge of WBG activities	12		13		22		1		5		58	
(2) Specific knowledge of one or more IFC projects	6		4		2		0		2		16	
(3) Specific knowledge of one or more IDA or IBRD projects	12		1		12		2		4		35	
	%+	#	%+	#	%+	#	%+	#	%+	#	%+	#
1. EXTRACTIVE INDUSTRIES DEVELOPMENT												
Need	67%	15	87%	15	76%	21	100%	2	50%	6	75%	59
Effort	21%	14	64%	14	56%	18	100%	2	33%	6	48%	54
Success	14%	14	47%	15	42%	19	50%	2	0%	5	33%	55
2. DISTRIBUTION OF PUBLIC REVENUES												
Need	80%	15	67%	15	82%	17	100%	3	60%	5	76%	55
Effort	17%	12	33%	12	41%	17	67%	3	25%	4	33%	48
Success	0%	10	27%	11	38%	13	33%	3	0%	5	21%	42
3. SUSTAINABLE DEVELOPMENT												
Need	86%	14	71%	14	74%	19	100%	3	80%	5	78%	55
Effort	8%	12	36%	11	50%	18	67%	3	60%	5	39%	49
Success	0%	12	13%	8	44%	16	33%	3	25%	4	23%	43
4. ENVIRONMENTAL IMPACTS												
Need	88%	17	93%	14	90%	21	100%	3	80%	5	90%	60
Effort	38%	13	83%	12	50%	20	67%	3	80%	5	58%	53
Success	15%	13	58%	12	53%	19	67%	3	40%	5	44%	52
5. SOCIAL IMPACTS												
Need	88%	17	86%	14	86%	21	100%	3	60%	5	85%	60
Effort	14%	14	60%	10	55%	20	33%	3	60%	5	44%	52
Success	7%	15	44%	9	50%	16	33%	3	40%	5	33%	48
6. GOVERNANCE AND TRANSPARENCY												
Need	94%	17	86%	14	68%	19	100%	3	80%	5	83%	58
Effort	21%	14	64%	11	44%	18	33%	3	33%	3	41%	49
Success	8%	13	22%	9	44%	18	33%	3	0%	4	26%	47
7. INVESTMENT CLIMATE AND ECONOMIC LINKAGES												
Need	71%	14	100%	12	83%	18	100%	3	80%	5	85%	52
Effort	30%	10	82%	11	61%	18	100%	3	67%	3	62%	45
Success	22%	9	33%	9	40%	15	100%	3	33%	3	38%	39

Response is greater than 60%

161

(continued)

Responses pertaining to IFC	Perception Survey Results - By Workshop							
QUESTIONS	Rio de Janeiro		Budapest		Mozambique		Total	
Responses primarily based on:								
(1) General knowledge of WBG activities	13		20		25		58	
(2) Specific knowledge of one or more IFC projects	2		13		1		16	
(3) Specific knowledge of one or more IDA or IBRD projects	12		13		10		35	
	%+	#	%+	#	%+	#	%+	#
1. EXTRACTIVE INDUSTRIES DEVELOPMENT								
Need	**74%**	19	**68%**	19	**81%**	21	**75%**	59
Effort	**60%**	15	**53%**	19	35%	20	48%	54
Success	**69%**	16	32%	19	5%	20	33%	55
2. DISTRIBUTION OF PUBLIC REVENUES								
Need	**87%**	15	**67%**	21	**79%**	19	**76%**	55
Effort	33%	12	24%	17	42%	19	33%	48
Success	33%	9	13%	16	24%	17	21%	42
3. SUSTAINABLE DEVELOPMENT								
Need	**88%**	16	**79%**	19	**70%**	20	**78%**	55
Effort	**67%**	12	29%	17	30%	20	39%	49
Success	45%	11	13%	15	18%	17	23%	43
4. ENVIRONMENTAL IMPACTS								
Need	**94%**	18	**80%**	20	**95%**	22	**90%**	60
Effort	**62%**	13	**67%**	18	50%	22	**58%**	53
Success	57%	14	**53%**	17	29%	21	44%	52
5. SOCIAL IMPACTS								
Need	**95%**	19	**75%**	20	**86%**	21	**85%**	60
Effort	46%	13	31%	16	**52%**	23	44%	52
Success	46%	13	25%	16	32%	19	33%	48
6. GOVERNANCE AND TRANSPARENCY								
Need	**78%**	18	**80%**	20	**90%**	20	**83%**	58
Effort	47%	15	44%	16	33%	18	41%	49
Success	46%	13	19%	16	17%	18	26%	47
7. INVESTMENT CLIMATE AND ECONOMIC LINKAGES								
Need	**100%**	16	**71%**	17	**84%**	19	**85%**	52
Effort	**73%**	15	**64%**	14	50%	16	**62%**	45
Success	**62%**	13	38%	13	15%	13	38%	39

Response is greater than 60%

Attachment 5C   **Perceptions of WBG Staff Surveyed**

The survey of WBG staff included 66 questions and room for comments. The questions were designed to get the views of staff on the relative importance of issues for EI-dependent countries and to determine if they feel that the WBG addresses them adequately.

- *Revenue Generation*—generating higher fiscal revenues from EI production activities
- *Revenue Distribution*—fair allocation of fiscal revenues among central/federal governments, subnational (provincial/district/municipal) governments, and local communities (villages, indigenous)
- *Revenue Utilization*—allocation of fiscal revenues from EI for developmental priorities
- *Mitigating Negative Environmental Impacts*—from past EI activities or new ones
- *Mitigating Negative Social Impacts*—from past EI activities or new ones

- *Capacity-Building for EI Sector Management*—including policy/legal/technical/business issues
- *Improving the Investment Climate*—legal/regulatory framework, property rights
- *Improving Transparency and Governance*—more public disclosure, less rent-seeking

The survey also asked staff to provide views on the level of coordination among IFC, MIGA, and the World Bank; on risk aversion toward EI; and on the constraints on the WBG's involvement in EI. Questionnaires were sent out by e-mail, and respondents were given about a month, until February 24, 2003, to respond. The 66 persons (69 percent) who responded have, on average, worked for WBG for about eight years (10 years for World Bank respondents and about 6 years for IFC and MIGA) and indicated familiarity with 48 EI-dependent countries.

JOINT OPERATIONS EVALUATION DEPARTMENT/GROUP/UNIT STAFF SURVEY RESULTS

Questions	IFC Staff			IBRD Staff			MIGA Staff			Total		
	Positive	High	Total	Positive	High	Total	Positive	High	Total	Positive	High	Total
1. Importance												
Revenue Generation	86%	62%	29	87%	83%	23	90%	70%	10	87%	71%	62
Revenue Distribution	86%	54%	28	77%	55%	22	88%	50%	8	83%	53%	58
Revenue Utilization	83%	59%	29	83%	57%	23	89%	67%	9	84%	59%	61
Mitigating Negative Environmental Impacts	86%	41%	29	77%	32%	22	100%	67%	9	85%	42%	60
Mitigating Negative Social Impacts	86%	45%	29	78%	39%	23	89%	56%	9	84%	44%	61
Capacity-Building for EI Sector Management	83%	38%	29	87%	39%	23	89%	56%	9	85%	41%	61
Improving the Investment Climate	93%	54%	28	88%	63%	24	90%	30%	10	90%	53%	62
Improving Transparency and Governance	93%	57%	28	88%	71%	24	90%	30%	10	90%	58%	62

(continued)

2. CAS—adequately addresses EI issues

Revenue Generation	86%	14%	21	78%	35%	23	100%	40%	5	84%	27%	49
Revenue Distribution	60%	20%	20	50%	20%	20	80%	40%	5	58%	22%	45
Revenue Utilization	65%	20%	20	71%	38%	21	80%	20%	5	70%	28%	46
Mitigating Negative Environmental Impacts	77%	27%	22	80%	20%	20	80%	60%	5	79%	28%	47
Mitigating Negative Social Impacts	76%	24%	21	76%	29%	21	60%	60%	5	74%	30%	47
Capacity-Building for EI Sector Management	68%	11%	19	76%	0%	21	80%	0%	5	73%	4%	45
Improving the Investment Climate	86%	32%	22	91%	27%	22	80%	20%	5	88%	29%	49
Improving Transparency and Governance	80%	25%	20	70%	35%	23	100%	60%	5	77%	33%	48

3. EI projects/operations—adequately address EI issues

Revenue Generation	92%	36%	25	88%	35%	17	100%	78%	9	92%	43%	51
Revenue Distribution	46%	8%	26	56%	19%	16	78%	22%	9	55%	14%	51
Revenue Utilization	54%	13%	24	67%	28%	18	78%	0%	9	63%	16%	51
Mitigating Negative Environmental Impacts	100%	62%	29	89%	50%	18	100%	67%	9	96%	59%	56
Mitigating Negative Social Impacts	96%	54%	28	78%	44%	18	88%	13%	8	89%	44%	54
Capacity-Building for EI Sector Management	83%	26%	23	88%	44%	16	89%	33%	9	85%	33%	48
Improving the Investment Climate	67%	21%	24	82%	35%	17	90%	30%	10	76%	27%	51
Improving Transparency and Governance	54%	8%	26	80%	35%	20	56%	11%	9	64%	18%	55

4. Interventions outside the EI sector—adequately address EI issues

Revenue Generation	69%	25%	16	74%	32%	19	86%	57%	7	74%	33%	42
Revenue Distribution	63%	0%	16	**39%**	17%	18	100%	14%	7	59%	10%	41
Revenue Utilization	47%	0%	15	42%	16%	19	86%	29%	7	51%	12%	41
Mitigating Negative Environmental Impacts	89%	33%	18	63%	26%	19	100%	44%	9	80%	33%	46
Mitigating Negative Social Impacts	88%	29%	17	41%	12%	17	75%	38%	8	67%	24%	42
Capacity-Building for EI Sector Management	67%	0%	15	50%	6%	18	75%	13%	8	61%	5%	41
Improving the Investment Climate	65%	12%	17	89%	39%	18	100%	0%	9	82%	20%	44
Improving Transparency and Governance	76%	6%	17	60%	20%	20	89%	0%	9	72%	11%	46

5. Non-lending interventions—adequately address EI issues

Revenue Generation	75%	6%	16	67%	29%	21	75%	0%	4	71%	17%	41
Revenue Distribution	60%	13%	15	50%	30%	20	100%	0%	4	59%	21%	39
Revenue Utilization	60%	20%	15	65%	25%	20	75%	0%	4	64%	21%	39
Mitigating Negative Environmental Impacts	84%	32%	19	43%	22%	23	100%	0%	4	65%	24%	46
Mitigating Negative Social Impacts	84%	32%	19	50%	21%	24	100%	25%	4	68%	26%	47
Capacity-Building for EI Sector Management	95%	15%	20	55%	18%	22	83%	33%	6	75%	19%	48

Improving the Investment Climate	94%	6%	18	77%	36%	22	83%	33%	6	85%	24%	46
Improving Transparency and Governance	68%	16%	19	68%	41%	22	80%	0%	5	70%	26%	46

6. Coordination across WBG is adequate

	48%	46%	25	52%	13%	23	100%	50%	8	57%	18%	56

7. The Global Product Group for Oil, Gas, and Mining has helped to improve the following:

Coordination between IFC and WB on sectoral issues	88%	46%	24	71%	29%	14	88%	0%	8	83%	33%	46
Strategic integration of sectoral and macro interventions	58%	11%	19	58%	8%	12	100%	0%	7	66%	8%	38
Quality of sectoral ESW and non-lending interventions	55%	0%	11	67%	8%	12	100%	0%	4	67%	4%	27
Sectoral knowledge-sharing across regions	90%	40%	20	67%	25%	12	83%	0%	6	82%	29%	38
Overall quality of service to clients	76%	19%	21	67%	0%	12	80%	0%	5	74%	11%	38
Other	100%	100%	1	67%	0%	3	100%	0%	1	80%	20%	5

8. WBG avoided good projects in EI due to safeguards concerns from the following:

WBG management	86%	14%	14	86%	21%	14	100%	50%	6	88%	24%	34
WBG task managers	70%	0%	10	38%	23%	13	60%	40%	5	54%	18%	28
Client country government	30%	20%	10	29%	14%	14	0%	0%	5	24%	14%	29
EI public agencies/enterprises	56%	11%	9	21%	7%	14	75%	25%	4	41%	11%	27
Private investors	54%	15%	13	29%	7%	14	40%	20%	5	41%	13%	32

9. Factors that constrain WBG's ability to assist client countries in enhancing EI's contribution to sustainable development:

Inadequate linkage between EI sector activities and sustainable development	42%	4%	24	50%	23%	22	56%	0%	9	47%	11%	55
Inadequate availability of staff with appropriate skills	32%	0%	25	59%	27%	22	22%	0%	9	41%	11%	56
Pressure for rapid processing of credits/funding/guarantees	38%	5%	21	38%	24%	21	44%	22%	9	39%	16%	51
Inadequate level of support from the Bank's Country Department/Country Management Unit	52%	10%	21	55%	20%	20	29%	0%	7	50%	13%	48
Inadequate level of support from the Global Product Group for Oil, Gas, and Mining	8%	4%	24	33%	20%	15	0%	0%	6	16%	9%	45
Inadequate level of support from the client government	63%	17%	24	38%	19%	21	17%	0%	6	47%	16%	51
Inadequate level of support from project implementor (sectoral agency or private sponsor)	24%	0%	21	25%	6%	16	50%	13%	8	29%	4%	45
Other	100%	0%	3	100%	100%	2	100%	100%	1	100%	50%	6

(continued)

Rating Scale—Question 1:

1 = Not at all Important

2 = Moderately Important

3 = Important

4 = Highly Important

High = % responding 4.   Positive = % responding 3 or 4

Rating Scale—Questions 2–9:

1 = Strongly disagree

2 = Disagree

3 = Agree

4 = Strongly agree

High = % responding 4.   Positive = % responding 3 or 4

Italics = Response is less than 40%

Bold = Response is less than 60% and 40% or more

	TABLE 2. STAFF SURVEY: RESPONDENT PROFILE				
	Organization				**% of all respondents**
	World Bank	**IFC**	**MIGA**	**Total**	
Task Managers	12			12	18
Investment Officers		24		24	36
Regional Economists	14	6		20	30
Underwriters		1	5	5	8
Other		4	5	5	89
Number of respondents	26	30	10	66	100
Number of surveys distributed	51	33	12	96	
Response rate (%)	51%	91%	83%	69%	

Source: http://www.ifc.org/enviro

The following social and environmental safeguards policies apply to extractive industries projects, as appropriate:

Environmental Safeguards Policies:

- OP 4.01 Environmental Assessment—October 1998
- OP 4.04 Natural Habitats—November 1998
- OP 4.36 Forestry—November 1998
- OP 4.37 Dam Safety—September 1996 (IFC now reportedly uses a 1999 draft policy, but it is not in the public domain)
- OP 7.50 International Waterways—November 1998
- OP 7.60 Disputed Territories—June 2001

Social Safeguards Policies:

- OD 4.20 Indigenous Peoples—September 1991
- OD 4.30 Involuntary Resettlement—June 1990
- OPN 11.03 Cultural Property—September 1986
- IFC's Statement on Child and Forced Labor—March 1998

OP 7.60, OD 4.20, OD 4.30, and OPN 11.03 remain as World Bank policies, while the others have been modified and updated to better correspond with the IFC business model.

Guidelines contained in the PPAH or updated http://www.ifc.org/enviro/enviro/pollution/guidelines.htm:

- General Environmental Guidelines (1993 and 1998)
- General Health and Safety Guidelines (1998)
- Base Metal and Iron Ore Mining (1998)
- Coal Mining and Production (1998)
- Oil and Gas Development—Onshore (1998)
- Oil and Gas Development—Offshore (2000)
- Mining and Milling—Underground (1995)
- Mining and Milling—Open Pit (1995)
- Hazardous Materials Management Guidelines (2001)

The PPAH also includes other guidelines on environmental management, fire safety, waste minimization, pollution prevention, air pollution control and wastewater management, cleaner production, risk assessment, trans-boundary issues (GHG), and pollution management of various chemicals—all of which may also be relevant in a specific project. A "precious metals" guideline is still pending.

IFC has specific requirements for Public Disclosure and Public Consultation, depending upon the categorization of the project.[277]

Consultation could be defined as a wider continuous process of participation of all stakeholders in the decisions throughout the formulation and execution of a project leading to a sustainable development for the population in the area. Consultation, formally, is part of the environmental impact assessment of the project. In practice, it is a tool for managing two-way communication between the developer and the public, in general, and the local community, in particular.

Consultation should be understood as a means to achieve certain goals and not as a goal in itself. Its basic purpose is to improve decisionmaking and build understanding by actively involving individuals and organizations with a stake in the project. This involvement will increase the project's long-term viability and will enhance its benefits to locally-impacted people and other stakeholders.

The process of consultation and participation should include precise agreements that could be adapted and monitored throughout the life of the project. Consultation should have an impact on the project design and implementation. It should be started by the appropriate government agency prior to licensing or contracting of the area and should be continued by an oil company that assumes the operation from the early seismic works through drilling operations, development and exploitation, and formal abandonment. When possible, the consultation process should be witnessed by a third party (i.e., the ombudsman office and/or an association of environmental NGOs).

Emerging Best Practices on Consultation

A list of best practices comprises the following points: Consultation requires exchange of information, collaboration, and mutual understanding of the parties involved. It often proceeds through cultural barriers, drops bad past legacies, and ends up creating confidence and trust.

It is essential to identify the representatives of key stakeholders and local authorities, including existing alliances, social structures, and possibly prevailing conflicts among local groups and/or external groups and NGOs. Where indigenous peoples have their own representative organizations, such organizations should be the channels for communicating their preferences.

Governments have an important role in establishing first contact with the indigenous population, gathering adequate social and cultural information, and introducing the new contractor. This kind of information is usually in the hands of academia and NGOs rather than the government's alone. Governments and the concerned private companies should make an effort to gather and review this information as early as possible.

Consultation should include the provision of information on the project in a timely, complete, and culturally appropriate fashion. It should lead to a meaningful dialogue and provide recorded results, including the views and recommendations of the indigenous peoples for the protection of the environment and the mechanisms put in place for their participation.

Mechanisms should be devised for direct participation by indigenous peoples in decisionmaking on aspects of the project that affect them. Such participation shall take place throughout project design, implementation, monitoring, and evaluation.

Proper consultation requires developing local capacity to interpret the technicalities of environmental studies, understanding the impact of international markets, developing long-term solutions, and being able to effectively communicate complex issues across cultural barriers. It requires time to obtain consensus on an adequate community relations program. Resulting delays could create conflicts if contract terms are not properly established.

Consultation—by the government prior to the contract or by the company as part of the environmental impact assessment of any important operation—requires the preparation of typical business plans, including identification of objectives, responsibilities, and inputs to be accomplished by each stakeholder.

Some Practical Recommendations

To organize a consultation: Designing meaningful consultations with indigenous peoples depends upon several factors, including the national, legal, and political context; the linguistic and cultural characteristics of the indigenous groups; and the degree of interaction and relationships with the regional and national societies and external social actors (that is, missionaries, school systems, local traders, and loggers). It also depends on the nature of their traditional social organizations and leadership patterns and the groups organized to represent the interests of indigenous peoples. Despite these differences, there are some general principles for organizing and conducting meaningful consultations with indigenous peoples. These include the following:

1. Using facilitators who know the indigenous languages and the indigenous cultures;
2. Creating appropriate settings and locations for the consultations, preferably in the territories and settlements where indigenous peoples live;
3. Providing background information on the proposed project in a language and format that the population understands (e.g., simple diagrams and charts in the native languages, maps, videos, 3D models);
4. Recognizing the time frames of indigenous peoples, especially in terms of decision-making, that are often different from those of outsiders;
5. Respecting indigenous leadership patterns and religious beliefs and ensuring that elders and other traditional authorities have the opportunity to express their points of view;
6. Recognizing that in some cases there may be different factions within a community with contrasting views on national development projects and establishment of

methodologies for the peaceful resolution of conflicts and differences;
7. Providing resources (e.g., food, shelter, travel funds) so persons can attend the consultations from distant villages or their representatives can attend consultations in district, provincial, or national capitals;
8. Ensuring that interpreters are provided for indigenous participants when consultations are held in district, provincial, and national capitals;
9. Supporting the local and regional indigenous leadership to improve communications with their communities and to be able to follow up the consultation process; and
10. Dealing with gender issues.

To manage a consultation process: At any point of the project life, the project developer should take into consideration the following steps:

1. Plan ahead—to identify the project risks, the parties to be involved, and the stakeholders' interests and institutional goals; to understand past experiences, if any; and to effectively fulfill regulations.
2. Test your proposals—to ensure that the key stakeholders understand the project impacts and benefits and would be able to voice their concerns and input alternative approaches. Prepare good responses to obvious questions.
3. Invest time and money—the schedule and budget of the project should properly include the consultation effort. Involve consultants and permanent staff with appropriate qualifications.
4. Involve senior and local managers—their direct participation will make the entire company understand the importance of integrating the stakeholders concerns.
5. Hire and train the right personnel—a community liaison advisor with direct access to management and certain negotiation capacity should be appointed and would be responsible for hearing the local concerns. The advisor could also work with community liaison officers, depending on the size of the project.

6. Maintain overall responsibility—manage consultants and subcontractors carefully to avoid bad feelings from affected people who will not differentiate contracted personnel from the company itself.

7. Coordinate all related activities—to provide consistency in the information conveyed by all company staff to all outside stakeholders.

8. Build dialogue and trust—develop two channels of communication, preferably in the local language. Particular attention should be given to women and less powerful groups, and actively include them in a culturally appropriate way into the dialogue. It is important to maintain the personnel who interact with the stakeholders. As in personal relationships, continuity and familiarity build trust.

9. Manage expectations—avoid unrealistic expectations. Be clear in describing the project impact and what it could deliver, trying not to overstate the benefits.

10. Work with governments—inform and consult with relevant government departments regarding the activities, risks, and opportunities of the project and the required permits. Work closely with local authorities who often have long-established relations with the local communities and who could delineate responsibilities between the local municipalities, the community leaders, and the project sponsor.

11. Work with NGOs and community-based organizations—identify and liaise, particularly with those who represent the affected people. NGOs have vital expertise and local knowledge and could be sounding boards for project design and mitigation efforts. Initial research is important to understand local power dynamics and to ensure that NGOs truly represent and convey the community interests.

12. Prepare an action plan—consolidate in an action plan the agreed projects, including timing and indicators for monitoring.

Government responsibilities: Within the process of consultation, government responsibilities could be grouped in the following list:

1. To set adequate regulations

2. To provide land tenure rights

3. To keep a database with sociocultural information available to interested companies

4. To carry out the first consultation

5. To contract areas allowing enough time for preparing adequate environmental impact assessments involving effective public consultations

6. To facilitate the process of consultation between industry and indigenous peoples, ensuring due representation of the parties and providing validity to the agreements reached

7. To establish proper links between the companies' community relations program, the communities' Planes de Vidal, and the regional development plans with respect to education, health, infrastructure, defense, and the activities of other productive sectors in the region

8. To supervise the execution of agreed plans and audit accounts

9. To mediate in case of conflicts

Operations Evaluation Unit:
Evaluation of MIGA's Experience

1. Introduction

MIGA has supported investments in EI projects since its inception in 1988 by providing guarantees to foreign investors against political risks[278] and, to a lesser extent, by offering technical assistance and advisory services. The involvement of foreign investors in EI projects has the potential for great benefits to the host countries and can significantly contribute to the private sector development agenda of resource-rich developing countries. At the same time, such investments have given rise, in some instances, to concerns about potential negative impacts on environment and affected communities, as well as about the sustainability of positive impacts. In that regard, MIGA, like the rest of the WBG, has come under increased scrutiny by its stakeholders.

In order to review the WBG's past experience and to inform its future strategy for the sector, the WBG's three evaluation units[279] have conducted a joint evaluation of Bank Group activities in EI. This independent evaluation reviews the WBG assistance to the development of EI and its contribution to economic, social, and environmental outcomes. The objective is to evaluate the development effectiveness of WBG activities in the EI sector and to draw lessons from the WBG experience to inform its future role in the sector. The study covers the process of extracting oil, gas, coal, minerals, and metals from the earth and their initial processing or concentration. The downstream utilization of these resources or issues related to the global impact of the consumption of EI products were not examined.[280] In parallel to this joint evaluation, WBG management commissioned an external EIR to advise the Bank Group on its future role in EI, in response to stakeholder concerns.

This report by MIGA's OEU presents the findings of an evaluation of MIGA guarantee projects in the EI sector. Section 1 describes the evaluation process and criteria for evaluation and methodologies used. It also presents an overview of the characteristics and evolution of MIGA's EI portfolio. Section 2 assesses the consistency of MIGA EI projects with environmental and social safeguard policies. Section 3 assesses the development impacts of a sample of evaluated EI projects. Section 4 reviews MIGA's role and effectiveness in the EI sector. Section 5 presents conclusions of the evaluation and makes recommendations for MIGA's future involvement in EI projects.

Evaluation Methodology and Approach

OEU's evaluation activities for this joint evaluation consisted of the following:

- An overview of MIGA's EI portfolio,
- A review of safeguard policy consistency for a sample of MIGA EI projects,[281]
- An update and validation of previously evaluated projects,
- Two case studies of mining sector projects, and
- A staff survey of underwriters involved in EI projects.

The overview of MIGA's EI portfolio covered 100 percent of projects guaranteed in the EI sector (with active and inactive guarantees) from FY90 through the first half of FY03 (December 31, 2002). These 31 projects (corresponding to 61 guarantee contracts) were used to describe the evolution and salient features of MIGA's EI portfolio.[282]

The objective of the safeguards review was to assess the consistency of MIGA guarantees in the EI sector since inception of operations in FY90 with current relevant environmental and social safeguard policies and the adequacy of measures to mitigate adverse environmental and social impacts. OEU evaluated the consistency of projects with MIGA's interim safeguard policies and procedures at two points for each project: at approval and during implementation (under guarantee or, if the guarantee had been cancelled, at the time of cancellation).

For the safeguards review, OEU selected a sample of 12 MIGA projects[283] in the EI sector (or 39 percent of EI sector projects with a total of 26 guarantees) with characteristics representative of MIGA's EI portfolio. Thus, OEU reviewed both early and more recent projects underwritten by MIGA, spanning a period of 12 years (FY90–01). The sample consisted of nine mining sector projects, of which four were gold, one cobalt, three copper (/zinc), and one coal, as well as three oil and gas projects. Projects in environmental categories 'A' (nine) and 'B' (three) were reviewed. The sample included projects in which other development institutions or insurers were involved (such as the IFC, European Investment Bank, Overseas Private Investment Corporation, Export Development Canada, and Export Finance and Insurance Corporation) and some in which MIGA was the sole participant. The review covered projects where MIGA guaranteed majority owners as well as minority owners or lenders. Finally, the sample was balanced in terms of projects with active guarantees (five) and those cancelled by the investor or lender (seven).

In addition to the safeguards review, OEU carried out a desk review to update and validate evaluations of six mining projects undertaken by MIGA's former evaluation unit. These six projects, five gold mines and a facility extracting cobalt from tailings, had been visited in FY90–FY00. These relatively mature projects were underwritten by MIGA in the early to mid-1990s (FY92–FY96). This desk review, using the most recent information available, sought to address four evaluation criteria: (i) the project's financial sustainability, (ii) the project's economic sustainability, (iii) the project's contributions to private sector development, and (iv)

MIGA's role and effectiveness. The update and validation consisted of a review of MIGA underwriting and evaluation files and information available in the public domain relating to various aspects of the projects.

OEU also undertook two evaluation case studies, both in Latin America, that involved site visits. The first case applied OEU's new guarantee project evaluation methodology, including a cost-benefit analysis, whereas the second case study focused on environmental, social, and community aspects.

Finally, OEU conducted a survey of a group of MIGA staff involved in underwriting EI projects, soliciting staff's perceptions on important issues in EI and obstacles to more MIGA involvement in the EI sector to compare those perceptions with OEU's findings from project evaluations. (OED and OEG have used the same survey to obtain views from World Bank and IFC staff.)

Altogether, OEU covered 15 out of 31 MIGA EI projects through the safeguards review, validation and update, or case studies. This is equivalent to 48 percent of MIGA's EI portfolio. Attachment 2 provides an overview of the projects reviewed by OEU.

Portfolio Overview: MIGA Activities in the Mining and Oil and Gas Sectors

MIGA began supporting mining projects in 1990, at the start of its operations. In fact, the first two projects ever to receive MIGA coverage were in the mining sector, and in its first year of operations, mining accounted for 76 percent of MIGA's aggregate liability.

As of December 31, 2002, MIGA had insured 24 mining and 7 oil and gas projects, for a total of 31 EI projects.[284] (A complete list of MIGA EI projects since its inception are in Attachment 1.) MIGA was relatively active in mining in the 1990s but has not insured mining projects since FY01. By contrast, MIGA began insuring oil and gas investments relatively late, in the mid-1990s (see Figure E1). In terms of MIGA's cumulative aggregate liability, mining has overshadowed oil and gas (of the total liability issued in EI of almost $1.5 billion, mining accounts for 74 percent and oil and gas for 26 percent). Overall, 13 percent

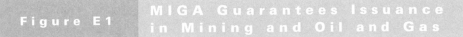

Figure E1 — MIGA Guarantees Issuance in Mining and Oil and Gas

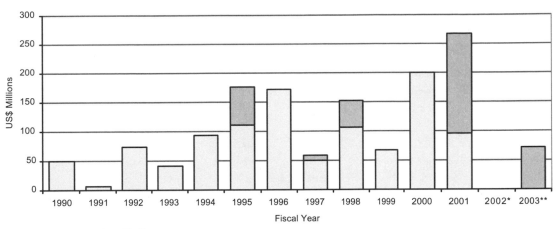

□ Mining (U.S.$M) ■ Oil and Gas (U.S.$M)

* No guarantees issued in EI
**As of 12/31/2002

of MIGA's cumulative issued liabilities were in EI. As MIGA operations grew and it diversified its portfolio into other sectors, fewer EI projects were underwritten, and as existing coverage expired or was cancelled, the share of EI in MIGA's outstanding portfolio gradually decreased (see Figure E2). As of December 31, 2002, this figure dropped to approximately 11 percent (6.6 percent for mining and 4.3 percent for oil and gas), or $552 million, in absolute terms.

MIGA coverage corresponded to an estimated foreign direct investment (FDI) of $10.2 billion

Figure E2 — MIGA Exposure in Mining Declining

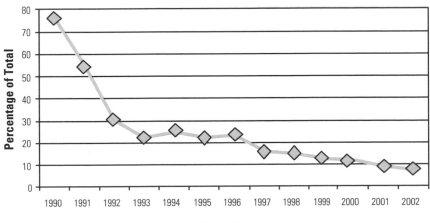

**MIGA Guarantees —
Mining Projects as a Percentage of MIGA Total Gross Exposure**

for mining projects and an estimated $5.1 billion for oil and gas. The total FDI facilitated in EI accounts for 32 percent of the overall estimated FDI facilitated by MIGA since its inception.

Extractive industries projects, especially greenfield projects, often entail large capital investments. Even privatizations and modernizations, which represent about half of the mining projects that MIGA has insured, required significant investments. This tends to produce a higher level of MIGA exposure per project, $47 million on average, compared with the MIGA average ($28 million). MIGA's exposure ratio, measured as the share of its gross exposure to the FDI facilitated by MIGA projects, is about 10 percent for EI (mining: 11 percent, oil and gas: 7 percent), whereas the overall ratio for MIGA is 23 percent. MIGA has extensively used opportunities for reinsurance and coinsurance with public or private political risk insurers for its projects in the EI sector, thereby limiting MIGA's net exposure.

Half of MIGA's mining projects have been gold mines (12 projects), and another 8 have been copper mines. In terms of coverage issued, MIGA mining projects have been concentrated in Latin America and the Caribbean (45 percent) and Africa (27 percent), followed by the transition economies in the former Soviet Union (16 percent). About half of the mining projects in Latin America have been privatizations or expansions, whereas almost all other projects in other regions have been greenfield operations. All mining projects in Africa have been located in IDA-eligible countries. Two more mining operations were located in IDA-eligible countries in Europe and Central Asia and Latin America and the Caribbean.

The majority of oil and gas projects insured by MIGA were new investments in existing production fields. Regionally, oil and gas projects have been fairly evenly distributed, in terms of MIGA's liability, between Latin America, Europe and Central Asia, Middle East and North Africa, and Africa, and have been evenly distributed between onshore and offshore fields.

MIGA's EI portfolio was concentrated in countries with a higher risk profile because demand for MIGA coverage originates from investors' unfavorable perception of political risk in host countries. There is often a correlation between the perceived risk in a country and governance; that is, political risks are likely to be more prominent in weaker governance environments. This in turn means that the need for MIGA guarantees is higher in countries where governance tends to be weaker. While there are no generally accepted governance ratings, Transparency International's (TI) corruption perception index provides a proxy for one dimension of governance in countries where MIGA had EI project guarantees. The 2002 TI rankings include 20 countries in which MIGA has had EI projects. The unweighted average score for countries with MIGA EI involvement is 3.58 (on a scale of 0 to 10, with MIGA EI scoring from 1.9 to 7.5), which is identical to the average score of all developing countries (79) covered by the corruption perception index. This means that MIGA EI projects, on average, were in countries where perceived governance levels were similar to the average level in its developing member countries. Governance issues are important for EI-dependent countries and are addressed by the joint evaluation at both the sectoral and country levels in the OED/OEG/OEU Main report.

Since FY00,[285] MIGA has not supported any new mining projects, and it has insured only three new oil and gas projects. While the reasons for this slowdown were not systematically assessed by this evaluation, it is likely due to (i) a decline in the number of applications received by MIGA (signaling either a lack of private investor interest or investment opportunities in these sectors given the fall in metal prices and other adverse global developments, or political risk insurance not being critical for their investment, or lack of attractiveness of MIGA instruments to investors) and (ii) a need for more rigorous project assessments during underwriting and, thus, delayed decisionmaking. MIGA may have been more careful and selective as well, given that EI sector projects often mean high underwriting costs, increased scrutiny, complex environmental and social issues, and some criticism by stakeholders or nongovernmental organizations with potential risks and implications for MIGA's reputation.[286]

A MIGA Contract of Guarantee, the agency's

key legal instrument, is issued for a period of 3 to 15 years, subject to the needs of the investor. Most contracts have a minimum duration of three years, after which the investor may cancel the guarantee on the premium anniversary date, with 30 days' advance notice to MIGA.

Cancellations of MIGA EI Projects

As of December 31, 2002, 299 of the cumulative total of 619 contracts issued by MIGA (i.e., 48 percent) remained active. In the extractive industries, 21 of the 61 contracts (i.e., 34 percent) were still active. These correspond to 11 projects out of a total of 31 extractive industries projects that obtained MIGA guarantees since 1990, implying a high cancellation rate of 66 percent for MIGA EI projects. This is most likely due to the relative seniority of extractive industries projects (especially mining projects) in MIGA's portfolio (most contracts have outlasted the three-year minimum contract period).

Those contracts in extractive industries, associated with 20 projects in all, that were cancelled by investors or expired, remained active for a median time of 4.0 years, with a range of 0.66 to 7.25 years.[287] As of December 2002, the oldest EI project in MIGA's portfolio, a mining project, had been insured for 11 years.

Reasons for observed cancellations of guarantee contracts for EI projects include, in decreasing order of occurrence, the following: (i) self-insurance (investors become comfortable with the host country political risk level, which means that the MIGA guarantee has served its useful purpose), (ii) replacement of MIGA insurance with private or national insurers, (iii) repayment of loans, (iv) commercial failure of the project enterprise, (v) transfer of shares by the guarantee holder to investors who have not requested a guarantee from MIGA, and (vi) financial restructuring, leading to replacements of existing contracts.

Technical Assistance, Advisory and Mediation Services, and Claims

MIGA's technical assistance and advisory services have focused on mining and in the past have aimed at assisting countries in formulating strategies and techniques to attract FDI in the sector.

The program consisted of three core activities. The objective of the first, capacity-building, was to improve the effectiveness of the host country's mining promotion agencies through strategy workshops and policy seminars for government officials. Second, investment facilitation activities, including six conferences on African Mining Investment, brought together potential investors and government leaders to catalyze projects in Africa. Finally, in information dissemination, using a predominantly Internet-based approach (such as the Investment Promotion Agency Network[288]), MIGA provided information on mineral potential, policy and legislation, infrastructure, financial services, basic country information, investment opportunities "who's who," new developments, and geological maps. Because MIGA's technical assistance and advisory services have not been evaluated, OEU is not able to report on the effectiveness of these activities.[289]

MIGA has not received or paid any claim related to an EI project. It has mediated two investment disputes involving mines, in Angola and Ukraine, for investors without MIGA guarantees.

2. Review of MIGA's EI Projects for Consistency with Safeguard Policies

This section summarizes the findings of a review to assess the consistency[290] of MIGA's extractive industry projects with current applicable environmental and social safeguard policies and the adequacy of measures to mitigate adverse environmental and social impacts.[291] This evaluation has focused on safeguard policies because the project's environmental and social performance is one of the most critical aspects of EI projects, and a failure to comply with applicable safeguards may have negative impacts on communities and the environment, thus undermining MIGA's development mandate. The section identifies specific issues emerging from the sample of projects reviewed in relation to (i) the application of the safeguards to the private sector, (ii) MIGA's unique mandate (within the WBG) as an insurer of political risks, and (iii) the adequacy of the safeguard oversight framework that has been adopted by MIGA management. The review is based on a comprehensive evaluation methodology that was developed and tested in a parallel OED study. It covers a sample of 12 MIGA EI projects in the mining and oil and gas sectors[292] approved between FY90 and FY01.

MIGA's framework for assessing the compliance of its guarantee projects with environmental policies and guidelines has evolved significantly over time. Prior to adopting its own policies and guidelines, MIGA applied World Bank environmental and social policies[293] and guidelines to its projects. An internal document indicated that MIGA had committed to "ensure that [its projects] conform to the environmental standards adopted by other members of the World Bank Group" since 1991 and initially did so using specialized IFC staff. The creation of an in-house environmental unit by MIGA in late 1997 was an important milestone for improving the Agency's capacity to address environmental issues. This unit has been responsible for setting up in-house procedures, formulating and revising policies, undertaking project assessments, and selective monitoring.[294] In May 1999, the Board approved MIGA's own specific EA and disclosure policies and procedures that reflect its business as an investment insurer for the private sector. They took effect with all new definitive applications received after July 1, 2000. In May 2002, MIGA's Board approved the adoption of its own interim issue-specific Safeguard Policies. MIGA's Web site[295] notes, "In carrying out its review and evaluation, MIGA considers:

- the project's ability to comply with the appropriate guidelines found in the World Bank Group's *Pollution Prevention and Abatement Handbook;*
- compliance of the project with host country environmental requirements; and
- consistency of the project with MIGA's safeguard policies regarding the following specific issues: natural habitats; forestry; pest management; dam safety; projects on international waterways; involuntary resettlement; indigenous peoples; and physical cultural resources."

Until late 1997, IFC environmental and social specialists were used to review MIGA projects for WBG safeguard policy consistency, as MIGA did not have its own in-house capacity due to its small size.[296] Even after MIGA's environmental unit was created, IFC experts continued to be called upon for their advice on certain projects. In some mining projects that were reviewed, IFC was also an investor and/or lender, and MIGA deferred to IFC experts on safeguard compliance matters in such cases. From an evaluation perspective, including projects for which IFC experts carried out MIGA's due diligence, and has provided valuable insights into the functioning of this earlier arrangement and its efficacy for MIGA, which could also be useful for future MIGA projects in which IFC may be involved.

The WBG safeguard policies contain a long list of requirements. For the purposes of this independent evaluation of consistency of MIGA projects with safeguard policies and guidelines, a set of basic criteria was developed reflecting key policy requirements and the necessary steps involved in meeting them. These criteria are summarized in Attachments 3a and 3b. This approach is similar to the one developed and used for a sample of World Bank EI projects by OED[297] in evaluating the compliance with WBG safeguards policies. They are based on MIGA's specific environmental assessment and disclosure policies and procedures, as well as the interim issue-specific safeguards,[298] as approved by MIGA's Board in 1999 and 2002, respectively, which differ somewhat from those of the World Bank to reflect MIGA's business model. MIGA's 2002 safeguards have adapted World Bank safeguards to the private sector. This has involved some simplifications and clarifications and in no case a tightening of World Bank safeguards.

This review was the first of its kind for MIGA projects and was undertaken to determine the status of a representative sample of EI projects on environmental and social fronts, using current standards. Using the most recent MIGA policies as criteria for consistency, rather than WBG policies and guidelines in effect at the time of approval of guarantees, enabled OEU to review the entire sample using the same criteria. OEU recognizes that the application of the safeguard policy framework has evolved considerably in MIGA since issuing the first guarantee in 1990 and that not all of the policies had the same degree of specificity. Furthermore, the Bank's and MIGA's procedures evolved over time as well. MIGA, as a member of the WBG, had subjected itself to WB policies and guidelines since the inception of the Agency and more explicitly since 1991, prior to adopting its own policies. Therefore, all projects covered by this review were subject to the WB policies at the time of their Board approval. MIGA's Board had the expectation that the projects it concurred with were fundamentally consistent with applicable WB policies and guidelines. For reasons of methodological soundness, this report does not refer to compliance (in its strict or legal meaning) across a period of 12 years (MIGA's operational history), but rather it assesses projects' consistency. The intention of this study was to learn about the extent to which MIGA EI projects were (and are) consistent with current applicable MIGA safeguard policies and guidelines. This approach also reflects the forward-looking nature of this evaluation and can inform decisions about possible future EI projects MIGA may be involved in.

The review focused on consistency with safeguards at two phases in the guaranteed investment cycle:

- *Consistency with Safeguards at Board Approval:* To what extent did the guaranteed investment comply or agree with the requirements of the current MIGA safeguard policies and guidelines at the time of Board approval?
- *Consistency with Safeguards under Guarantee:* To what extent did the project fulfill or agree with the conditions and requirements of the safeguard policies and guidelines (currently in force) during investment implementation and adequately implement the safeguard management/action plans that had been identified at approval?

The review found that 73 percent of the EI projects in the sample were substantially[299] consistent with current MIGA safeguard policies at the time of MIGA Board approval. This ratio increased to 88 percent during implementation, while the project was still under guarantee or at the time of cancellation of the guarantee. More-over, safeguard policy consistency showed an improving trend over the period of 1990–2001 for the sampled projects, for both stages—at approval and during project implementation (see Figure E3).

Safeguard Issues Prior to Board Approval

For 82 percent of the projects, the EAs, including analysis of alternatives and baseline studies, were well prepared by the time of Board approval.[301] However, this has not always translated into well-prepared EMPs or Environmental Management System (EMS) provisions in the sponsor's project organization and contracting arrangements during construction, which are the principal means for operationalizing the protective measures proposed under the EAs. The main problems of safeguard consistency identified at approval (see Table E1 and Attachment 5a) are (i) poor public consultation and disclosure in approximately half of the projects, (ii) inadequate provisions for safeguard compliance in Contracts of Guarantee in more than two-thirds of the projects, and (iii) deficiencies in application of issue specific safeguards, where relevant, such as involuntary resettlement (two-thirds of the projects), indigenous peoples (in all projects), natural habitats (in two-thirds of the projects), and dam safety (one-quarter of the projects).[302]

The projects reviewed included cases where (i) specific safeguards were not explicitly identified in the documents in the files, or were identified late in project processing (sometimes even after Board approval); (ii) instructions given to clients regarding specific safeguard requirements were not clear; (iii) requirements were not adequately communicated to consultants preparing EAs; and (iv) internal documents and clearances for Board approval were not sufficiently clear about which safeguard policies or environmental guidelines were applicable. The more common reasons for these problems identified by the review were (i) MIGA getting involved too late into the process; (ii) lack of social sector expertise in identifying applicable safeguards; (iii) underwriters not having the experience or necessary background, leading to poor initial communications with clients before

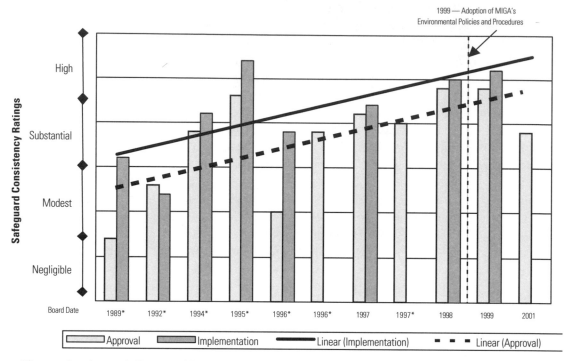

Figure E3 — Safeguard Consistency Ratings for MIGA Projects Show an Improving Trend[300]

* Guarantees for projects noted with an asterisk (*) are no longer active.

environmental staff got involved; (iv) institutional pressures to meet guarantee volume objectives for the fiscal year, which may have prevented some critical environmental verification (e.g., updating previous clearances if time elapsed was significant, additional site visits when needed); and (v) changes in project scope and design between Board approval and issuance of Contracts of Guarantee without further safeguard evaluation. The potential value added MIGA could provide tends to be downplayed at the underwriting and marketing stages of a prospective guarantee. It is unclear why in some of the projects reviewed safeguard policies were not triggered early enough—or not at all—in the underwriting process. Reviewed projects also provide some positive examples, suggesting that when safeguard policy issues are handled expeditiously and efficiently with clients, MIGA's intervention provides value added and a level of comfort.

The EAs that were reviewed varied in quality from relatively mediocre to the highest international standard. The scope and comprehensiveness of 82 percent of the EAs reviewed met basic MIGA requirements, as outlined in Attachment 3a. Some were developed over several years with many refinements and improvements added in the process and included extensive inputs from a variety of independent experts and reviews by competent regulatory authorities, as well as project-affected communities and NGOs. Cases were noted where MIGA (or IFC) experts provided important inputs during the process of EA review, which considerably improved their quality. There were other examples where their inputs were too late and had to be addressed after project approval. In one case, independent consultants hired by the major lenders identified a long list of deficiencies in the EA, which was initially prepared by one of the investors.

Table E1	Safeguard Consistency Summary for MIGA EI Projects at Board Approval (Based on a Review of 11 MIGA EI Projects)

Criterion	Applicable to (no. of projects)	Addressed *substantially* or *higher* (percent of projects)[a]
Cultural property protection proposed	7	100%
Comprehensive environmental assessment	11	82%
Comprehensive environmental and social baseline survey	11	82%
Comprehensive dam safety measures proposed	4	75%
Adequate environmental action plan proposed	11	73%
Adequate analysis of feasible alternatives	11	73%
Project sponsor's environmental management system adequate	11	64%
Public disclosure/consultation addressed	9	56%
Comprehensive and implementable resettlement plan/community development program prepared	9	33%
Natural habitats protected or offsets provided	6	33%
Contract of guarantee for implementation of safeguard	11	27%
Policies/guidelines adequate comprehensive and implementable indigenous peoples plan prepared	3	0%
Overall safeguard consistency	11	73%

Note: Four projects could not be reviewed as no monitoring reports were on file.

a. Four rating categories were used: negligible, modest, substantial, and high. See Attachment 3a for more details.

Addressing Mine Closure. The main issue in the application of the 1995 *Mining and Milling Guidelines—Open Pit* noted during the review was the requirement for preparation of a Mine Closure and Restoration Plan. It was not clear in the guideline when such a plan had to be prepared, at what level of detail, and when the investor needed to start accumulating funds for mine closure (as required in the 1998 version of this guideline). In some of the cases reviewed, the plan was required at the time the EA was prepared, but in others it was not until later, during project implementation, that MIGA (or IFC) made it clear that the plan was needed. Some clients argued that it was too early for them to prepare such plans at the final feasibility stage and include them in the EA, while others recognized that mine reclamation should be a progressive process and incorporated into the mine development plans (and financial plans) to minimize costs and reduce environmental (and social) impacts. In these cases, the plans were revised and adjusted during the operational phase as more experience was gained.

Public consultation and disclosure of environmental and social impacts was one of the weakest areas of safeguard consistency for the reviewed projects, with only about half substantially meeting MIGA's requirements.[303] In some projects, MIGA and IFC experts took great care to ensure that the clients were aware of their EA public disclosure obligations. In other cases, insufficient guidance was provided, and, as a result, too little attention was given to this matter. Some EAs were deficient in describing the public consultation process, while others were forthcoming and noted improvements that resulted from the process. Cases were noted where project decisions had already been made and the public disclosure process was seen as a pro-forma exercise, defeating the purpose of the MIGA policy. There were no cases where the MIGA disclosure policy delayed guarantee processing.

The review found that only one-third of the projects had adequate provisions for safeguard enforcement in the Contracts of Guarantee,[304] although even these did not refer to the individual safeguards that applied. In three more recent cases, the specific applicable Environmental Guidelines were indicated and attached to the contracts. The review of clearance memos also indicated a lack of clarity on the specific safeguard policies that applied to projects prior to approval. In only a few cases has MIGA included any specific environmental and social reporting requirements by its clients in its contracts.

OEU did not include ratings for one project selected for the safeguard review because of a lack of relevant information verifying the adequacy of the project's environmental classification. MIGA Management has taken action to provide the documentation, and OEU will complete the review of this project upon receipt of the relevant documents.

Safeguard Issues During Project Implementation

As noted above, there was notable improvement in the safeguard performance of the sample of extractive industry projects during their implementation (see Table E2 and Attachment 5b). Of particular note is the high level of performance in (i) implementing Environmental

Action Plans (EAP)/EMPs, (ii) carrying out environmental and social monitoring,[305] (iii) operating Environmental and Health and Safety Management Systems, and (iv) generally improved consistency with specific safeguard policies, with the exception of the natural habitats policy. Public consultation and disclosure, a key area, continued to fall short of good practice in one-third of the projects reviewed, in particular in three Category 'A' projects underwritten before FY00, when MIGA's Environmental Review Procedures and Disclosure Policies went into effect. Reporting on safeguard policy consistency by clients and monitoring and evaluation by MIGA could also be improved.

The most important factor in ensuring safeguard compliance is a committed investor with the capacity to implement the environmental, health and safety, and social mitigation and monitoring programs that are required under the project and spelled out in the EAs.

One case illustrated what can go wrong if management and organizational structure set up for project management during the construction phase become too autonomous and disconnected from the environmentally and socially responsible policies and procedures of the individual investors. The case also showed that a company can learn from experience. It was only after receiving public complaints against the project that MIGA came to realize the seriousness of the situation and fielded a mission to assist the investor in restoring its public image and helping it to act as a responsible corporate citizen. This case also clearly illustrates both MIGA's positive contribution in this process and the need for MIGA to take a more proactive approach in evaluating clients' organizational and management arrangements to satisfy itself that they are adequate for implementing responsible environmental and social policies from the very start of project construction. Risks and costs associated with consequences for inadequately addressed social and environmental issues, for both MIGA and the investors, are high and increase throughout the life of the project (see Box E1).

Environmental Management Plans/Environmental Action Plans. Environmental and

Table E2	Safeguard Consistency Summary for MIGA EI Projects Under Guarantee (Based on a Review of 11 MIGA EI Projects)	
Criterion	**Applicable to (no. of projects)**	**Addressed *substantially* or *higher* (percent of projects)[a]**
Environmental action plan/environmental management plan fully implemented by sponsor	8	100%
Environmental and social monitoring fully implemented by sponsor	8	88%
Sponsor's project implementation environmental management system effective	8	88%
Resettlement plan/community development program fully implemented	7	86%
Full compensation of project affected people	6	83%
Cultural property protected	6	83%
Dam safety measures implemented	4	75%
Indigenous peoples plan fully implomonted	3	67%
Continuing public disclosure and consultation	8	63%
Reporting on safeguard policies by sponsor adequate	10	60%
Monitoring and evaluation of safeguard policies by MIGA adequate	10	60%
Natural habitats protected or offsets provided	6	50%
Overall safeguard consistency	8	88%

Note: Four projects could not be reviewed as no monitoring reports were on file.

a. Four rating categories were used: negligible, modest, substantial, and high. See Attachment 3b for more details.

social action plans are the key outputs from the preparation and approval stages of MIGA projects. There are good examples among MIGA projects reviewed where these action plans have been taken seriously by investors—usually those in which the investors were directly involved in their preparation and finalization. There were other cases where the action plans were prepared by independent consultants without full endorsement by investors. EMP/EAPs were substantially implemented by all of the investors for the projects reviewed, in some cases with persistent prodding by MIGA's (or IFC's) environmental and social experts. Some investors incorporated the EMPs into their EMS monitoring and auditing programs to ensure that they were fully implemented. In such cases, variances from the plan were noted, as were action plans drawn up to fulfill these requirements.

Land acquisition and resettlement was substantially accomplished according to the requirements of MIGA's involuntary resettlement policy

Box E1	A Company Learns How to Handle Social and Environmental Issues

The evolution of this project's handling of social and environmental issues, and MIGA's role in the process, provides important lessons. During the early construction phase of 1998–99, priority was given to earliest possible project completion and cost efficiency. The contractor coordinated only with the project management side and had no line of communication with the company's operations side, which was responsible for the eventual operation of the mining facility, including environmental protection and community relations. As a result, concerns and messages coming from the company's operations side during the construction phase were not addressed by the project management, resulting in a gap between expectations of the local community and actions of the project. It also generated several social and environmental problems:

- An accelerated resettlement program of more than 40 indigenous families carried out inadequately during March and April 1999, which led to social discontent, was a clear indication that a culture of social responsibility had not yet permeated project management and organization.
- In terms of governance, not much effort was devoted to strengthening local organizations.
- Economic linkages to the local economy were not activated, as no initiatives were taken to implement programs of local employment, training, or procurement.

- No appropriate mechanism was implemented to ensure timely advice to those communities and persons who received substantial amounts of money for their land in a noncash economy.

This situation led to complaint letters to MIGA, which sent a mission to the field to investigate the matter in May 2000. Reacting to the widespread dissatisfaction in neighboring communities, the company began working on community relations and took corrective action in early 2000. MIGA's involvement at this precise time appears to have had a positive effect, changing the priorities and attitude of project management with respect to community and environmental issues. However, the management structure was modified only after project construction was completed in mid-2001. In mid-2002, one year after production start-up, the company implemented a new organizational structure more consistent with the social and environmental concerns of a modern mining company. Under the new structure, the chief executive officer is responsible for the operational, financial, and environmental aspects, as well as community relations. This new unified structure facilitates coordination and teamwork among different departments and the articulation of a common objective for operational and social and environmental areas. It should enable the company to address environmental and social issues more proactively in the future.

in 86 percent of the projects reviewed. This was a great improvement over the situation at project approval, when only 33 percent of the projects had adequately prepared resettlement plans. It reflects a conscientious effort by MIGA (and IFC) to bring these projects into conformance with the social safeguard policies during the implementation phase. However, there were deficiencies in applying the policies, which should be noted for future reference and attention. In regard to those projects where land acquisition and resettlement occurred before MIGA involvement, the policy requires monitoring and evaluation of its implementation and then, upon completion, an assessment of the outcomes to see

if the objectives of the policy have been met in the process. This was not carried out.

In two-thirds of the projects, investors were active in implementing community development activities to mitigate the impacts of their operations on local communities. In projects where IFC was also involved, it promoted these activities to investors, while MIGA played a critical catalytic role in one project. The community development programs have focused on improving services such as health, education, and water supply and sanitation services in project-affected communities, and they have promoted economic development, including job creation, training, and credit for small-scale business activities and improved agricultural practices.

With regard to other specific safeguards, closer attention by investors to indigenous peoples' issues during implementation resulted in substantial consistency in two of the three projects with the requirements of this safeguard policy. Tailings dam safety has been a concern that has been highlighted by well-publicized failures, so it is not surprising that most mining companies are sensitive to this issue and take it seriously. Seventy-five percent of the projects reviewed with dam heights in excess of 10 to 15 meters were substantially consistent with this safeguard policy at Board approval, as well as during implementation. The most serious concerns during implementation were leaking dams and sealing problems at abutments, which required pump-back of the leaked tailings water; failure in one case to remove trees and tree roots from the tailings impoundment, which compromised the integrity of the dam foundations; poor construction practices without adequate supervision; and poor operating practices that allowed ponding in front of dam walls. One of the mining projects previously evaluated by MIGA experienced a tailings dam failure while under MIGA guarantee, releasing large quantities of cyanide-contaminated water into a downstream river system. In this case, MIGA was a reinsurer, and it lacked the legal ability to apply and monitor its safeguard policies.[306] In another instance, crates of cyanide fell into a river in a traffic accident while being transported to the mine site. Since these incidents, MIGA has paid closer attention to safety matters in the transportation of hazardous substances for EI projects.

The only safeguard for which the consistency outcomes were not appreciably improved during implementation was the natural habitats policy. Only half of the projects substantially conformed with this policy during implementation, although one project was taking steps to meet the requirements when it was prematurely shut down and put on a care and maintenance basis.

The review also found that three MIGA-guaranteed projects were vulnerable to social unrest, which may have been exacerbated by security-related incidents leading to claims of violations of individual rights. In those three projects, MIGA did not separately consider issues related to conflict in the context of the projects as part of its underwriting. However, MIGA's development mandate encompasses a concern for such potential negative impacts on individuals in host countries. This is also a political risk issue with the potential to affect both the project (increased conflict) and MIGA (claims brought under war and civil disturbance coverage, as well as reputational risk). Another MIGA project entailed a dispute with a neighboring country regarding ownership of the resource. MIGA treated this issue thoroughly in its political risk assessment.[307]

The variety of reporting mechanisms that were noted in the projects provide good lessons on the quality and usefulness of the information provided for assessing environmental and social risks and safeguard consistency of projects under guarantee. Examples of good reporting were provided by (i) independent experts hired by senior lenders, (ii) independent auditing experts hired by the investor, (iii) investor head-office auditing teams, (iv) monthly or quarterly reporting by clients to lenders and MIGA, and (v) MIGA and IFC environmental and social specialists in mission reports and internal memos. MIGA does not require AMRs from its clients. Reporting on social impacts and compliance with social safeguards continues to be weak in MIGA's reporting system, although there were some good examples in the case studies of independent auditing of involuntary resettlement and indigenous peoples plans.

There was a frequent and steady flow of monitoring reports from clients or independent consultants hired by senior lenders or bilateral investment insurers in 60 percent of projects reviewed. In about half of the projects, MIGA benefited from an independent review of the project EA by consultants hired by senior lenders or bilateral investment insurers. The independent review requirements of the senior lenders and bilateral investment insurers focused only on the environmental and health and safety aspects of the proposed investments, except in one case in which social issues were also addressed. In none of the cases did MIGA hire outside independent expertise to carry out its due diligence work on the projects reviewed, relying on the investor, or other external agencies, to finance this work. The downside to this arrangement is that MIGA does not have any control of the scope of the consultants' work, the quality of the consultants hired, or the frequency and timeliness of their reporting. The main deficiencies in the independent assessments have been on the social issues, except in a few cases where such expertise has been specifically hired by investors to evaluate their resettlement and social programs. There were no monitoring reports in MIGA files for one Category 'A' project and one Category 'B' project, even though they had been under implementation for more than three years.

MIGA has limited in-house capacity to adequately monitor and influence social safeguard outcomes. For the sampled projects where IFC was involved in the financing arrangements, MIGA delegated monitoring of environmental and social aspects to IFC, which carried out a systematic supervision of the projects, including site visits (on behalf of both MIGA and IFC). Social specialists have been involved in field visits from the beginning of project processing in only one case. The observed pattern has been a delayed involvement (including field visits), often after Board approval, resulting in increased project cost and delays and generating dissatisfaction among project stakeholders. Investors have benefited considerably from environmental and social specialists' site visits and advice in IFC/MIGA projects. Investors have expressed their appreciation for these inputs, in particular for dealing with land acquisition, resettlement, and community development issues, where the WBG has substantial experience and competitive advantage.

3. Development Impacts of MIGA EI Projects

The findings on the development impacts of MIGA EI projects presented in this section are drawn from six MIGA projects in the EI sector evaluated between FY99 and FY00 and one case study conducted in FY02–03. The six have been updated and validated through a desk review to arrive at rating categories consistent with OEU's new evaluation methodology, whereas the case study applied this new methodology for the first time to a project evaluation.[308]

All projects, most of them gold mines (and one copper and one cobalt extraction/processing), were approved in the early to mid-1990s, when gold prices were higher than $350 per ounce. Metals prices, including gold, fell precipitously in the second half of the 1990s. The price of gold fell to below $300 per ounce toward the end of the 1990s, greatly reducing, and in some cases totally eliminating, returns to equity investors.

Quality of underwriting and risk assessment: An analysis of the underwriting of the seven projects found that MIGA's assessment of the projects' financial viability was generally thorough and based on the best information available from the clients at that time, although assumptions on metals prices, volume, and quality proved to be optimistic. All seven project assessments also provided an estimated ERR, but none of the cases explained the underlying assumptions of the ERR calculation, so that it was not possible to judge their validity (or calculate a comparable ex-post ERR). Some instances were noted where backward linkages appeared somewhat overestimated (e.g., in the purchases of fuel or electric power, where value added is extremely low), as was the case for infrastructure improvements (some deterioration in infrastructure was neglected, whereas other improvements had very little impact due to the remoteness of the location). In another case, credit was claimed for health and educational services available only to employees, which is considered a standard compensation package. On risk assessments, all project analyses went into substantial detail on the three major political risks MIGA insured, and most of the problems related to these risks were fully identified and appraised. However, there was no discussion of the potential risk from a low financial return if the government owned a significant share of the company (one project).

In general, during the underwriting of the reviewed projects, there was a compartmentalized approach defined by the source of the information. For example, financial analysis and projections, as well as anticipated economic data, were provided by investors; partial development analysis was carried out by MIGA underwriters; environmental and social issues were addressed by investors with MIGA inputs; and risk analysis was undertaken by MIGA underwriters. EI projects reviewed were complex, involved large investments and revenues for the host governments, and had important environmental and social implications, subjecting them to close public and international scrutiny. Thus, they required a more up-front and in-depth analysis and a holistic understanding of financial, economic, social, and environmental aspects from a developmental perspective.

The Risk Management Committee, established as a result of the Guarantees Business Process Review undertaken in 1998, brings together guarantees, legal, environmental, financial, and risk aspects during the decision-making stage for potential guarantees. While it has provided a forum for the discussion of many aspects of the newer EI projects covered in this evaluation, these discussions are not adequately informed by full assessments of the social issues and developmental impacts frequently encountered in complex projects in the EI sector.[309]

Business Performance and Financial Sustainability: Low Metals Prices Suppressed Profitability of EI Projects

Financial returns in all seven projects were affected by the fall in metals prices. In assessing financial benefits, all projects had assumed that metals prices would remain stable over the project lifetime. The commodity price margins within which the projects were expected to be profitable widely varied. Only one of the projects was still financially profitable at the gold prices that prevailed during the latter part of the 1990s and through mid-2002. The evaluated cobalt project was hit hardest and placed on care and maintenance in late 2002 until such time as the metal's price returned to near its pre-project level. Two of the evaluated projects had moderately satisfactory ratings for financial sus-

tainability, two were rated moderately unsatisfactory, and three had an unsatisfactory rating.

Revenues to host governments from equity holdings have been disappointing, and little is known about their use. Low metals prices, coupled with significant cost overruns and/or lower-than-anticipated ore quality in some projects, resulted in low financial returns to equity holders. In cases where governments held equity in compensation for providing a proven gold reserve, this has had a profound impact on their return to equity and expectations of significant revenues were not fulfilled. In at least some cases, governments have been aggrieved that they have received little or no benefits from the valuable natural resources that they have allowed foreign companies to exploit. Clearly, the more a government relies on proceeds from equity ownership rather than taxes and royalties, the greater its dependency on good financial outcomes of the mine. Analyses of the developmental impacts of EI projects by MIGA underwriters, in general, have made no attempt to assess the use of EI revenues by governments, focusing mainly on the private investment project itself. (The Main Report of this joint OED/OEG/OEU evaluation addresses the issue of the use of EI revenues by governments for the World Bank Group.)

Economic Sustainability: Financial Performance Limits Economic Benefits

Overall, economic sustainability was marginally better than financial sustainability for these projects, with two projects rated moderately satisfactory, three others rated moderately unsatisfactory, and two rated unsatisfactory for economic sustainability.

Economic sustainability of these projects also largely depended on the price of the mineral resource, moving in parallel with financial sustainability and profitability. This is because the profitability of the project not only influences the amount of resources the project has available for supporting local community initiatives, but, more importantly, it is a major determinant of the mine life. The volume of economically mineable resources (and therefore the number of years that the mine will operate and provide jobs and other benefits to the country/community) is highly dependent on the price of these resources.

The most important benefits of these projects to their host countries were in the areas of employment creation, often in remote and depressed areas; training; and government revenues. The seven projects created, on average, 710 jobs, with a range of 0[310] to 1,375. Except for two projects, local employment at the time of evaluation was higher than initially anticipated. One of the exceptions is an operation that was put on care and maintenance due to its unprofitability under current metal prices. All evaluated projects allocated resources to training (an average of US$1,200 per employee per year). Although aggregated annual government revenues fell short of initial expectations by more than 50 percent, the contributions to local and central government budgets were still significant (averaging between US$5 and US$10 million per year) for most projects. Within the scope of this evaluation, OEU did not assess the effectiveness of the use of EI revenues by the host country governments (nor was there a baseline analysis of these issues in MIGA underwriting documents), as it is beyond the reach of private sector projects that MIGA guarantees. All evaluated projects have supported local government financing and local initiatives to varying degrees. In more general terms, projects with a nearby labor pool and communities were more successful in generating direct economic benefits for those communities. There is evidence that projects that allocated more funds to local authorities and affected populations were more favorably viewed and had fewer social problems than those where most of the funds went to central government activities.

Private Sector Development: Supporting Countries' Private Sector Development Agendas

The majority of the evaluated projects made positive contributions to private sector development in their host countries. Five projects were rated moderately satisfactory, and two were rated moderately unsatisfactory.

All of the projects were consistent with and supported the private sector strategies of their host countries. Most projects under review were in countries where private investors had been hesitant to make large investments, either because there had been only limited experience working with new governments, or because investors' experience in previous projects with earlier governments had led to significant difficulties. In another case (see Box E2), the project was the first and largest mining development in the country, following a comprehensive sector reform, with an important demonstration effect for other projects. Each investment was expected to generate a substantial increase in private investment in the country's mining sector.

Government relations with project entities remained good in all the projects reviewed, and, other things being equal, the experience of the projects would have supported further investment in the sector. However, this expectation has not been fulfilled, probably because of the fall of metals prices through most of the late 1990s and the more recent global slowdown, which curbed investor interest in this complex sector. However, there was evidence that some mining investments guaranteed by MIGA in a particular country were viewed as pioneer investments, thereby changing foreign investors' perceptions about its investment climate and leading to increased foreign investments in other sectors in the country.

In addition to demonstration effects and follow-up investments in some cases, the projects all enhanced private ownership in the host countries and contributed, to varying degrees, to the development of downstream linkages. Some projects had local business development programs in place to increase the amount of local purchases, as significant backward linkages were rarely automatic, and specific programs appeared to be needed to maximize such linkages. In addition, evaluated projects supported some infrastructure improvements, some of which benefited adjacent communities and regions.

Box E2	**Demonstrating the Viability of Mining**

This project, underwritten in the second half of the 1990s, is the largest mining project in the host country involving mining and copper/gold ore processing at the mine site to recover copper and gold in concentrate, as well as gold doré. It was the first mining project following a major change in government policy designed to encourage development of a mining industry and to diversify the economy and exports. MIGA provided coverage against losses due to transfer restriction, expropriation, and war and civil disturbance for a minority equity investor and a shareholder loan. The MIGA coverage was part of a much larger political risk insurance package provided by national insurance agencies, covering commercial risks. MIGA's political risk insurance coverage supported a loan package on highly favorable terms, which encouraged the equity investors to make large investments in a new mining country. MIGA's role in facilitating this investment was thus rated *satisfactory*.

The project's objectives were consistent with the World Bank's strategy and support for mining sector reform, which helped set up a legal and fiscal framework—considered best practice—to encourage the development of the mining industry. Development of the sector, however, was hampered by the economic downturn and declining metals prices, leading to a drop in investment in the sector. However, the ability of the project to establish and operate a large-scale mine, albeit at relatively modest financial and economic returns, has given confidence to other potential investors in the industry. This has encouraged additional exploration and investment in other mining projects. Overall, the PSD impact of the project was rated *moderately satisfactory*.

The project's financial rate of return is expected to be below the rate initially estimated by the investors. This difference is due to (1) cost overruns in constructing the mine and processing facilities, (2) lower ore content, and (3) lower-than-expected metals prices. The estimate for the economic rate of return was similarly revised downward, but it is somewhat higher than the financial rate of return because of taxes paid (although these were lower than anticipated) and is enhanced by wage payments to previously unemployed workers and by the training provided. The project's economic sustainability was rated *moderately unsatisfactory*. A number of additional benefits arose from the mine: an electrical connection for a nearby city, making electricity available at lower prices; rehabilitation of transport infrastructure linking the region with a port, which is usable by others; and social expenditures for education and community programs.

The main environmental concerns were related to the selection of the right-of-way for support infrastructure, where it was necessary to avoid sensitive and important natural habitats, as well as cultural heritage sites. The mining operations are well designed for total capture and evaporation in the tailings reservoir of process tailings water and all-site run-off water. The tailings dam has been designed and is being operated and inspected to conform to MIGA dam safety standards. The environmental performance of this project was rated *moderately satisfactory*.

Although the social impact of the mine has been relatively benign, the expectations of the local population for employment opportunities and backward linkages to local businesses have remained unfulfilled. This reflects, in part, a failure of national and regional governments to prepare the local population to take advantage of opportunities created by the development and operation of the mine and the failure of the company to initiate a dialogue with adjacent communities and the government to build stakeholder support and to reach a consensus on human and regional development the project could foster.

4. MIGA's Role in EI Projects: Contribution, Effectiveness, and Staff Perceptions

One of the objectives of this evaluation was to assess MIGA's role in EI projects. The safeguard review, update and validation of previously evaluated projects, and case studies all looked at MIGA's contribution and effectiveness. MIGA's business is distinct from that of the Bank and IFC. "MIGA neither invests, grants nor lends money to investors, nor does it propose or design projects. Like any other form of insurance, investors and lenders who want this coverage pay premiums."[311] Clearly, because MIGA offers political risk insurance, a primary dimension of its contribution is expected to be the facilitation or enabling of FDI in countries and sectors where perceptions of political risk are high. However, as a member of the WBG, MIGA's potential to add value is broader than that of a traditional insurer and encompasses environmental, social, and developmental impacts of the projects it insures. In reference to this role, MIGA has also noted that "in order for investments to provide development opportunities for local communities, the projects must be environmentally and socially sound. Therefore, in carrying out its mission, it is MIGA's policy that all the foreign investments that it insures are carried out in an environmentally and socially responsible manner."[312] Against this background, defining the value MIGA adds, as a member of the WBG, is even more important.

With respect to the environmental and social dimensions of EI projects, MIGA's role has evolved over the period covered by this evaluation, with a clearly improving trend. More recently, the concept of MIGA's role has been more appropriately articulated as its "value added" to the projects it guarantees. The findings of this evaluation indicate that there are areas where MIGA has added substantial value for some projects, while for others, MIGA's role has been more that of a traditional insurer (i.e., limited to providing political risk coverage). The latter is more likely when guarantee holders are lenders or minority partners and less so if they are majority owners or operators.

MIGA's Contribution and Effectiveness

This subsection draws on findings from the evaluated projects to assess to what extent and in which ways MIGA had contributed to their improvement or success. These findings show that MIGA's role and the degree and nature of its contributions varied widely, as the agency changed its approach over the period covered by this evaluation.

Where Was MIGA's Value Added Lowest?

Business performance of projects. As expected from its Operational Regulations and

role as an insurer, this review has found that MIGA plays no direct role in the financial performance of EI projects, although the agency provides a potential safety net against the impact of political risks. (While a reduction in political risks may have the potential to lower the cost of capital and enhance financial performance indirectly, an analysis of this relationship was not carried out in the scope of this evaluation.) As an insurer with the primary mandate to facilitate investment, MIGA does not participate in the operational or financial management of the project, and, thus, its room for action is very limited. Nevertheless, the financial viability of its guarantee projects is highly relevant for MIGA's long-term financial sustainability, as poor financial performance can lead to early cancellation of guarantees.

Project development impact/outcome. The development impacts of evaluated projects, as presented in previous sections, have varied. Once a guarantee is issued, MIGA does not normally influence the development impact of the project and has not done so in any of the projects reviewed. (In one project, MIGA had a positive role in community and environmental issues. See Box E1.) Moreover, no follow-up development information about the reviewed projects existed in MIGA's files, except if it had an ex-post evaluation (i.e., the six validated projects). The key role is therefore for MIGA to select projects with high potential development impact through the underwriting process.

Where Was MIGA's Value Added Highest?

Facilitating foreign investments. The provision of political risk insurance is a core tool for MIGA to facilitate FDI and the basis for the agency's most important value added. Evaluated EI investments were primarily in countries in which private foreign investors had been reluctant to make large investments because of either limited experience with new governments or difficulties faced by previous investments in that country or sector. In these cases, MIGA's political risk insurance was important for enabling investment flows into the mining and oil and gas sectors and in some cases has led the way for other investments in the host countries. MIGA has acted as a facilitator of investments, often with other partners, that otherwise would have been delayed or avoided. MIGA insurance was essential for most projects evaluated, given their location in countries with high political risks and low governance scores, and large sunk costs associated with investments in EI projects. In some cases, investments would not have gone forward without MIGA's involvement.

Environmental and Social Safeguards. Apart from reducing political risk for investors, the other area where MIGA has added value was in the incorporation, and/or enforcement of safeguards in EI projects and the advice MIGA experts (or those performing this function on MIGA's behalf) have provided to clients. All EI projects reviewed have to some degree benefited from the incorporation of environmental and social safeguards, even though not all of the projects have attained a level of full consistency with MIGA safeguard policies. The association with the World Bank Group has been perceived by most investors both as an umbrella for their projects and as a source of knowledge and best practice on environmental and social aspects. In some cases, international investors have applied their own high standards consistent with international best practice.

In one case (a high-profile project with environmental and social ramifications), because the sponsor requested that MIGA provide coverage that would address land rights disputes, MIGA (with advice from IFC) followed the land negotiations process in great detail and obliged the sponsor to provide detailed information on both the consultation process and the results of the land usage agreement. MIGA then verified the validity of the process and results with government and civil society organizations at national, regional, and local levels. In another case, MIGA's value added came during project implementation rather than at the design stage (see Box E1).

In some projects, MIGA delegated environmental and social safeguards aspects to its partners, who took the responsibility for due diligence. These arrangements worked reasonably well (and were cost-effective) for MIGA when the partner adhered to similar environmental and social policies and guidelines (e.g., IFC). However, when a partner carrying out due diligence on MIGA's behalf had lower standards than MIGA, it led to unsatisfactory results. This was the case in one project reviewed, where MIGA's reinsurance agreement predated the new MIGA practice by which the reinsured project must adhere to MIGA's environmental standards.

The results from several projects also demonstrate that well-designed plans for minimizing social impacts can greatly reduce social conflicts, thereby reducing the occurrence of some of the risks MIGA guarantees. Thus, there is a strong business case for MIGA to add value by remaining engaged and providing more proactive social and environmental advice to its clients involved in extractive industries projects.

Staff Perceptions

WBG EI staff survey results: Divergence of Operations Evaluation Unit findings from MIGA staff perceptions. The WBG EI survey was administered to relevant Bank, IFC, and MIGA staff. In MIGA, all current MIGA staff who have been directly involved with EI projects (either as underwriters or project managers) were asked to respond to the survey (the same set of questions was given to World Bank and IFC staff involved in EI sector projects).[313] MIGA responses to the survey (Box E3) show some important differences from OEU evaluation findings of EI projects. One notable divergence is in the area of addressing environmental and social aspects of EI projects: all (9 out of 9) MIGA staff who responded felt that the issue of mitigating environmental and social impacts was highly important and, at the same time, all (9 out of 9 who responded) also felt that these issues had been adequately addressed in MIGA-guaranteed EI projects. However, OEU's safeguards review indicated that about 27 percent of EI projects had substantial gaps and were not fully consistent with environ-

Box E3	Main Messages from Responses by MIGA Staff in WBG EI Survey

The survey was administered to all MIGA staff (12) previously involved in EI projects, with a response rate of 83 percent (10 out of 12). While the absolute numbers are small (as MIGA itself is small, with a total of 78 International staff), it represents the statistical population of MIGA staff who have worked on the EI sector projects. In parallel, the same survey was sent to 51 World Bank staff, with 26 responding (51 percent of EI staff), and to 33 IFC staff, with 30 responding (91 percent). (Because not all respondents provided answers to all questions, the total number of respondents to specific questions are noted below.)

Importance of EI-related issues for EI-dependent countries: Almost all MIGA and WBG respondents agreed with the importance of all EI issues the survey questionnaire had identified. In particular, *all* (9 out of 9) MIGA respondents agreed with the importance of mitigating negative environmental and social impacts. On the other hand, the investment climate and governance and transparency were considered highly important by only one-third (3 out of 9) of MIGA respondents, whereas a higher share (two-thirds) of IFC and World Bank respondents felt these were highly important in EI projects.

Extent to which EI projects address EI-related issues: The majority of MIGA respondents and about two-thirds or more of all WBG respondents felt that WBG projects collectively and adequately addressed all major issues, except the improvement of transparency and governance. Moreover, all (9 out of 9)

MIGA respondents felt that the mitigation of negative environmental impacts (same proportion for IFC) and revenue generation had been adequately addressed in past EI projects.

Coordination across WBG for the EI sector: All (8 of 8) MIGA respondents considered the coordination across the WBG as adequate, while only 48 percent of IFC respondents and 52 percent of World Bank respondents considered the level of coordination as sufficient.

Avoidance of EI projects due to safeguards concerns: Among the possible sources of avoidance of potential EI projects due to safeguard concerns, MIGA respondents identified WBG management (6 out of 6) and EI public agencies/enterprises (3 out of 4) as the top two leading causes. While all WBG respondents also cited WBG management as a primary cause, only 21 percent of World Bank respondents and 56 percent of IFC respondents considered EI public agencies/enterprises an important factor.

Factors constraining the ability of WBG staff to assist client countries in EI sector: More than half of MIGA respondents (5 out of 9) cited the inadequate linkage between EI sector activities and sustainable development as the major factor constraining their ability to assist host countries in the EI sector. In addition, less than one-third of MIGA respondents cited inadequate availability of staff with appropriate skills, inadequate level of support from the Bank's Country Department/Country Management Unit, and inadequate level of support from the client government.

mental and social safeguards.[314] One possible explanation for this divergence is the relatively short tenure of the respondents in MIGA. This could have influenced their views in focusing on the current, rather than historical, perspective. However, 7 out of 10 MIGA respondents were also directly involved in five projects covered in this review, increasing the relevance of their answers.

The joint WBG evaluation (as reflected in the Main Report) identified the lack of adequate coordination among the three WBG organizations as a problem that constrains the delivery

of better results in EI projects. However, all (8 out of 8) MIGA respondents indicated that, in their view, the level of coordination was adequate, which may suggest a desire to preserve MIGA's operational "autonomy" (i.e., not getting too involved with WBG operations/processes). These results are also likely to be a reflection of the differences in products, clientele, and procedures between the Bank and MIGA, where staff see opportunities for coordination as inherently limited to policy and strategy matters. Similarly, very few (2 out of 7) MIGA staff felt that there was a need for better support from

World Bank country units, in contrast to IFC's staff perceptions.

MIGA respondents (6 out of 6) also felt that WBG (World Bank, IFC, and MIGA) management is the most likely cause for avoiding good EI projects due to perceived risks and the time needed to address safeguard concerns. These responses indicate that staff find WBG management is overly cautious and also some (4) believe that public agencies interfere with, rather than facilitate, MIGA's work. On the other hand, none of the respondents felt that concerns from host countries about safeguards were a source for avoiding good EI projects.

5. Findings and Recommendations

MIGA's activities in the extractive industry sectors have evolved significantly in the period under review (in particular since 1997), improving its operations at approval and during implementation and learning from its experience in underwriting 31 projects. Noteworthy milestones are its Business Process Review, the creation of an in-house environmental unit, the environmental assessment and disclosure polices, the approval of interim issue-specific safeguard policies, and the updating of its guarantee contract language and reinsurance practice.

MIGA's approach over the years has followed the guidance of its Convention, Article 2 of which states that "the objective of the Agency shall be to encourage the flow of investments for productive purposes." Article 12 requires the Agency to satisfy itself as to "the economic soundness of the investment and its contribution to the development of the host country" and to the "consistency of the investment with the declared development objectives and priorities of the host country." These objectives also underpin MIGA's need to use environmental and social standards for the projects it insures. As standards for successful development have become more complex and sophisticated, MIGA has adapted its safeguard policies and its analyses of the development impact of projects. MIGA continues to refine and augment the scope of its selection criteria. The findings and recommendations listed in this section are intended to contribute to this process.

Findings

Portfolio

Extractive industry projects and guarantees constitute a declining share of MIGA's portfolio. Mining was originally the largest share of MIGA's guarantees, making up more than half of its portfolio. Extractive industries now constitute about 11 percent (6.6 percent mining and 4.3 percent oil and gas), and MIGA continues to be engaged in the sector.

Application of Environmental and Social Safeguards

Consistency of project performance with safeguards has generally been greater during implementation than at approval, and the trend in safeguard performance has been improving over time. On average, the rate of substantial consistency with MIGA's safeguard policies of EI projects improved from 73 percent (at Board approval) to 88 percent (during implementation or at guarantee cancellation). This likely reflects the expansion of MIGA's efforts and of its capacity in safeguard areas since 1997.

- **At Board approval, the greatest areas of weakness in safeguard performance** have been in consultation and disclosure, inadequate incorporation of safeguard issues in contracts of guarantee, and in specific elements, including resettlement, indigenous peoples, natural habitats, dam safety, and lack of clarity on mine closure provisions.
- **During implementation, the greatest areas of weakness in safeguard performance** have been in consultation and disclosure, final assessment of resettlement implementation, and natural habitats. Reporting on social impacts and social safeguard compliance has also been weak.

Insufficient attention paid to consistency with social safeguards is the most sensitive and critical issue in extractive industries projects. Only one-third of the sampled projects that involved indigenous peoples and resettlement and community development issues had prepared a comprehensive and implementable Resettlement Plan (RP) or Community Development Program (CDP). Not a single reviewed project (where these safeguards were applicable) had a comprehensive and implementable IPP at Board approval.

None of the contracts issued for the projects under review specified the safeguard policies that applied, and only a few indicated the WBG's environmental, health, and safety guidelines that applied. Although all recent MIGA contracts allow MIGA to terminate the contract if the project does not comply with MIGA's environmental polices and guidelines and there has been a more consistent effort in reference to this requirement since 1999, this may not be sufficient to ensure investors' awareness of specific applicable policies and guidelines.

MIGA has not consistently required environmental and social monitoring reports from its guarantee holders in its contract of guarantee. In two-thirds of the reviewed projects, senior lenders, bilateral agencies, or the major investors provided regular monitoring reports on environmental (and sometimes social) issues that allowed MIGA to monitor safeguard compliance. However, in four projects there were no follow-up monitoring reports from investors, leaving MIGA in a vulnerable position regarding safeguards implementation.

Committed investors with the capacity to implement mitigation and monitoring programs have been an important factor in ensuring better safeguard compliance.

Internal Capacity

Environmental performance was treated more thoroughly by MIGA in the second half of the 1990s than in the first half, especially after the creation of an environmental unit. MIGA relied on environmental and social experts of IFC or of other parties in the project

before establishing its own unit. In 6 of 12 projects reviewed, independent monitoring and reporting initiatives were taken by either senior lenders or other insurers and not by MIGA. In some earlier projects, there was no explicit contractual obligation and no recourse to MIGA for the project to comply with safeguard policies. MIGA environmental specialists visited 5 of the 12 projects reviewed, following the establishment of the in-house environmental unit. MIGA could have had greater impact on improving project performance had it taken a more proactive approach earlier in its history.

MIGA's due diligence model (and current capacity) is not sufficient to adequately address social aspects of extractive industries projects. The current MIGA approach of gearing the processes of monitoring and supervision, directing its resources and staff selectively to projects after problems emerge, is not appropriate for dealing with complex social issues often associated with EI sector projects. Systematic and proactive monitoring, including site visits by MIGA experts, to identify the nature of possible gaps in safeguards and potential problems is a critical element of the due diligence process. It is particularly important to assess the social risks at critical project cycle milestones, which cannot be adequately done through desk reviews.

MIGA's delayed involvement in extractive industries projects has meant missed opportunities to add value or to improve projects' environmental and social performance. One consequence is that projects' environmental and social management systems are not in place at the start of project construction; this can lead to adverse social and environmental impacts due to the lack of control over the work of contractors. This is the most critical period for investors in their relationship with project-affected communities, and any good will that has been generated during their previous dealings (and promises) with the community can quickly sour, leaving investors with a difficult legacy to overcome when the project becomes operational.

Development Impacts and Underwriting

The evaluated extractive industries sector projects generally have produced positive economic impacts in host countries, but investor returns have been disappointing. Actual financial returns to investors were lower than originally anticipated, due to decreasing metals prices in the late 1990s, as well as cost overruns and lower ore quality than expected. The projects provided jobs, training, revenues to the government, and funds to community initiatives and had demonstration effects for private sector development. Host governments have received less revenue than they expected because of the poorer-than-expected economic and financial performance of extractive industry projects.

MIGA's underwriting for extractive industries projects reviewed was generally thorough, and project assessments were based on the information available from the clients at that time, although their components could have been better integrated. Analysis was compartmentalized by the sources of the information (e.g., investors, MIGA underwriters, and environmental specialists). While most elements are combined when projects are assessed, economic and social analyses and impacts have not been well integrated. EI projects reviewed were complex, involved large investments and revenues for the host governments, and had important environmental and social implications, subjecting them to close public and international scrutiny. Thus, they required a more holistic understanding of financial, economic, social, and environmental aspects from a developmental perspective.

Security-related incidents in MIGA-guaranteed extractive industries projects involving allegations of violations of individual rights can pose particularly high risks for MIGA. Some reviewed MIGA projects experienced incidents where alleged violations of individual rights occurred in connection with site security. Such violations can increase risks to MIGA-guaranteed projects (increasing conflict and affecting operations)

and to MIGA itself (reputational risk, as well as claims brought under civil war and disturbance and expropriation coverages). Even though issues related to human rights are part of MIGA's due diligence process when they have an impact on covered risks, greater awareness during underwriting by MIGA staff and ensuring that they are adequately dealt with by investors would better address such risks.

Lack of a systematic and post-contract follow-up of developmental impacts in extractive industry projects. MIGA does not have a system that monitors developmental impacts to identify shortcomings after contract signing and to manage risks from the developmental perspective.

MIGA's Role in Extractive Industries Projects

Most of the evaluated projects were in difficult countries with weak governance, as well as high perceived political risks, where MIGA's political risk insurance was deemed essential for investments to go forward. Thus, MIGA added value as an insurer by facilitating and enabling foreign direct investment in these large and complex projects.

Surveyed MIGA staff who have been involved in underwriting extractive industry projects are supportive of MIGA's environmental and social standards and feel that MIGA is doing a sound job in applying these standards to its projects. These staff see no need for increased coordination with the Bank and IFC on extractive industries projects.

In some projects, MIGA delegated environmental and social safeguard due diligence to its partners. These arrangements worked well when the partners adhered to similar policies and guidelines. But if a partner had lower standards than MIGA (such as in an older reinsured project), it led to unsatisfactory results and left MIGA vulnerable.

MIGA's particular value added as an insurer of extractive industries projects is

in the environmental and social standards it brings with its guarantees. This aspect of its insurance is appealing to many investors, as it helps them manage their own nonfinancial project risks. Hands-on assistance and advice is possible and desirable in extractive industries projects, and it is appreciated by clients.

There is a strong business case for MIGA to add value by providing substantive and continued social and environmental advice to extractive industries clients after contract signing. The results from several projects demonstrate that well-designed plans for minimizing social impacts can greatly reduce social conflicts, thereby mitigating the political risks MIGA guarantees, whereas their absence can lead to serious problems.

Recommendations

MIGA's support to EI sector projects has the potential to generate positive development results. MIGA should continue underwriting EI projects while strengthening its value added to meet stakeholders' expectations. MIGA's safeguard policies provide the basis, and an opportunity, for contributing to the development effectiveness of EI projects it guarantees.

Recommendation 1: Strategy and Rules of Engagement

MIGA needs to recognize and promote the potential benefits it brings to EI projects through its internationally recognized and comprehensive set of safeguard policies and its environmental and social impact mitigation services. MIGA's engagement with EI projects should move beyond compliance with its environmental and social safeguard policies toward the promotion and achievement of the development effectiveness of these projects. This requires the following:

Recognizing that MIGA has the opportunity to add value to EI projects by adopting an explicit business strategy focused on providing proactive environmental and social advice to its guarantee clients that brings EI projects closer to best practices in the industry, with the goal of achieving sustainable development. This requires strengthening the economic and social

components in MIGA's work in addition to the environmental component. This calls for a more proactive, forward-looking approach to servicing clients that goes beyond the current practice of intervening only when events warrant it.

Strengthening the upstream involvement of environmental and social issues in MIGA's underwriting decisionmaking process. This entails consistently identifying applicable safeguard policies to clients as early as possible in the underwriting process and using risk assessments early on to identify where failures in the safeguard system may occur to avoid adverse impacts on the environment and local communities. MIGA needs to make a greater effort to work with clients to ensure compliance with its environmental and social safeguard policies and guidelines at the time of Board approval. In addition, MIGA needs to consider how its work in assessing, underwriting, and supervising its guarantee projects can go beyond the monitoring of compliance with safeguards toward promoting development effectiveness in its projects.

Associating with investors committed to sustainable development and avoiding those who are unable to provide MIGA with timely environmental and social monitoring reports during implementation. MIGA should satisfy itself before engaging in new EI projects that the investor understands its environmental and social responsibilities and demonstrates ownership at the top management level to community development and mitigating environmental and social impacts. The project enterprise's organizational structure, policies, and stated mission should be consistent with these goals.

Recommendation 2: Policies, Procedures, and Enforcement Mechanisms

MIGA should strengthen its internal policies and support them with appropriate procedures and guidelines for staff to ensure accountability. This requires the following:

Establishing internal requirements for MIGA's timely engagement and systematic monitoring to maximize environmental and social benefits. This will entail avoiding projects where MIGA cannot address environmental or social issues to improve the outcome due to its late participation. Site visits by MIGA's environmental and social experts should be required as early as possible in its involvement in Category 'A' and other high-risk projects to assess which policies are applicable. MIGA should not rely exclusively on assessments and reports of non-WBG institutions.

Incorporating standards recognizing the rights of individuals relating to security arrangements at EI projects into its policies and operational regulations.

Making better use of MIGA's Contracts of Guarantee to enable the Agency to facilitate compliance with its policies and standards. In addition to the current requirement to comply with safeguard policies and environmental and health and safety guidelines, for future projects MIGA should ensure that the contracts clearly and explicitly state which environmental and social safeguard policies and guidelines apply to the project under guarantee and establish thresholds and conditions for timely and effective compliance. When applicable, contracts should also specify requirements for implementation of Environmental Management Plans, RPs, CDPs, and IPPs. As required by the involuntary resettlement and indigenous peoples policies, MIGA should ensure that investors prepare RPs, CDPs, and IPPs before project approval rather than leaving them to implementation.

Establishing necessary mechanisms to ensure systematic, timely, and regular monitoring and supervision of safeguard compliance of MIGA EI guarantee projects (e.g., MIGA should require in its Contracts of Guarantee timely environmental and social monitoring reports from its guarantee holders during the project implementation phase). MIGA should also require sponsors to set up environmental and social project management systems at a sufficiently early stage to effectively monitor impacts, including during the construction stage.

Recommendation 3: Internal Organization
MIGA should update its business model by clearly assigning the locus of responsibility for better integration of economic, environmental, and social issues in MIGA operations. This is needed in order to support other departments in the achievement of these objectives and to provide guidance to operational staff, as well as for the analysis and monitoring of economic, environmental, and social issues in an integrated manner. This requires the following:

Scaling up the analysis of developmental impacts of prospective projects and integrating new concepts in harmony with the rest of the World Bank Group. In so doing, MIGA should closely cooperate with the other members of the WBG to benefit from synergies, complementarities, and expert knowledge, with the objective of promoting a holistic approach to EI projects. This will also require building internal capacity by both recruiting needed economic skills and providing appropriate training to current staff.

Establishing an internal system that allows a more integrated and timely monitoring of developmental impacts of guaranteed projects.

Upgrading and expanding the role of environmental and social specialists and, at the same time, building internal social skills capacity to effectively enable the application of social safeguards in MIGA projects.

Formalizing the practice of ensuring that MIGA environmental staff are involved in projects beyond the submission of clearance memos, and requiring that MIGA environmental and social staff provide inputs to guarantee and legal documentation to incorporate any environmental and social concerns. In addition, MIGA underwriting staff should be required to keep environmental and social specialists appraised of all relevant changes beyond Board approval and contract signing.

Recommendation 4: Legacy of Active EI Projects
MIGA needs to review its portfolio of active EI projects to identify potential or actual deficiencies in the application of safeguard policies and to swiftly take appropriate remedial actions. This should involve the following:

Identifying projects that may not be consistent with safeguard policies. In particular, where resettlement and land acquisition has taken place without follow-up audits to determine compliance with WBG policies regarding resettlement, third-party audits should be required. Similarly, where indigenous peoples have been affected without the provision for Indigenous Peoples Plans to mitigate the impacts, sponsors should be asked to prepare and implement such plans. Providing briefings on potential problems with sensitive projects, a system currently used by MIGA, is useful but not sufficient. MIGA should take appropriate remedial actions to address existing safeguard deficiencies in extractive industry projects that are still active in MIGA's portfolio.

Making every effort to encourage consistency with MIGA's safeguard policies in active extractive industries projects with reinsurance agreements predating the new MIGA practice. New agreements require that environmental and social standards applied by partners are consistent with MIGA's own safeguard policies and guidelines.

Attachment 1	MIGA Guarantee Projects in the Extractive Industries, FY1990–2003 (as of December 31, 2002)

Project enterprise	Guarantee holder	Host country	Sector	Fiscal year	Maximum aggregate liability (US$)	Status	FDI (US$)
1. **Freeport Indonesia, Inc.**	Freeport-McMoRan Copper & Gold, Inc.	Indonesia	Mining	90	50,000,000	Cancelled	499,813,000
2. **Compania Minera Mantos de Oro**	Placer Dome, Inc. (Export Development Corporation [EDC])	Chile	Mining	90	49,770,000	Cancelled	335,000,000
3. **Compania Minera Cerro Colorado S.A.**	Rio Algom Limited	Chile	Mining	91	5,000,000	Cancelled	310,000,000
	OPIC (Citibank/Credit Suisse)			92	22,500,000		
4. **Omai Gold Mines Ltd.**	Cambior Inc. (EDC)	Guyana	Mining	92	36,720,000	Active	162,000,000
	Cambior Inc. (EDC)			92	13,158,000		
5. **Alumina Partners of Jamaica**	Hydro Aluminum Jamaica a.s.	Jamaica	Mining	93	20,223,000	Cancelled	336,974,000
6. **Kasese Cobalt Company Limited**	La Source Compagnie Minière SAS.	Uganda	Mining	93	5,000,000	Cancelled	95,400,000
	La Source/Mine Or S.A./ Barclays Metals Ltd.			93	5,000,000		
	La Source			96	3,600,000		
	Banff Resources Ltd.			98	1,908,020		
	Banff Resources Ltd. & La Source SAS			98	47,480,000		
7. **Ghanaian-Australian Mines Limited**	GSM Gold Limited	Ghana	Mining	93	9,850,000	Cancelled	71,600,000
8. **Minera Yanacocha**	Compagnie Minière Internationale Or	Peru	Mining	94	1,404,000	Cancelled	82,081,387
	Newmont Mining Corporation			94	2,160,000		
	Newmont Mining Corporation			94	5,616,000		
	Compagnie Minière			94	5,040,000		
	Internationale Or			94	18,961,000		
	Union Bank of Switzerland						
	Union Bank of Switzerland			95	5,700,000		
	Newmont Mining Corporation			95	14,408,387		
	Mine Or S.A.			95	6,404,000		
9. **Compania Contractual Minera Candelaria**	Sumitomo Corporation	Chile	Mining	94	19,800,000	Cancelled	527,400,000
10. **Newmont-Zarafshan Joint Venture**	Newmont Gold Company	Uzbekistan	Mining	94	40,000,000	Cancelled	110,000,000
	Newmont Gold Company			95	10,000,000		

(continued)

Project enterprise	Guarantee holder	Host country	Sector	Fiscal year	Maximum aggregate liability (US$)	Status	FDI (US$)
11. Sociedad Minera Cerro Verde, S.A.	Cyprus Climax Metals Company	Peru	Mining	95	50,000,000	Cancelled	141,000,000
12. British Gas Overseas Holdings (British Gas Tunisia)	British Gas plc	Tunisia	Oil & Gas	95	65,000,000	Cancelled	627,000,000
13. Magma Tintaya S.A.	BHP Copper Inc.	Peru	Mining	95	24,000,000	Cancelled	328,000,000
14. Southern Gold (Bahamas) Limited, Lihir Gold Limited	R.T.Z. Overseas Holdings Limited (Rio Tinto Zinc—RTZ)	Papua New Guinea	Mining	96	10,000,000	Cancelled	892,000,000
	Union Bank of Switzerland			96	66,600,000		
15. Kumtor Gold Company	Cameco Corporation (EDC)	Kyrgyzstan	Mining	96	45,000,000	Active	335,000,000
	Cameco Corporation (EDC)			2001	39,330,000		
16. Societe d'Exploitation des Mines d'Or de Sadiola S.A.	AngloGold	Mali	Mining	96	50,000,000	Cancelled	267,000,000
17. Drummond Limited	Drummond Company, Inc.	Colombia	Mining	97	35,000,000	Cancelled	235,000,000
18. Minera Alumbrera Limited	Minera Alumbrera Ltd. (Export Finance Insurance Corporation [EFIC])	Argentina	Mining	97	12,000,000	Active	1,033,000,000
	Rio Algom Limited			97	2,000,000		
19. Hydrocarbon Research Block Rhourde Yacoub	Compañia Española de Seguros de Crédito a la Exportación S.A.	Algeria	Oil & Gas	97	10,000,000	Cancelled	240,000,000
20. Zafiro Offshore Field	UMC Equatorial Guinea Corporation	Equatorial Guinea	Oil & Gas	98	24,000,000	Cancelled	995,500,000
21. Cerro Vanguardia S.A.	Minorco S.A.	Argentina	Mining	98	5,000,000	Cancelled	202,600,000
22. Minera Los Pelambres	Marubeni LP Holding B.V.	Chile	Mining	98	31,263,750	Cancelled	1,114,000,000
23. Companias Asociadas Petroleras S.A.	El Paso Energy International Company	Argentina	Oil & Gas	98	22,580,000	Active	538,000,000
	El Paso Energy International Company			98	17,617,500		
24. ICV-Inertes de Cabo Verde, Ltda.	Secil-Companhia Geral De Cal e Cimento, S.A	Cape Verde	Mining	98	540,000	Active	1,709,000
	Secil-Companhia Geral De Cal e Cimento, S.A			98	660,000		
	Sociedade de Empreitadas Adriano S.A.			98	540,000		
	Sociedade de Empreitadas Adriano S.A.			98	660,000		
25. Compania Minera Antamina S.A.	Citicorp	Peru	Mining	99	60,702,000	Active	2,106,000,000
	Noranda Inc.			99	2,550,000		
	Rio Algom Limited			99	2,550,000		
	Teck Corporation			99	1,700,000		
	Mitsubishi Corporation			2000	16,250,047		
	Mitsubishi Corporation			2000	23,709,953		

Project enterprise	Guarantee holder	Host country	Sector	Fiscal year	Maximum aggregate liability (US$)	Status	FDI (US$)
26. Omolon Gold Mining Inc.	Kinam Gold, Inc.	Russia	Mining	2000	27,420,000	Cancelled	226,900,000
27. Kahama Mining Corporation Limited	Societe Generale Barrick Gold Corporation	Tanzania	Mining	2000 2001	115,830,000 56,250,000	Active	505,300,000
28. Omsukchansk Mining & Geological Company	New Arian Resources Corporation	Russia	Mining	2000	2,250,000	Active	96,000,000
	New Arian Resources Corporation	Russia	Mining	2000	2,250,000	Active	96,000,000
	Standard Bank London Limited			2000	14,900,000		
29. Barracuda & Caratinga Leasing Company, B.V.	Itochu Corporation, Mitsubishi Corporation	Brazil	Oil & Gas	2001	12,000,000	Active	1,740,000,000
	Deutsche Bank AG New York Branch			2001	60,000,000		
30. ZAO Stimul	Victory Oil B.V.	Russia	Oil & Gas	2001	100,000,000	Active	71,201,160
31. ROMPCO (Pty) Ltd.	Sasol Gas Holdings	Mozambique	Oil & Gas	2003	45,000,000	Active	857,000,000
	Sasol Petroleum International (Pty) Ltd.			2003	27,000,000		
				Total	**1,479,605,657**		**15,082,478,547**

Extractive industries projects:

Active projects: 11

Cancelled projects: 20

Oil & gas projects:

Oil & gas projects: 7

Active oil & gas projects: 4

Mining projects:

Mining projects: 24

Active mining projects: 7

		MIGA Extractive Industries Projects Evaluated by OEU
Attachment 2		

	FY	Environmental category	Safeguards review	Evaluation of developmental impact	Case study
1.	1990	A	✓		
2.	1992	A		✓	
3.	1993, 1996, 1998	A	✓	✓	
4.	1993	(A)ᵃ	✓		
5.	1994	A		✓	
6.	1996	A	✓	✓	
7.	1996	A		✓	
8.	1996	A	✓	✓	
9.	1997	A	✓		
10.	1997	A	✓		✓
11.	1998	B	✓		
12.	1999	A	✓		✓
13.	2000	A	✓		
14.	2001	B	✓		
15.	2001	B	✓		

a. No formal category was assigned. The project was assumed to have been Category 'A.'

Number of active projects: 7

Number of cancelled projects: 8

Criterion	Requirements
Comprehensive Environmental Assessment	Applies to both majority and minority owners and lenders (designated herein as "sponsors") —required for all 'As' and for 'Bs' if host country legislation require or any of the environmental issues identified in the screening process warrant special attention. Comprehensive EA includes: (i) natural environment, social aspects, human health and safety, major hazards, transboundary/global and cumulative/induced impacts; (ii) prevent, minimize, mitigate or compensate for adverse environmental and social impacts and enhance positive impacts; (iii) potential for independent environmental advisory panel in case of highly risky or contentious project; (iv) properly defined area(s) of project impact; (v) for expansion or modernization projects the entire plant is subject to an EA (usually including an environmental audit); (vi) privatization projects require environmental audits; (vii) EAs (including environmental audits) to be carried out or reviewed by independent consultants; and (viii) compliance with more stringent of host country or MIGA environmental and health and safety standards or guidelines.
Adequate analysis of feasible alternatives	Proper analysis of project alternatives including: (i) without project alternative; (ii) where appropriate other sector alternatives; (iii) alternative sitings for facilities and routings of infrastructure corridors; (iv) alternative technologies and mitigation arrangements; and (v) analysis of feasible alternatives.
Comprehensive Environmental and Social (E&S) baseline survey	Full description (with adequate support data) of the climatic, geological, topographical, physical, chemical, biological and socio-cultural-economic environment of the area of project impact as a basis for an adequate analysis of project impacts and future monitoring of the efficacy of the mitigation measures incorporated into the project.
Adequate EAP or EMP proposed	A detailed plan of the set of mitigation, monitoring and reporting measures proposed to be taken during project implementation to eliminate adverse environmental or social impacts, offset them, or reduce them to acceptable levels—required for all 'As' and 'Bs.'
Project sponsor's EMS adequate	Comprehensiveness of environmental, social and safety management system proposed by the sponsor (including contractors) to fully implement the EAP or EMP, as well as appropriateness of proposed measures to strengthen these arrangements.
Public disclosure/consultation addressed	(i) consultation with local affected parties and local interest groups during EA process; (ii) disclosure of information in a timely manner and in a language and form understandable and accessible to local groups; (iii) for 'A' projects final EA reports disclosed locally and through the World Bank Info-shop at least 60 days before MIGA Board approval.
Comprehensive and implementable RP/CDP prepared	(i) avoid or minimize involuntary physical resettlement or economic displacement; (ii) directly affected and displaced persons should be: (a) informed of their options and rights regarding land acquisition and resettlement as well as alternatives that are available; (b) compensated for their losses at full replacement cost prior to the actual move; (c) assisted with the move and supported during the transition period in the resettlement site; and (d) assisted in their efforts to improve their former living standards, income earning capacity, and production levels, *or at least to restore them*. Particular attention should be paid to the needs of the poorest groups to be resettled; (iii) Land, housing, infrastructure, and other compensation should be provided to the adversely affected population, indigenous groups, ethnic minorities, and pastoralists who may have usufruct or customary rights to the land or other

(continued)

Criterion	Requirements
	resources taken for the project. The absence of legal title to land by such groups should not be a bar to compensation; (iv) alternative or similar resources provided to compensate for the loss of access to community resources; (v) in new resettlement sites or host communities improve, restore or maintain accessibility and levels of service for the displaced persons and host communities; (vi) minimize impacts on host communities including consultation with these communities; (vii) consult and involve affected people in planning, and implementation; (viii) community level impacts require preparation of community development programs to improve the economic and social well-being of the affected communities as well as the affected households; (ix) preparation of a resettlement plan (RP), or other resettlement instrument (e.g., resettlement framework) as agreed with MIGA; and (x) disclosure of RPs involving more than 50 households or 250 people.
Comprehensive and implementable IPP prepared	Appropriate identification of indigenous groups in project area, namely those having: (a) close attachment to ancestral territories and the natural resources in them; (b) self-identification and identification by others as members of a distinct cultural group; (c) presence of customary social and political institutions; (d) economic systems primarily orientated to subsistence production; and (e) indigenous language. Ensure: (i) avoidance and mitigation of adverse impacts; (ii) informed participation of the indigenous peoples themselves; (iii) culturally appropriate compensatory measures or social and economic benefits; and (iv) in consultation with indigenous peoples preparation of an Indigenous Peoples Plan.
Natural habitats protected or offsets provided	(i) Project does not significantly convert/degrade a critical habitat; (ii) natural habitats are correctly identified; (iii) alternative analysis examines alternatives to significant conversion; (iv) if conversion can- not be avoided, impact are minimized, mitigated and offset requirements are examined.
Comprehensive dam safety measures proposed	**New Dams:** Safety measures from design to operation for dam and associated works, including for: (i) dams >15 meters in final height; (ii) for special case (flood prone, seismic area, difficult foundations, toxic materials, etc.) dams between 10 and 15 m; and (iii) for dams initially under 10 m if expected to become large dams during construction, require the following: (a) reviews by independent expertise throughout design and construction of dam and for start of operations; (b) plan for construction, supervision and quality assurance, plan for instrumentation, an Operation and Maintenance (O&M) plan, and an emergency preparedness plan; (c) construction by fully qualified companies under proper supervision; (d) periodic safety inspections after completion of construction; **Existing Dams:** (i) independent dam specialist(s) to evaluate safety status, performance history and owner's operation/maintenance procedures; and (ii) specify remedial works or safety-related measures to upgrade dam to an acceptable standard of safety. **Tailings Dams and Ash Lagoons:** (i) this policy applies to such dams in excess of 10 m if: (a) the impoundment is cross-valley structure; or (b) after construction of a starter dam, the impoundment structure is made of whole tailings; or (c) standard testing methods indicate net acid generating potential of tailings or ash. However generic safety measures designed by qualified engineers are adequate for such dams less than 10 m in height, if tailings or ash have no net acid generating potential and impoundment is: (a) located in relatively flat terrain, highly arid areas or in permafrost zones; and (b) not subject to inflow from streams or rivers: (ii) stream

Criterion	Requirements
	diversions and spillways to be designed for 100 yr. flood; and (iii) preparation of closure and abandonment plans.
Cultural Property protection proposed	(i) avoid harm to significant, non-replicable cultural property or with the help of qualified experts mitigate such impacts if loss is judged to be minor or otherwise acceptable; (ii) sponsor addresses protection/management of cultural property in project area including "chance finds"; (iii) sponsor meets host country regulations/laws (or adheres to best practice in the absence of host country laws); and (iv) sponsor consults with relevant stakeholders in documenting presence and significance of physical cultural resources.

The set of requirements for each criterion of safeguard policy compliance were rated according to the following scale:

- **High:** the set of requirements were fully met, or expected to be fully met, with no shortcomings
- **Substantial:** the set of requirements generally were met, or expected to be met, with only minor shortcomings
- **Modest:** the set of requirements were met, or expected to be met, but with significant shortcomings
- **Negligible:** the set of requirements were not met, or expected not to be met, due to major shortcomings

Criterion	Requirements
EAP or EMP fully implemented	Assess how effectively the EAP or EMP has been implemented by the sponsor and note any gaps and deficiencies. Note how well EAP or EMP implementation progress has been documented and reported in a timely manner. Note any deviations from the original plan and if these were appropriate considering the circumstances.
E&S monitoring implemented	Assess if the EAP's or EMP's E&S monitoring plan has been implemented according to the timing proposed. Assess if the monitoring results are substantiating the effectiveness of the E&S mitigation measures or not. Note if the results are being used to take corrective measures if needed.
Sponsor's project implementation EMS effective	Determine if the sponsor has implemented the environmental, social and safety management system proposed in the EAP or EMP. Assess the effectiveness of the proposed institutional strengthening measures to improve this system and whether the system has active sponsor management support. Assess its sustainability in the longer term.
Continuing public disclosure and consultation	Determine the extent to which project affected groups and other stakeholders continue to be consulted and involved during the implementation phase of the project. Assess if there have been any complaints by project affected people and how these complaints were dealt with by the Borrower.
Full compensation of project affected people (PAPs)	Assess if displaced persons have been: (a) compensated for their losses at full replacement cost prior to the actual move; (b) assisted with the move and supported during the transition period in the resettlement site; and (c) assisted in their efforts to improve their former living standards, income earning capacity, and production levels, or at least to restore them.
RP/CDP fully implemented	Determine if the RP/CDP has been fully implemented by the sponsor. Assess if the sponsor has adequately monitored and evaluated the activities set forth in the RP/CDP. If upon termination of the contract of guarantee the RP/CDP has not been fully implemented assess what follow-up actions the sponsor proposes to meet the objectives of the plan and if these are adequate.
IPP fully implemented	Determine if the IPP has been fully implemented by the sponsor. Assess if the sponsor has adequately monitored and evaluated the activities set forth in the IPAP. If upon termination of the contract of guarantee the IPAP has not been fully implemented, assess what follow-up actions the sponsor proposes to meet the objectives of the plan and if these are adequate.
Natural habitats protected or offsets provided	Assess if sponsor has taken all necessary measures to limit any significant conversion/degradation of critical natural habitat and/or provide offset requirements as proposed in the EA. Assess the sustainability of these measures once the project has been implemented.
Dam safety measures implemented	For new dams covered by the policy, assess if the safety measures recommended by the independent dam expert(s) throughout investigation, design and construction of dam and start-up of operations were implemented. Evaluate effectiveness of plans for construction, supervision and quality assurance, as well as for instrumentation, O&M and emergency preparedness. Assess the results of periodic safety inspections after completion of construction. For existing dams, assess if the safety measures proposed by the independent dam specialist(s) have been implemented as proposed and note any deviations.

(continued)

Criterion	Requirements
Cultural property protected	Assess if appropriate measures were taken by the sponsor to avoid harm to significant, non-replicable cultural property and provide protection/management of cultural property in project area including "chance finds" according to best practice or host country regulations/laws.
Reporting on safeguard policies by sponsor adequate	Determine if MIGA has specified a comprehensive set of safeguard policy performance indicators that are appropriate for the project under implementation. Assess the timeliness and effectiveness of the reporting of indicators and their evaluation by the sponsor and MIGA, noting any deficiencies. Assess if the following requirements have been met: (i) MIGA ensures that contract of guarantee includes an obligation to carry out the EAP/EMP and includes as additional conditions specific measures under the EAP/EMP, as appropriate for facilitating effective monitoring on EMP implementation; and (ii) the sponsor's obligations to carry out the RP/CDP and/or IPP (or other instrument agreed with MIGA) and to keep MIGA informed of implementation progress are provided for in the contract of guarantee.
Monitoring and evaluation (M&E) of safeguard policies by MIGA adequate	MIGA reviews regular monitoring reports on safeguard compliance provided by the sponsor and notes any areas of concern for follow-up with sponsor. MIGA bases supervision of the projects environmental/social/safety aspects on the findings and recommendations of the EA, including measures set out in the legal agreements, any EMP and other project documents, and ensures that supervision missions contain adequate environmental and social expertise. During supervision MIGA reviews sponsor's implementation progress (incl. progress reports) and assesses Borrower's compliance with agreed environmental actions, particularly the implementation of environmental and social mitigation, monitoring and management measures. If compliance is unsatisfactory, MIGA discusses with sponsor actions necessary to correct non-compliance and follows-up on the implementation of such actions.

The set of requirements for each criterion of safeguard policy compliance were rated according to the following scale:
- **High:** the set of requirements were fully met, or expected to be fully met, with no shortcomings
- **Substantial:** the set of requirements generally were met, or expected to be met, with only minor shortcomings
- **Modest:** the set of requirements were met, or expected to be met, but with significant shortcomings
- **Negligible:** the set of requirements were not met, or expected not to be met, due to major shortcomings

Safeguard Policy	Trigger
Environmental Assessment—Category 'A' (May 1999)	Adverse environmental and social impacts that are sensitive, diverse or unprecedented and likely to be significant beyond the project fenceline.
Environmental Assessment—Category 'B' (May 1999)	Projects whose impacts are limited in number, less adverse than those of Category 'A,' and can be addressed by compliance with MIGA's environmental guidelines or through application of recognized pollution prevention and abatement measures (or recognized best management practices).
Natural Habitats (Interim 2002 policy)	Significant conversion or degradation of natural habitats, or loss or modification of habitat in protected areas.
Involuntary Resettlement (Interim 2002 policy)	Involuntary taking of land resulting in (i) relocation or loss of shelter; (ii) loss of assets or access to assets; or (iii) loss of income source or means of livelihood.
Indigenous Peoples (Interim 2002 policy)	Conflicts with or adverse impacts on indigenous peoples, tribes or ethnic minorities whose social and economic state restricts their capacity to assert their interests and rights in land and other productive resources.
Dam Safety (Interim 2002 policy)	Safety of new or existing dams, including tailings dams > 10 meters in height.
Forestry (Interim 2002 policy)	Sustainable forestry practices.
Cultural Property (Interim 2002 policy)	Adverse, irreversible impacts on cultural or natural sites having archeological, paleontological, historical, religious or unique natural aesthetic value.
Pest Management (Interim 2002 policy)	Significant use of pesticides.
Projects on International Waterways (Interim 2002 policy)	Notification of projects with significant and adverse impacts on international waterways in respect to the quantity and quality of water flows to other riparian states, or will significantly and adversely affect present or likely future water use by other riparian states.

Attachment 5A	Safeguard Policy Consistency Ratings of MIGA EI Projects at Approval

					Project Name						
Description	**M**	**O**	**A**	**F**	**J**	**D**	**H**	**L**	**C**	**I**	**K**
EA Category[1]	**A**	**B**	**A**	**A**	**A**	**A**	**A**	**A**	**A**	**A**	**B**
MIGA Client Category	**Maj**	**Maj**	**Maj**	**Maj**	**Min**	**Maj**	**Maj**	**Maj**	**Maj**	**Maj**	**Min**
Comprehensive environmental assessment[2]	S	S	M	H	H	S	S	H	M	S	S
Adequate analysis of feasible alternatives	H	H	N	H	S	M	S	H	M	S	H
Comprehensive E&S baseline survey	S	S	N	H	S	S	S	S	M	S	S
Adequate EAP proposed	H	S	N	H	H	M	S	H	M	S	S
Project investor's EMS adequate	S	M	M	H	S	M	S	H	H	M	S
Public disclosure/consultation addressed	S		M	S	M	M	S	H	M	S	
Contract of guarantee for implementation of safeguard policies/guidelines adequate	H	S	N	M	M	M	M	S	M	M	M
Comprehensive and implementable RP/CDP prepared	S	M	S	M		M	M	M	N	H	
Comprehensive and implementable IPP prepared			M	M				N			
Natural habitats protected or offsets provided			M	S	M	M		H	M		
Comprehensive dam safety measures proposed					H		S	H	N		
Cultural property protection proposed	H	S		H	H	S	H	H			
Average score[3]	**3.4**	**2.9**	**1.7**	**3.3**	**3.1**	**2.3**	**2.9**	**3.4**	**2.0**	**2.9**	**3.0**
Overall rating	**S**	**S**	**M**	**S**	**S**	**M**	**S**	**S**	**M**	**S**	**S**

High (H); Substantial (S); Modest (M); and Negligible (N)

1. An EA may include an environmental impact assessment, environmental audit, and hazard or environmental risk assessment or a combination of these instruments.

2. MIGA's guarantee holders identified as Maj = Major project investor; Min = Minor project investor.

3. Scoring system used: H=4; S=3; M=2; N=1. If average score is > or = 2.5, then "S"; if < 2.5, then "M."

Attachment 5B	Safeguard Policy Consistency Ratings of MIGA EI Projects under Guarantee

	Project Name										
Description	**M**	**O**	**A**	**F**	**J**	**D**	**H**	**L**	**C**	**I**	**K**
EA Category	A	B	A	A	A	A	A	A	A	A	B
MIGA Client Category[a]	Maj	Maj	Maj	Maj	Min	Maj	Maj	Maj	Maj	Maj	Min
EAP/EMP fully implemented by investor	S		S	H	H	S	S	S	S		
E&S monitoring fully implemented by investor	H		S	H	H	M	S	H	S		
Investor's project implementation EMS effective	S		S	H	S	M	S	H	H		
Continuing public disclosure and consultation	H		M	H	M	M	S	S	S		
Full compensation of PAPs	S			H		M	S	S	S		
RP/CDP fully implemented	H		H	H		M	S	S	S		
IPP fully implemented			M	S				S			
Natural habitats protected or offsets provided			M	H	S	M		H	M		
Dam safety measures implemented					H		S	H	M		
Cultural property protected	H			H	H	M	S	H			
Reporting on safeguard policies by investor adequate	H		M	S	M	S	S	H	S	N	N
M&E of safeguard policies by MIGA adequate	S		M	S	S	M	H	S	S	N	N
Average score	3.6		2.6	3.7	3.2	2.2	3.1	3.5	2.9		
Overall rating	S		S	S	S	M	S	S	S		

a. MIGA's guarantee holders identified as Maj = Major project investor; Min = Minor project investor.

ENDNOTES

Foreword

1. Climate change has been covered in other WBG publications and evaluations. See www.worldbank.org/climate change and www.ifc.org/test/sustainability/docs/Climate_Change_IFC.pdf. The WBG's environmental strategy for the energy sector—*Fuel for Thought* (www.worldbank.org/html/fpd/energy/eee/FuelforThought.htm)—aims to mitigate the effects of and vulnerability to climate change.

2. For more information on the EIR, see www.eireview.org.

3. Concurrently, the CAO has been examining the extent to which IFC and MIGA have addressed sustainability concerns in recent extractive industries projects. See www.cao-ombudsman.org.

4. The Approach Paper and other supporting documents for this evaluation study are available on the Internet (www.ifc.org/oeg/EIEvaluation/eievaluation.html).

Chapter 1

5. This evaluation focuses on the impacts of extractive industries on developing countries. It does not address issues of downstream consumption, including important global impacts such as climate change, except for climate change impacts related to production, such as gas flaring.

6. This phenomenon—resource-rich countries falling far short of their developmental potential and even being worse off than resource-poor countries—has been termed "the paradox of plenty."

7. This relationship, which is statistically significant at the 95 percent confidence level (t-statistic = −2.39), illustrates a conclusion that is widely accepted in the literature. No claim is made that EI dependence is the sole determinant of a country's economic growth.

8. "Borrower" includes all countries eligible for borrowing from the WBG with a population greater than one million as of 2000, for which data is available. When nonborrower countries are included, the slope is also statistically significant (t-statistic = −2.82), and steeper (−0.038 vs. −0.032).

9. Seminal papers by Richard Auty (ed., 2001), Gelb (1988), Isham (2002), Sachs and Warner (1997), have discussed the evolution of thinking on the subject in recent years. See References in Annex C, Attachment 5.

10. Analysis in the 1960s focused on how to manage the macroeconomic impacts of resource export income, which raised domestic prices and made other exports less competitive internationally (the so-called Dutch disease). More recent analysis emphasizes poor use of fiscal revenues from resources.

Chapter 2

11. The portfolio of projects chosen for review consists of all EI projects approved during or after fiscal year 1993, the first full financial year after the WBG adopted revised safeguard policies. OED reviewed 76 Bank projects, comprising 48 closed (24 oil and gas, 24 mining) and 28 active projects (15 oil and gas, 13 mining).

12. The Bank's project completion reports are usually expected to assess economic benefits by calculating an economic rate of return or using a cost-effectiveness criterion to determine whether the project represented the expected least-cost solution to attain the identified benefits, but only 35 percent of the completion reports did so. Another 27 percent contained some quantification and valuation of benefits but no analysis of their cost effectiveness.

13. See Annex C, Chapter 3.

14. OEG's review is based on in-depth evaluations of a random, representative sample of 22 projects approved in calendar years 1991–96 (12 oil and gas, 10 mining), supplemented by "mini" desk-evaluations of all other projects either approved after fiscal year 1993 or still in IFC's portfolio. In total, OEG studied 45 projects or companies (23 oil and gas, 22 mining). Immature projects and projects with insufficient information (usually where IFC had exited early) are not included in these numbers, but OEG used them also to draw lessons and highlight issues.

15. See, for example, *WBG Work in Low-Income Countries Under Stress: A Task Force Report,* World Bank (2002).

16. See also Annex D, Attachment 4 for the perceptions of stakeholders outside and inside the WBG.

17. OEU reviewed six previously evaluated projects, all in mining (five gold, one cobalt) and conducted two additional in-field case studies of mining projects. Most of the projects were underwritten by MIGA in the early to mid-1990s. OEU also reviewed the consistency with safeguard policies of 12 projects (3 oil and gas, 9 mining). In total, OEU reviews covered 15 MIGA projects with active or cancelled contracts of guarantee (out of a total of 31 that MIGA guaranteed since 1990).

18. See Annex C, Chapter 5.

19. The CAS is the central vehicle for Board review of the WBG's assistance strategy for its borrower countries. The CAS is expected to (a) describe the WBG's strategy based on an assessment of the priorities in the country, and (b) indicate the level and composition of assistance based on the strategy and the performance of the country's project portfolio.

20. See Annex D, Attachment 4c for complete results of the staff survey.

21. See Annex C, Figure C10. However, following the launch of the WBG's Low-Income Countries Under Stress (LICUS) program in 2002, additional budget for activities designed to improve the policy and institutional framework has been allocated to many of these countries.

22. See Annex C, Chapter 5.

23. See Annex D, Chapter 6.

24. The sample of 38 projects was purposely chosen from the EI portfolio of 76 projects to include projects that were likely to have adverse environmental or social impacts and included 19 oil and gas and 19 mining projects. See Annex C, Chapter 4.

25. The policy on Environmental Assessment (OP 4.01) defines project categories as follows: 'A': likely to have significant adverse environmental impacts that are sensitive, diverse, or unprecedented
'B': potential environmental impacts are less adverse than for 'A'
'C': likely to have minimal or no adverse environmental impacts

26 In the absence of an established approach for assessing a project's degree of consistency with safeguards policy requirements, the evaluation has synthesized the policy requirements into a set of basic criteria and used it for the subject review. The criteria for consistency have been benchmarked against those used by the Inspection Panel reports on EI projects and discussed with the Quality Assurance and Compliance Unit (QACU) and the Legal Department. See Annex C, Chapter 4.

27. See Annex C, Chapter 4.

28. See Annex D, Chapter 4, "IFC's Results in Mitigating Negative and Enhancing Positive Impacts," which also explains the difficulties comparing the two data sets.

29. The review of safeguard policy compliance for MIGA EI projects covered 12 out of 30 MIGA projects with active and cancelled guarantees issued since MIGA's inception. The review was commissioned from an external expert and is the first of its kind for MIGA.

30. The project was rated "consistent" when the policy requirements were generally met, or expected to be met, with only minor shortcomings.

31. See Annex D, Chapter 4, "IFC Helping to Generate Sustainable Benefits."

32. Halting or reversing the spread of AIDS is one of the Millennium Development Goals. Initiatives in the WBG address HIV/AIDS, but addressing the issue in specific EI-projects is not mandatory. See also Annex D, Chapter 4 and Box D2.

33. See Annex C, Chapter 4, and Annex D, Chapter 3 and Box D1.

34. For example, the May 15, 2002, Toronto Declaration of the International Council of Mining and Metals (ICMM) states (on behalf of the mining industry): "orphan site legacy issues are important and complex. However, they are beyond the capacity of ICMM to resolve. Governments and international agencies should assume the lead role in addressing them."

Chapter 3

35. Here again, this relationship is statistically significant at the 95 percent confidence level (t-statistic = 2.44) and illustrates a conclusion that is widely accepted in the literature. No claim is

made that EI dependence is the sole determinant of a country's quality of governance.

36. In Figure 2, Chile and Botswana are shown at the top of the graph, near the center and toward the right, respectively.

37. For a definition of macro and sectoral governance, see Annex C, Chapter 6.

38. See Annex C, Chapter 6.

39. Corruption, one particular public financial management shortcoming, is a possible proxy measure.

40. That is, the use of public power in accordance with the law.

41. At this point, the position paper (www.-ifc.org/test/sustainability/docs/Revenue_Distri_Mgmt.pdf) focuses only on projects generating substantial revenues compared with the country's overall fiscal revenues, and the suggested steps are optional, not mandatory.

42. For all EA Category 'A' projects, the borrower is expected to consult project-affected groups, local NGOs, and so forth and disclose relevant material in a timely and culturally appropriate manner. The requirements are somewhat more rigorous for 'A' than for 'B' projects, and IFC requires public consultation only for some Category 'B' projects.

43. The "Extractive Industries Transparency Initiative" and an NGO campaign—"Publish What You Pay"—advocate disclosure.

Chapter 4

44. Given the size and complexity of the WBG, and the diversity of issues that needs to be addressed, it is expected that the responsibility for following up on these recommendations will not rest exclusively with the sector specialists; that is, the Energy and Mining Sector Board and the Oil, Gas, Mining and Chemicals Global Product Group. The Management Response is expected to identify the unit(s) responsible for following up each recommendation.

45. "Significant" should be considered both in absolute terms and in relation to total sector production, based on analysis of past experience, and may vary by country. Supporting increased investment could be either through investments by IFC, guarantees by MIGA, or assistance from the World Bank, in making the investment code more attractive, for example. A possible mitigating measure could be "ring-fencing" of fiscal revenues from EI projects for development purposes. MIGA should consider adopting a position on revenue management and distribution similar to IFC's.

46. For example, the Bank should help countries establish appropriate laws and regulations to mitigate negative environmental and social effects and build capacity to enforce them. Private sector projects supported by IFC and MIGA could serve as role models for environmental and social performance, transparency, and disclosure, and thus raise sector performance.

47. This recommendation also applies to countries that are expected to become resource-rich, through a large, WBG-supported project, for example. In all resource-rich countries, the WBG should also encourage client countries to include EI in their Poverty Reduction Strategy Papers.

48. In line with the Bank's performance-based allocation of IDA credits.

49. This recommendation is consistent with the LICUS approach mentioned in notes 11 and 17.

50. For example, for sectoral adjustment and technical assistance.

51. Such as, for example, advisory work funded by trust funds.

52. For example, in project completion reports for the Bank and in project supervision reports for IFC.

53. See Annex D, Chapter 4, "IFC Helping to General Sustainable Benefits" for more details.

54. Several stakeholders have already sought IMF and WBG assistance in advocating or requiring disclosure and in developing a reporting framework.

55. Such indicators could include, for example, health and safety statistics, gas flaring (or greenhouse gas emissions), adequacy of mine closure preparations (including funding) and oil transportation arrangements, hazardous materials management and emergency response plans, availability of infrastructure and services (e.g., health and education), and revenues generated for governments.

Annex A

56. Volume I is the overall summary of a joint OED/OEG/OEU sector review of the World Bank Group's activities; Volume II is OED's review of the Bank's activities; Volume III is OEG's review of IFC's activities; and Volume IV is OEU's review of MIGA's activities.

57. See *Background Paper—World Bank Group Activities in Extractive Industries,* Oil, Gas, Mining and Chemicals Department, World Bank/IFC, August 2001. This paper and other documents relevant to the WBG strategy are available at www.worldbank.org/ogmc.

58. *Resource-rich* countries are those in which EIs account for, or are expected soon to account for, more than 50 percent of government revenues and potentially include, for example: Algeria, Angola, Azerbaijan, Botswana, Chad, Congo (R), Congo (DRC), Equatorial Guinea, Gabon, Iran, Iraq, Kazakhstan, Libya, Nigeria, Oman, Syria, Sao Tome, Sudan, Timor-Leste, Turkmenistan, Venezuela, and Yemen. Countries with *substantial resources* are those in which extractive industries account for, or are expected soon to account for, 30 to 50 percent of fiscal revenues or exports and include potentially, for example: Bolivia, Cameroon, Central African Republic, Chile, Colombia, Ecuador, Egypt, Ghana, Guinea, Guyana, Indonesia, Jamaica, Jordan, Kyrgyz Republic, Mali, Malaysia, Mauritania, Mexico, Mongolia, Mozambique, Namibia, Niger, Papua New Guinea, Peru, Russia, Sierra Leone, South Africa, Suriname, Tanzania, Togo, Trinidad and Tobago, Ukraine, Uzbekistan, and Zambia. The usefulness of the two-tier approach and relevance of the specific thresholds will be reviewed in light of implementation experience; the corresponding country groupings will be periodically updated as necessary.

59. See *A Review of IFC's Safeguard Policies,* CAO, January 2003, *Insuring Responsible Investment?,* CAO, December 2002, and other reports accessible at: www.cao-ombudsman.org

Annex C

60. Ross (2001). However, it is important to note that while the issue of "whether or not mining *usually* promotes economic development remains unresolved, there is widespread agreement that rich mineral deposits provide developing countries with opportunities, which in some instances have been used wisely to promote development, and in other instances have been misused, hurting development." Davis and Tilton (2001).

61. Letter from Friends of the Earth International to Mr. James D. Wolfensohn, President of the World Bank Group (October 30, 2000).

62. The OED of the World Bank (IBRD and IDA), the OEG of the IFC, and the OEU of MIGA.

63. The EIR is headed by Dr. Emil Salim, former Minister of Environment for Indonesia. Additional information on the EIR can be found at www.eireview.org.

64. Seminal papers by Auty (2000), Gelb (1988), Isham (2002), and Sachs and Warner (1995), have discussed the evolution of thinking on the subject in recent years.

65. See Attachment 3 for an explanation of OED's project ratings scale.

66. The Approach Paper and other supporting documents for this evaluation study are available on the Internet (www.ifc.org/oeg/EIEvaluation/eievaluation.html).

67. The portfolio of projects chosen for review by this study consists of all extractive industries projects approved during or after FY93, the first full financial year after the WBG adopted revised safeguard policies. A total of 76 projects were reviewed, comprising 48 completed (24 oil and gas, 24 mining) and 28 active projects (15 oil and gas, 13 mining). Detailed discussion and statistical tables on the main characteristics of the project portfolio are provided in the background paper "Review of the Portfolio of World Bank Extractive Industry Projects."

68. See Attachment 4 for the complete list of background papers.

69. The five countries were chosen based on the relative importance of extractive industries in their economies, the intensity of Bank assistance they received, and for regional diversity.

70. The staff survey questionnaire was sent to 95 WBG staff involved in extractive industries projects and countries (WB: 51, IFC: 33, MIGA: 12) and responses were received from 69 percent (WB: 51%, IFC: 91%, MIGA: 83%).

71. The stakeholder survey questionnaire was distributed to 292 participants of the EIR's LAC, ECA, and AFR regional stakeholder workshops, and the response rate has been 26 percent (Rio: 25%, Budapest: 30%, Maputo: 24%). The EIR designed the regional workshops to be representative of WBG stakeholders. The participants represented governments: 25 percent, industry: 21 percent, civil society: 30 percent, the WBG: 11 percent, and others (academia, other multilateral organizations, etc.): 13 percent. Survey respondents represented government: 41 percent, industry: 21 percent, civil society: 25 percent, the WBG: 4 percent, and others: 9 percent.

72. World Bank (1984).

73. World Bank (1992).

74. The Bank has 10 safeguard policies: 8 deal with environmental and social concerns (OP/BP 4.01, *Environmental Assessment;* OP/BP 4.04, *Natural Habitats;* OP 4.09, *Pest Management;* OP/BP 4.12, *Involuntary Resettlement;* OD 4.20, *Indigenous Peoples;* OP 4.36, *Forestry;* OP/BP 4.37, *Safety of Dams;* and OPN 11.03, *Cultural Property*) and 2 deal with legal matters (OP/BP 7.50, *Projects on International Waterways* and OP/BP 7.60, *Projects in Disputed Areas*).

75. Fox, Onorato, and Strongman (1998).

76. Van der Veen et al. (1996).

77. The outcome rating denotes the extent to which the project's major relevant objectives were achieved, or are expected to be achieved, efficiently.

78. The institutional development impact denotes the extent to which a project improved the ability of a country or region to make more efficient, equitable, and sustainable use of its human, financial, and natural resources.

79. For projects completed during 1980–86, only 53 percent were rated for institutional development impact under the older performance ratings. They are therefore excluded from this comparison.

80. The sustainability rating denotes the resilience to risk of the project's net benefit flows over time.

81. For this review, the EI portfolio includes projects that are not primarily classified under the oil and gas or mining sector headings of the Bank's classification system but nevertheless contain significant EI-related components.

82. A more detailed discussion on the Bank's changing role, portfolio objectives, and quality of lending for the extractive industries is the "Review of the Portfolio of World Bank Extractive Industry Projects."

83. Under WB's OP 4.01 for Environmental Assessment, Category 'A' projects are those that are likely to have adverse environmental and social impacts that are sensitive, diverse, or unprecedented; Category 'B' projects are those with adverse impacts on human populations or environmentally important areas; Category 'C' is a residual category.

84. See Attachment 3 for an explanation of OED's project ratings scale.

85. That is, whether the project creates more net benefits to the economy than other mutually exclusive options. See OP 10.04: *Economic Analysis of Investment Operations,* World Bank (September 1994).

86. See OP 13.55: *Implementation Completion Reporting,* World Bank (July 1999).

87. The four completed structural adjustment loans in the sample were excluded from this analysis given the Bank's practice of not estimating ERRs or quantifying benefits for such projects.

88. *Guidelines for Preparing Implementation Completion Reports,* World Bank (1999). The earlier Bank policy on Project Completion Reports also required the preparation of an ex-post economic analysis.

89. This figure includes one Emergency Recovery Loan.

90. That is, a proxy for the opportunity cost of capital.

91. The fourth remaining SIL, Ethiopia's Calub Energy Project, was closed prematurely, precluding any meaningful ex-post economic analysis.

92. This figure includes one GEF grant.

93. The ERR for the Guinea Mining Sector Investment Promotion Project was estimated for the appraisal and re-estimated for the ICR.

94. This figure includes one Rehabilitation Investment Loan.

95. There is no reason to believe that the performance of extractive industries projects in this

regard is different than that of projects in other sectors.

96. The May 15, 2002, Toronto Declaration of the International Council of Mining and Metals states (on behalf of the mining industry): "orphan site legacy issues are important and complex. However, they are beyond the capacity of ICMM to resolve. Governments and international agencies should assume the lead role in addressing them."

97. Since the start of fiscal year 1993, the World Bank has approved 76 projects in the extractive industries or with significant components relating to extractive industries. As of June 30, 2002, 48 projects have been completed (24 oil and gas, 24 mining) and 28 projects are still active (15 oil and gas, 13 mining).

98. The purposive selection of projects that were likely to have significant adverse environmental or social impacts is consistent with the objective of the Safeguards Review, as the WBG's safeguard policies are applicable only to such projects. As a result, the validity of the findings is limited to such projects and should not be extended to those Category 'C' projects that were likely to have minimal or no adverse impacts or SALs, which are not covered by the safeguard policies.

99. As stated in the Bank's policy on Environmental Assessment (OP 4.01), to fall under Category 'A,' a project is deemed to be likely to have significant adverse environmental impacts that are sensitive, diverse, or unprecedented. Category 'B' is assigned to projects whose potential environmental impacts are less adverse than those for Category 'A.' Category 'C' is for projects that are likely to have minimal or no adverse environmental impacts. SECALs have been covered by the policy only since 1999. Earlier SECALs were uncategorized.

100. These requirements are recorded in Annex 1-A and 1-B of the Safeguards Review. The list is based on the latest version of the policies (as of June 30, 2002).

101. The individual project review worksheets were sent to the relevant project managers for fact checking.

102. It should also be noted that the extractive industries portfolio includes a higher share of TA and SECAL projects, whose classification has been subject to differing interpretation.

103. Given the small size of the sample, it was not feasible to evaluate any impact from the Bank's enhanced safeguards compliance system established in 1999.

104. See note 13 for additional information about the survey. The complete results are provided in Annex D, Attachment 6b.

105. The adequacy of the initial project screening and of Bank supervision were not themselves criteria for evaluating the adequacy of safeguards compliance at the project approval or implementation stage but factors that were tracked and assessed in parallel as part of the safeguards review.

106. That is, the process by which the EA category is assigned, the nature and extent of the EA or environmental analysis is decided, and the applicable safeguard policies are identified. Responsibility for the initial project screening resides with the project's task team, under the supervision of regional management, subject to clearance by the regional safeguards coordinator, under the oversight of the central QACU. Before 2000, responsibility for initial project screening was shared between the project's task team and the Bank's regional environment divisions.

107. Of the 11 projects, 6 were 'B' projects that should have been more appropriately categorized as 'A,' and 5 were 'C' projects that should have been more appropriately categorized as 'B.'

108. The Bank's Operational Manual lists seven investment lending instruments: SIL, Learning and Innovation Loan, TAL, Emergency Recovery Loan, Financial Intermediary Loan, Sector Investment and Maintenance Loan, and Adaptable Program Loan. The manual lists the following six adjustment lending instruments: Programmatic Structural Adjustment Loan, Poverty Reduction Support Credit, SECAL, SAL, Special Structural Adjustment Loan, and Rehabilitation Loan.

109. EIA, Sectoral EA, Regional EA, Environmental Audit, Hazard/Risk Assessment.

110. The five SECALs in Russia, Poland, and Ukraine were subject to careful environmental and social review. The remaining one is the

Madagascar Sector Reform Project, which should also have been categorized as an 'A' because of proposed new port facilities.

111. The mine closures supported by these SECALs were unprecedented in scale, diversity of environmental conditions, and the complexity of environmental, safety, and social issues. The past environmental and social neglect of these mining operations further aggravated the problems involved in their closure.

112. World Bank (1991).

113. As indicated earlier, there is no implication that the treatment of extractive industries projects in this regard is different from the Bank's practice in other sectors at the time, which was to interpret the EA Source Book with great flexibility. In recent years, management, the Inspection Panel, and the Bank's legal department have clarified that the EA Source Book is to be followed. The Safeguards Review is in line with this position.

114. However, Poland's Ministry of the Environment has not endorsed this conclusion.

115. *Environmental Assessment Sourcebook Update No. 2: Environmental Screening,* Environmental Department, World Bank, Washington, D.C. (April 1993).

116. Thailand: Second Gas Transmission Project.

117. The issue was settled amicably, but it took some time.

118. Cameroon: Chad-Cameroon Pipeline Project; Chad: Petroleum Sector Capacity Management Project.

119. As mentioned in Chapter 4, this may be related to the fact that many of the projects had been assigned to lower EA categories or applicable safeguards were not triggered at the initial project screening.

120. The PSR for the India Coal Sector Rehabilitation Project dated March 28, 2001, records a "Highly Unsatisfactory" rating in respect to compliance with the safeguard policy for Involuntary Resettlement (OD 4.30), prior to receipt of a complaint by the Inspection Panel (RQ01/2) on June 21, 2001.

121. The Bank's EA policy requires comprehensive environmental and social baseline surveys only for Category 'A' projects.

122. World Bank (2001d).

123. However, some allowance needs to be made for the evolving more rigorous interpretation of these policies, in a world that is ever more concerned about sustainable development, as noted in Chapter 2.

124. Here again, there is no reason to believe that the performance of extractive industries projects in this regard is different than that of projects in other sectors.

125. Other potential economic benefits include financial flows accruing to private investors, employees, local communities, and so forth, which represent compensation for risk capital, labor, and social and environmental services.

126. Beyond the allocation of fiscal revenues in line with national development priorities, an assessment of the efficacy of public expenditure for achieving sustainable development and poverty reduction was outside the scope of this evaluation. Such assessments are regularly included in OED's Country Assistance Evaluations.

127. As stated in BP 2.11, "The Country Assistance Strategy (CAS) is the central vehicle for Board review of the World Bank Group's assistance strategy for IDA and IBRD borrowers. The CAS document (a) describes the World Bank Group's strategy based on an assessment of priorities in the country, and (b) indicates the level and composition of assistance to be provided based on the strategy and the country's portfolio performance."

128. That is, those with negative GDP/capita growth during the 1990s.

129. The percentage was higher for better performing EI-dependent countries at 80 percent and lower for non-EI dependent countries.

130. Many of these countries fit the description of LICUS. As stated in the *LICUS Task Force Report* (World Bank 2002): "Low-income countries under stress are characterized by very weak policies, institutions, and governance. Aid does not work well in these environments...Yet neglect of such countries (by the development community) perpetuates poverty and may contribute to the collapse of the state, with adverse regional and even global consequences."

131. The five countries were chosen based on the relative importance of extractive in-

dustries in their economies, the intensity of Bank assistance they received, and for regional diversity.

132. Of the 60 CASs that were reviewed, 26 covered EI-dependent countries, and 4 of these were joint Bank-IFC-MIGA CASs.

133. Since 2002, the Bank's LICUS program (see note 72) has led to the allocation of additional budget to eligible countries for activities designed to improve the institutional and policy framework.

134. This relationship, which is statistically significant at the 95 percent confidence level (t-statistic = 2.44), illustrates a conclusion that is widely accepted in the literature. No claim is made that EI dependence is the sole determinant of a country's quality of governance. The figure includes all countries eligible for borrowing from the WBG with a population greater than one million as of 2000, for which data is available.

135. In Figure C11, Chile and Botswana are shown at the top, near center and to the right hand side, respectively.

136. *Governance and Development,* World Bank, Washington, D.C. (1992).

137. For example, the Bank has set up a project Web site with a comprehensive set of documents including (i) the Project Appraisal Documents for the three projects, (ii) the full set of Environmental Assessments and Environmental Management Plan documents, (iii) the Loan and Credit Agreements, (iv) Environmental Compliance Monitoring Group and International Advisory Group reports, and (v) up-to-date progress reports on project implementation. Many of these reports are in English and French to make them more broadly accessible. See http:www.worldbank.org/afr/ccproj/project/pro_document.htm.

139. The six countries were chosen for variation in region, size and importance of the EI sector, quality of governance, and intensity of Bank intervention in the sector.

139. For additional information on GRICS, see http://www.worldbank.org/wbi/governance/data.html#dataset2001.

140. Because abuse of individual rights, mostly in connection with site security arrange-

ments for project sites, has been alleged in connection with some EI projects—albeit none in connection with projects in the Bank portfolio under review—the Bank needs to consider its position on these issues. While extractive industry leaders and some governments subscribe to Voluntary Principles on Security and Human Rights, the Bank has no comparable guidance.

141. In recent years, the Bank's governance-related public expenditure and financial accountability sector work has rapidly evolved. Public Expenditure Reviews, Country Financial Accountability Assessments, and Country Procurement Assessment Reviews are now part of core economic and sector work in all borrowing countries. Follow-up to these core diagnostics in terms of policies and institutions and capacity-building is part of regular CAS preparation discussions.

142. The Mining TA project includes, among others, components for (a) policy and regulatory institutional strengthening of the Department of Mining and (b) institutional strengthening and capacity-building for the Internal Revenue Commission. The Gas TA project includes, among others, components to (a) enhance the monitoring and regulatory capacity of the Department of Petroleum and (b) facilitate the participation of local communities.

143. Notably a weak legislature and civil society, lack of freedom for the media, and lack of transparency of public accounts.

144. That is, the use of public power in accordance with law.

145. For example, through AAA, technical assistance projects, and other instruments that are primarily aimed at strengthening governance and management of environmental and social risks.

146. Given the Bank's very modest record with fiscal revenue management in EI-dependent countries (see Chapter 5) the number of such "test cases" is expected to be small.

147. The Management Response is expected to identify the unit(s) responsible for following up each recommendation.

148. Aspects to be addressed should include, inter alia, key policy issues, the Bank's role, and business implications (including resource issues and WBG coordination).

149. Management accepts the need to factor governance into its support for extractive industry activities and will work to improve its approaches, based on country circumstances. However, it does not feel that mandating for an entire set of countries a specific program to ensure that fiscal revenues are used for development priorities would be a practical solution.

150. "Significant" should be considered both in absolute terms and in relation to total sector production, based on analysis of past experience, and may vary by country.

151. In resource-rich countries, the WBG should also encourage client countries to include EI in the Poverty Reduction Strategy Papers.

152. In line with the Bank's performance-based allocation of IDA credits.

153. This recommendation is consistent with the LICUS approach mentioned in Chapter 5.

154. Such as on mine closure, safety of dams, forced and child labor.

155. Such as those related to consultation and disclosure, community development, security, hazardous materials management, acid rock drainage, gas flaring, and transportation of oil, for which the good practice guidelines that have been issued need to be complemented by supporting language in the policies.

156. Several stakeholders have already sought IMF and WBG assistance in advocating or requiring disclosure and in developing a reporting framework.

157. Such indicators could include, for example, health and safety statistics, gas flaring (or greenhouse gas emissions), adequacy of mine closure preparations (including funding) and oil transportation arrangements, hazardous materials management and emergency response plans, availability of infrastructure and services (e.g., health and education), and revenues generated for governments.

Annex D

158. As in IFC's guidelines, "environmental" aspects include worker health and safety.

159. Environmental effects could be local (e.g., impacts on water quality) or global (e.g., contribution to greenhouse gases through gas flaring).

160. IFC does not have a Board-approved sector strategy for EI, but its investment departments discuss their strategies annually with IFC management. While these sector strategies are not normally disclosed, IFC has started to publish regional strategies for mining (www.ifc.org/mining/region/region.html). IFC ceased to invest in oil and gas exploration in fiscal year 1992, but this was due to poor results and the difficulties of assessing exploration risks. Exploration projects in mining are very rare, but IFC has invested at very early stages (exploration or pre-feasibility study).

161. See, for example, *The oil and gas industry from Rio to Johannesburg and beyond—contributing to sustainable development* (2002), by the International Association of Oil and Gas Producers (OGP) and the International Petroleum Industry Environmental Conservation Association (IPIECA). Other initiatives in the mining sector, for example, the Mining, Minerals and Sustainable Development Project (MMSD), came to similar conclusions.

162. For example, the ICMM is working with the Global Reporting Initiative (GRI) to develop sustainability indicators for the mining industry. Ultimately, this is expected to result in a consistent and coherent module for reporting on sustainable development for mining companies.

163. Mining and Minerals Sustainability Survey (2001).

164. This and other comparisons of "evaluated" projects relate to a random, representative sample of 22 IFC projects (12 oil and gas, 10 mining) approved 1991–96 and evaluated 1996–2001 (results in Attachment 4b) using IFC's standard evaluation framework. For desk reviews of all 45 "studied" projects—22 oil and gas and 23 mining projects approved since fiscal year 1993 or still in IFC's portfolio—a similar but simplified ratings framework was used (Attachment 4e, results in Attachments 4c and 4d).

165. The results of all studied projects are not strictly comparable, as they have a different maturity profile—older and younger—than the evaluated projects. Also, there are no comparators in IFC's portfolio, as IFC does not track and rate development results on a portfolio basis. The number of projects is too small to analyze trends.

166. See, for example, *World Bank Group Work in Low-Income Countries Under Stress: A Task Force Report* (2002), http://www1.worldbank.org/operations/licus.

167. "Significantly" used in this report implies statistically significant using a 90 percent confidence interval.

168. Until 1996, IFC effectively valued resources at zero. Since then, IFC has started to deduct the net present value of the economic benefits generated from the resource over the projected life as depletion premium. This may differ substantially from how governments or investors might value the resource, which will depend on many factors, such as country and resource risk.

169. Adequate economic returns do not always mean large government revenues. See below on distribution.

170. There are many different taxation regimes. For an excellent overview, see *Global Mining Taxation Comparative Study* (J. Otto, 2000) or *Review of Legal and Fiscal Frameworks for Exploration and Mining* (Koh Naito, Felix Remy, John P. Williams, 2001). On oil and gas, see www.ifc.org/ogmc/pdfs/DanielJohnston.pdf.

171. Oil features higher royalties—and other forms of "rents"—than mining. Royalties in mining affect the cutoff grade and can thus easily make otherwise attractive deposits unviable; in oil this is less likely, as marginal costs are low compared with the resource value. Rents are the excess of pre-tax benefits over cost, including the minimum return on capital required to attract investment.

172. We surveyed over 50 people at the EIR Planning Workshop, and about half responded (Attachment 6a). Broad and balanced representation of stakeholders was one of the workshop's goals.

173. Examples include questioning the appropriateness of favorable tax exemptions and swap arrangements.

174. The Inspection Panel for the Chad-Cameroon pipeline claimed "it was unable to find any analysis justifying the allocation of revenues between Chad and the Consortium [of investors]." World Bank management stated that it was not a party to the confidential agreement between Chad and the Consortium, but that the reasonableness of the agreement had been independently studied, and that it had made certain Chad received independent expert advice.

175. This appears to be changing. IFC has started to track development results in supervision, and some recent Board Reports for EI projects identify government revenues as one of the indicators to be tracked.

176. See, for example, *Breaking the Conflict Trap: Civil War and Development Policy,* draft WBG Policy Research Report (2003), http://econ.worldbank.org/prr/CivilWarPRR.

177. *Review of Legal and Fiscal Frameworks for Exploration and Mining* (Koh Naito, Felix Remy, John P. Williams, 2001) compares the fiscal regimes of 23 countries. *Global Mining Taxation Comparative Study,* Institute for Global Resources Policy and Management and Colorado School of Mines (second edition, March 2000, James Otto et al.) compares the effects of taxation on "model" copper and gold mines. An unofficial note on the WBG's Web site, "Best Practices in Dealing with the Social Impacts of Oil and Gas Operations," on management of government revenues, cites numerous reference documents and concludes that international practice of the government's "take" in oil and gas is about 45 percent to 50 percent at the low end and 80 percent to 85 percent at the high end.

178. For example, a host government has requested an independent "fairness" assessment of an existing contract with an IFC client company. Routinely providing a resolution mechanism where conflicts between governments and investors arise may help settle disputes, and is now often incorporated in agreements between investors and governments. However, years after the contract was signed, it is even more difficult to assess how reasonable a distribution is, and renegotiating contracts later will also discourage potential future investors. Annex C (Chapter 5 and Box C11) discusses issues related to the acceptability of benefit distribution.

179. The WBG hosted a workshop on petroleum revenue management (www.ifc.org/ogmc/petroleum.htm) in October 2002; the IMF hosted a similar conference in June 2002.

180. Chad (2000), Chile (1957), Gabon (1982), Ghana (1984), Guinea (1982), Guinea-Bissau

(1989), Kyrgyz Republic (1995), Mauritania (1968), Russian Federation (1993), Tajikistan (1996), Uzbekistan (1994), Zimbabwe (1981). EI projects have been among the first investments in several other countries.

181. The benchmark for a satisfactory business success is whether the real (inflation-adjusted), after-tax financial rate of return exceeds a company's estimated weighted average cost of capital.

182. Attachment 3 contains more information on IFC's EI investment activities.

183. Before that, the World Bank reviewed the environmental aspects of IFC's projects, using guidelines initially published in 1984 and revised in 1988.

184. Available online at http://www.ifc.org/enviro/EnvSoc/childlabor/childsafeguard.htm.

185. Available online at http://www.ifc.org/enviro/enviro/pollution/guidelines.htm.

186. Ibid.

187. Category 'A' projects are "likely to have significant adverse environmental impacts that are sensitive, diverse, or unprecedented." They require EIAs that normally cover (a) environmental and social baseline conditions; (b) potential environmental and social impacts (direct and indirect), including opportunities for enhancement, cumulative impact, and other anticipated developments; (c) systematic comparison of feasible alternatives, sites, technologies, and designs; (d) preventive, mitigating, and compensatory measures; (e) capacity for environmental and social management and training programs; (f) detailed results of the public consultation and disclosure program; and (g) monitoring. They usually quantify capital and recurrent costs, environmental and social staffing, training, monitoring requirements, and the benefits of proposed alternatives and mitigation measures. See www.ifc.org/enviro/EnvSoc/ESRP/esrp.htm.

188. For example, a feasibility study for a project that would—if implemented—be categorized as 'A' was categorized as 'C' (no impact); an exploration project potentially affecting a nature reserve and indigenous people was categorized as 'B.' The CAO's safeguard policy review found that decisions about categorizations "may be inconsistent and non-transparent." IFC's Environment and Social Development Department conceded that consistent categorization was difficult. This suggests a need for better guidance, transparency, and peer review.

189. For a more detailed description of the Millennium Development Goals, see www.developmentgoals.org. We did not have sufficient data to analyze performance for the important goal of poverty reduction. Also, OEG's analysis did not control for other factors that may affect achievement of Millennium Development Goals, such as, for example, income per capita.

190. Twenty-two projects were approved 1991–96 and evaluated 1996–2001, 10 in mining and 12 in oil and gas.

191. There was insufficient information to rate the twelfth project, as IFC had exited from the investment.

192. The portfolio analysis is mainly based on desk reviews, even though some of the results were verified through OEG's 13 field visits. It excludes 14 projects that were considered immature and 5 projects from which IFC had exited and insufficient information for an overall assessment was available. It also summarizes ratings for multiple projects in the same company and takes into account longer-term developments than the typical five-year span of the more detailed evaluations. See Attachments 4e and 4f.

193. Ratings for the sample of evaluated projects were not updated to incorporate new information, to remain comparable with those of non-EI projects in the same sample and allow for meaningful statistical analysis. For the studied projects, such new information was incorporated. For example, in several cases, material problems had later been corrected and OEG considered that the earlier shortfalls were not material enough to warrant a rating less than satisfactory. Also, the evaluated sample included 1991–92 projects, some with environmental problems, that were no longer considered in the studied portfolio (approvals since 1993 and current portfolio).

194. For example, some companies have established a zero flaring goal. Shell's and BP's sustainability reporting is considered among the best in the oil industry. See www.sustainability.com for the Top 50 corporate reports.

195. IFC's 2001 offshore guidelines require the following: minimize low pressure and eliminate high pressure flaring (or justify where this is not possible), eliminate continuous venting and minimize emergency venting, and calculate GHG emissions annually. The World Bank's 1998 onshore guidelines simply state, "minimize flaring" but "flaring is preferable to venting."

196. See www.worldbank.org/ogmc/global_gas.htm.

197. The code can be found at www.cyanide-code.org/thecode/thecode.PDF.

198. IFC's policy requires that "all its operations are carried out in an environmentally and socially responsible manner."

199. *Community Development Resource Guide for Private Companies,* IFC (2000), http://www.ifc.org/enviro/Publications/Community/IFC_CDR_Guide.pdf. Also, the World Bank Mining Department hosted a conference on Local Management of Mineral Wealth, June 2002.

200. Examples of SME linkage programs in EI include Chad-Cameroon Pipeline; Kyrgyz Republic—Kumtor Gold Mine; Mozambique—Mozal Aluminum Smelter; Nigeria—Niger Delta Contractor Credit Facility.

201. An IFC specialist for social development expressed some frustration that investment staff sometimes resist community development plans because they are not mandatory (unless the project involves resettlement).

202. A UNEP study, *The Role of Financial Institutions in Sustainable Mineral Development* (2002), recommended benchmarking projects against international standards, such as the WBG guidelines (www.mineralresourcesforum.org/docs/pdfs/zemek.pdf). A 2001 study for Japan's Ministry of the Environment considered WBG guidelines to be the highest among international financial institutions (http://www.env.go.jp/en/jeq/v006-04.pdf). Industry associations (OGP/IPIECA's 2002 study, *Key questions in managing social issues in oil & gas projects,* www.ipieca.org/downloads/social/impact_assessment.pdf) recognize that WBG policies and guidelines set de-facto standards where others do not exist—for example on resettlement. These positive views were confirmed by OEG's own evaluations, research, and interviews.

203. *The Environmental and Social Challenges of Private Sector Projects: IFC's Experience* (2002), http://www.ifc.org/publications/pubs/loe/loe8/loe8.html.

204. This can put IFC in a difficult position, because it does not disclose the environmental performance of projects. For example, one client claimed compliance even though an evaluation had just established material noncompliance. Clearly, IFC cannot verify claims of nonclients.

205. Available online at http://ifchq14.ifc.org/Apps/OSD/IOToolkit.nsf/Resource?OpenFrameSet.

206. See, for example, the guidance notes at www.ifc.org/enviro/EnvSoc/ESRP/Guidance/guidance.htm.

207. Banks adopting the so-called "Equator Principles"—a voluntary set of guidelines based on the social and environmental policies of IFC and the World Bank—are ABN AMRO Bank, N.V.; Barclays PLC; Citigroup, Inc.; Credit Lyonnais; Credit Suisse Group; HVB Group; Rabobank; Royal Bank of Scotland; WestLB AG; and Westpac Banking Corporation.

208. IFC did not update safeguard policies during the CAO review of these policies.

209. Interestingly, many of these issues are covered in the best practices for oil and gas compiled with input from different stakeholder groups and hosted on the World Bank's Web site. However, these best practices (www.worldbank.org/ogsimpact) are unofficial and not even well known within IFC.

210. www.hrw.org/corporations.

211. www.state.gov/www/global/human_rights/001220_fsdrl_principles.html.

212. The World Bank's Operational Policy 7.60 (OP 7.60, June 2001), *Projects in Disputed Areas,* relates to disputes among countries, not within a country.

213. No assessment of the environmental effects of eight projects was possible: in five, IFC no longer had an investment and had insufficient information before exiting; in one, the sponsor does not have the contractual obligation to report because IFC has only an equity investment; in two, projects had not begun commercial operations. Even for newer equity investments, IFC is not always able to contrac-

tually require compliance with its environmental policies and guidelines—but IFC's review procedures do not distinguish between investment instruments.

214. For example, OEG's *Annual Review of IFC's Evaluation Findings: FY2001, in OEG Findings* (April 2003) (http://www.ifc.org/oeg/OEG_Findings_042103.pdf).

215. An exception is one project where IFC had put in place funds for mine closure before exiting and controlled their use even after the exit. IFC is now handing over the responsibility to oversee use of the funds to the local regulatory agency.

216. For example, World Bank sector adjustment loans in Ghana and Peru helped support capacity-building for proper environmental governance in EI. But due to insufficient funds, it is unclear whether the monitoring regimes will be sustainable.

217. For example, by securing International Standards Organizations (ISO) 14001, BS8800, and/or National Occupational Safety Association (NOSA) ratings.

218. For example, one IFC client did not complete a baseline study and thus experienced major difficulties when faced with claims of pollution, and land and agriculture degradation; another client reportedly completed a baseline study but was subsequently unable to locate it.

219. For example, villagers claimed a company had not compensated for the destruction of a long-standing village, but photographic evidence showed the village did not exist before mining activities were announced; numerous claims of stream and drinking water pollution could be disproved by evidence of prior conditions.

220. NGOs have criticized IFC, saying that it cannot demonstrate that EI projects reduce poverty and improve living standards. In the past, IFC has not consistently tracked changes in environmental and, particularly, socioeconomic indicators. OEG observed negative impacts in some projects it visited—but clear improvements in others.

221. While these guidelines apply in principle only to coal, iron ore, and base metal projects, IFC has in practice also applied them to other mining projects. Reserving money is not required in the general 1995 open pit and underground mining guidelines, another example illustrating the need to update IFC's guidelines. These are the guidelines relevant for precious metal mining, the largest share of IFC's mining portfolio.

222. For example, in one portfolio project it was doubtful whether and how funding for mine closure could be secured, and in another IFC did not know whether a mine had been closed in line with IFC requirements. Supervision documents do not consistently address whether mine closure plans and funding are in place.

223. In *It's not over when it's over: Mine closure around the world* (2002), the mining policy group of the WBG's global product group has suggested several options for dealing with this problem, such as "closure bonds," warranties, securities, and insurance.

224. Ibid. The publication recognizes that many aspects of mine closure are beyond the private sector's control but recommends several steps that mining companies should undertake.

225. IFC asked the client to redress the problem, but the client chose to prepay IFC's loan instead.

226. In another project, the reputation of an IFC client suffered because of a tailings dam break at an adjacent mine.

227. For example, while IFC has strongly advocated the *Business Case for Sustainable Development,* IFC's guidance for nominees to corporate boards does not specify whether they are expected to promote the sustainability concept.

228. For example, ASM is a major issue in several mining projects in Africa.

229. See Annex C on what the World Bank has done and can do with respect to ASM, the collaborative group on ASM (http://wbln1018.worldbank.org/IFCEXT/casmsite.nsf) in which the WBG participates, and the MMSD working paper on ASM (www.iied.org/mmsd/activities/small_scale_mining.html).

230. For IFC's current disclosure policy, see www.ifc.org/enviro/enviro/Disclosure_Policy/disclosure.htm.

231. IFC's disclosure policy is ambiguous: it requires that the summary of project information and environmental review summary be updated

when there are material changes, but it does not specify whether this also applies after Board approval. In practice, IFC did not always update these documents where later changes occurred.

232. In its current form, the AMR is highly technical, sometimes running into hundreds of pages and would not necessarily lend itself for publication. A less technical summary of key indicators of environmental, social, health, and safety performance (standardized to the extent possible) may be preferable.

233. Trust and validity can be increased when the community participates in the monitoring activities and in the design of the baseline data collection, gets trained in sampling and analytical techniques, and participates in the recording and archiving of the data. Such measures could proactively increase trust or may be necessary once trust is lost.

234. Examples include an updated environmental action plan for La Colorada (Mexico) and an updated environmental management plan for Konkola Copper Mine (Zambia).

235. This is true not only for EI, but for IFC's entire portfolio.

236. For example, Kumtor in the Kyrgyz Republic (www.cameco.com/operations/gold/kumtor/index.php) or MBR, a Brazilian company: (www.mbr.com.br/eng/meioambiente/meioambiente.asp).

237. Disclosure of financial information, including revenues generated for governments, is covered in the next section.

238. Available from the WBG bookstore or online at www.ifc.org/enviro/Publications/Practice/practice.htm.

239. For Category 'A' projects, IFC's 1998 procedures require that "The project sponsor continues to consult with relevant stakeholders throughout project construction and operation, *as necessary*, to address environmental assessment related and other issues that affect them. IFC requires the project sponsor to report on ongoing consultation as part of its annual reporting requirements" (emphasis added).

240. For example, one IFC client did not effectively consult the community and key players at the outset. An accident with hazardous material spill soured community relations, cost the company millions of dollars, and created major and costly problems; it may result in preventing them from developing an important deposit on the concession. The company started an active social assistance program, but it came late.

241. IFC has prepared a checklist for improved public consultation, "Doing Better Business through Effective Publish Consultation and Disclosure: A Check Sheet" (Attachment 6).

242. This is particularly the case where governments get revenues based on production or revenue (e.g., royalties), not on profitability. In addition, in several projects, notably in Europe and Central Asia and Africa, the government retroactively changed fiscal rules or contractual arrangements.

243. OEG used the 2001GRICS published by the World Bank Institute. It measures perceptions of a large number of respondents, and, as with any such indicator, individual country rankings are subject to large margins of error. Countries were sorted using a composite of the average ratings for voice and accountability, political stability, government effectiveness, regulatory quality, rule of law, and control of corruption, and then were divided into quartiles. Results are similar using Transparency International's 2002 Corruption Perceptions Index. However, IFC staff attested that IFC had not invested in several projects due to country governance concerns.

244. For example: IMF Economic Issue 6: *Why worry about corruption*. (Paolo Mauro, 1997). Also: IMF Economic Issue 12: *Roads to nowhere: How corruption in public investment hurts growth* (Hamid Davoodi and Vito Tanzi, 1998).

245. Transparency International ranks them in the top third on corruption, ahead of several industrialized countries.

246. "Good" control of corruption—government effectiveness, voice and accountability, political stability, and rule of law—was defined as the top half of the World Bank Institute's "GRICS-II" data. Too few (4 of 45 studied projects) of IFC's EI investments were in countries with good control of corruption to conduct meaningful statistical analysis.

247. Ranking in terms of "successful" was based on returns (in NPV terms). "Highest corruption" countries were those in the bottom

quartile of Transparency International's 2002 Corruption Perception Index.

248. Rankings for control of corruption by quartile of the World Bank Institute's "GRICS-II" data.

249. Bribery in business sectors: www.transparency.org/cpi/2002/bpi2002.en.html#sectors.

250. See www.oecd.org and the section on corruption.

251. For example, the United States with the Foreign Corrupt Practices Act of 1977.

252. For more details, see www.worldbank.org/afr/ccproj.

253. Revenue distribution and management in IFC projects: www.ifc.org/test/sustainability/docs/Revenue_Distri_Mgmt.pdf.

254. See http://www.ifc.org/ogmc/socialandeconomicimpact.htm.

255. The "extractive industries transparency initiative" (www.dfid.gov.uk/News/News/files/eiti_guide.htm) and "publish what you pay" (www.publishwhatyoupay.org) advocate disclosure.

256. See, for example, IFC's publication, *The Business Case for Sustainability* (www.ifc.org/test/sustainability/docs/TheBusinessCase.pdf) and its *2002 Sustainability Review* (http://www.ifc.org/ar2002/review/sustainability.html). See also the work of the Natural Resources Cluster of Business Partners for Development (www.bpd-naturalresources.org).

257. Over 90 percent of 33 staff responded. We did not survey managers and directors but interviewed them individually.

258. Fifty-two percent of IFC respondents saw this as a problem. Their comments included, "The big issue is that the WB country departments rarely give adequate priority to mining issues." "IFC/WB coordination happens only on an individual basis at staff level and on the director level, but the former is not very consistent."

259. Eighty-eight percent of 34 WBG respondents stated that the WBG avoided good EI projects due to safeguard concerns. This confirms the 2001 *Fourth Quality-At-Entry Assessment* by the WBG's Quality Assurance Group, which found that risk aversion resulted in dropping environmental components of projects. An anonymous World Bank survey respondent put

it bluntly: "The World Bank Management is extremely sensitive to developed country social and environmental NGOs."

260. This recommendation also applies to countries expected to become resource-rich, through a large IFC-supported project, for example, and where IFC intends to make investments more generally.

261. One form of public-private partnerships, as recommended in the WBG's *Private Sector Development Strategy* (2002) is "output-based aid" (OBA). OBA would use public funding, at least in part, but feature private provision of services. Some taxation schemes allowing tax credits for community development expenditures are similar to OBA.

262. For example, IFC should encourage disclosure of production-sharing agreements, concession, and privatization terms, as well as payments made to governments at different levels. Given that providing this information is even illegal in some countries and investors may have justified concerns about unilateral disclosure, the WBG should encourage country- or industrywide disclosure

263. "Significant" should be considered both in absolute terms and in relation to total sector production, based on analysis of past experience, and may vary by country.

264. IFC should continue to appraise projects by comparing their global competitiveness and review in-depth geological and metallurgical characteristics. IFC should also diligently check the background of sponsors and how concessions were awarded.

265. Current supervision of EI projects is significantly better than average, and these recommendations build on this strength.

266. This requirement should apply to all portfolio companies. For example, IFC should routinely ask clients for Annual Monitoring Reports, even where they are not required.

267. The requirements should encompass environmental and social risks, as well as financial risks (e.g., from hedging) and parallel what IFC normally addresses in its loan covenants.

268. IFC should encourage its clients to improve their practices in line with evolving good industry practices. Where clients do not

correct important shortfalls, IFC should call the loan, raise the issue at shareholders' meetings, or inform the local regulatory agency, or the press. IFC should consider developing guidelines on how active it should be as a shareholder.

269. Together with the World Bank and other stakeholders.

270. The policies and guidelines need to be comprehensive enough to capture all important environmental and social effects, local, regional, and global, as well as short- and long-term. Yet, they also need to be practical and reflect IFC's industry experience: they need to be realistic (achievable at reasonable cost), client-driven (adaptable to the client's other reporting requirements), and monitorable (sufficiently specific). To be practicable, the policies and guidelines should meet the business case for sustainability, that is, implementing them should be in a company's long-term commercial interest.

271. IFC could build on existing industry initiatives. Information on industry-specific indicators should include, for example, fiscal revenue generation, health and safety statistics (including HIV/AIDS prevention), gas flaring (or greenhouse gas emissions), adequacy of mine closure preparations (including funding) and oil transportation arrangements, hazardous materials management, and emergency response plans. It could also include data to capture private sector contributions beyond compliance, such as infrastructure, health, and education services. The reporting requirements should also include relevant sustainable development indicators, such as water quality, access to potable water or schooling, and income levels. Other documentation, such as aerial photography and videotaping of the site and surrounding areas, could help to later document improvements or deteriorations, and potentially reduce later disputes.

272. Such an assessment should be conducted as early as possible, and IFC should prepare guidance on what IFC and its clients should do when early consultations were not carried out or were insufficient.

373. For example, IFC could review the mine closure plans of all existing clients and share best practices among them.

274. From 1983 until 1991, IFC also financed oil and gas exploration, but the amounts involved were small ($60 million). It ceased to do so, mainly because of disappointing initial results.

275. Institutional Investor country credit ratings below 30 or without a rating. In this report such countries are referred to as "risky" countries.

276. Chad (2000), Chile (1957), Gabon (1982), Ghana (1984), Guinea (1982), Guinea-Bissau (1989), Kyrgyz Republic (1995), Mauritania (1968), Russian Federation (1993), Tajikistan (1996), Uzbekistan (1994), Zimbabwe (1981).

277. http://www.ifc.org/enviro/enviro/ Disclosure_Policy/disclosure.htm.

Annex E

278. The first guarantee issued by MIGA (1990) was in mining.

279. OED for the Bank, OEG for IFC, and OEU for MIGA.

280. See *Joint OED/OEG Evaluation of WBG Activities in the Extractive Industries Sector—Approach Paper*, p. 4 ff.

281. "MIGA project" refers to a MIGA-insured investment project. A single project may have several contracts of guarantee, depending on the number of investors/lenders requesting coverage, the type of investment insured (equity, debt), and the risks insured (expropriation, war and civil disturbance, transfer restriction, breach of contract, or a combination thereof). Because contracts of guarantee have a limited lifespan, the term "MIGA project" in this report also refers to a project that was insured by MIGA but for which coverage was either cancelled or has expired.

282. All 31 projects conform to the definition of EI sector projects in the context of this joint WBG evaluation, which is consistent with the classification used by MIGA.

283. For one project selected for the review, only a partial evaluation could be made.

284. In total, MIGA issued 51 Contracts of Guarantee in support of 24 mining projects and 10 contracts for 7 oil and gas projects.

285. Contracts of guarantee issued in FY01 in mining were for existing MIGA projects.

286. Also see results of MIGA staff survey.

287. The mean was 3.9 years and the standard deviation 1.55 years.

288. Accessible at www.ipanet.net or www.miga.org.

289. MIGA's early work in this respect was cited in the *Mining Journal* (January 1997) as an important factor leading to the resurgence in mineral exploration and mining project planning in Africa in the mid-1990s.

290. Because MIGA had not officially adopted its own safeguard policies from its inception, it is more appropriate to evaluate the "consistency" of its projects with these polices rather than "compliance."

291. Based on a review of MIGA EI projects' consistency with safeguard policies undertaken in conjunction with this evaluation.

292. Nine mining and three oil and gas projects, with one project undergoing incomplete review. Therefore, graphs in this section present the results for 11 projects.

293. The World Bank has 10 safeguard policies, of which 7 are covered in the present review: (OP/BP 4.01, *Environmental Assessment;* OP 4.30, *Involuntary Resettlement;* OD 4.20, *Indigenous Peoples;* OP 4.04, *Natural Habitats;* OP 4.37, *Safety of Dams;* OPN 11.03, *Cultural Property;* and OP/BP 7.50, *Projects on International Waterways.* The following three policies are not covered in the present review: OP 4.09, *Pest Management;* OP 4.36, *Forestry;* and OP/BP 7.60, *Projects in Disputed Areas.*

294. Shortly after MIGA obtained its in-house environmental expertise, a review of the portfolio was conducted to identify high-risk projects from an environmental and social standpoint, as well as priorities for potential monitoring site visits.

295. In its description of *Framework for Safeguard Policies at MIGA.*

296. IFC or WB environmental and social specialists reviewed 10 out of 12 projects covered in this safeguards review.

297. Roger J. Batstone, *Review of Implementation of Safeguard Policies of World Bank Extractive Industries Projects,* OED Background Paper World Bank (2003).

298. A list of MIGA safeguard policy triggers is shown in Attachment 4.

299. OEU rated consistency with safeguard policies using a scoring system with four categories: negligible, modest, substantial, and high, as defined in Attachments 3a and 3b. Projects were *substantially* consistent when the "set of requirements generally was met, or expected to be met, with only minor shortcomings."

300. While one guarantee project was approved by MIGA's Board in 1992 to cover the initial stages of project development, OEU's assessment of the consistency with safeguard policies was based on documents available when the project was approved by IFC's Board in 1996, as the scope and design of the project changed appreciably between 1992 and 1996. Assessment ratings were based on the full feasibility study and comprehensive EA, which were completed in 1995.

MIGA Management notes that if this unique case was excluded from the scoring in Table 1, the ratings would have been significantly higher in many categories.

OEU notes that it has selected a representative sample covering 39 percent of MIGA guaranteed projects and including various types of partnerships and arrangements for MIGA guarantees.

301. Assignment of environmental categories ('A' or 'B') was appropriate for all sampled projects, with the possible exception of one project 'N' for which documentation was incomplete.

302. MIGA Management notes that there is clear documentation in the files that shows that all the key concerns of the Indigenous Peoples Policy and the Involuntary Resettlement Policy were addressed at the planning level, at the minimum, in well over half of the applicable projects.

303. MIGA's EA disclosure policy requires that, "For all Category 'A' projects during the environmental assessment process, MIGA will require the project investor to consult, or to have consulted, project-affected groups and local nongovernmental organizations about the project's environmental impacts, and to take their views into account. The project investor should initiate such consultations as early as possible, and consult with such groups throughout project implementation, as necessary, to address project-related environmental and social issues that affect them." There is no requirement for public consultation in MIGA-approved Category 'B' projects.

304. MIGA's General Conditions of Guarantee have been revised over the course of the period that MIGA has been in existence and, hence, over the period that is covered by the projects under review. For all guarantee issued since 1999, MIGA has the right to terminate the contract if the project does not comply with MIGA's environmental policies and guidelines.

305. Due mainly to monitoring requirements of senior lenders and other bilateral insurance agencies.

306. The reinsurance agreement covering this project pre-dates the current reinsurance practice by which MIGA's environmental and safeguard policies must be adhered to if MIGA is to act as an reinsurer. In particular, MIGA will require that the primary insurer change its contract wording, if necessary, to meet MIGA's standards. All current MIGA reinsurance contracts include MIGA's right to terminate the reinsurance contract if the investor is not in compliance with MIGA's environmental and social policies and guidelines.

307. Unlike the World Bank, MIGA does not have a Projects in Disputed Areas safeguard policy.

308. The new evaluation framework approved by CODE in 2002 introduces systematic cost-benefit analysis to the evaluation of individual guarantee projects and harmonizes evaluation standards with those used by OEG. The development outcome of guarantee projects is evaluated in four different categories: Business Performance of the project, Economic Sustainability, Environmental and Social Impact, and Impact on Private Sector Development. OEU uses the following rating scale: Satisfactory, Moderately Satisfactory, Moderately Unsatisfactory, and Unsatisfactory.

309. Internal MIGA staff workshops undertaken in 2003 have identified similar shortcomings of the RMC process and other MIGA decisionmaking committees.

310. For a recently closed down project, OEU assumed a net job creation of zero.

311. From *Framework for Safeguard Policies at MIGA*. MIGA's external Web site: www.miga.org.

312. Op. cit. Ibid.

313. It should be noted that given the size of the Agency, the survey was administered to the entire population of current MIGA underwriters and project managers involved in EI projects. Thus, it was sent to 12 MIGA active staff, with a response rate of 83 percent (10 staff).

314. The CAO report *Insuring Responsible Investments? A Review of the Application of MIGA's Environmental and Social Review Procedures* (CAO03/07/2003, accessible at www.cao-ombudsman.org) also deals with the treatment of environmental issues but addresses procedural compliance rather than the more in-depth examination of compliance with individual safeguard policies, which OEU considered. Thus, it is not directly comparable with this staff survey, which specifically asked about the treatment and application of environmental issues in EI projects.